Living with Globalization

Living with Globalization

Paul Hopper

Oxford • New York

English edition
First published in 2006 by
Berg
Editorial offices:
First Floor, Angel Court, 81 St Clements Street, Oxford OX4 1AW, UK
175 Fifth Avenue, New York, NY 10010, USA

Berg is the imprint of Oxford International Publishers Ltd.

Library of Congress Cataloging-in-Publication Data
Hopper, Paul, 1963-
    Living with globalization / Paul Hopper.— English ed.
      p. cm.
    Includes bibliographical references and index.
    ISBN-13: 978-1-84520-192-0 (hardback)
    ISBN-10: 1-84520-192-2 (hardback)
    ISBN-13: 978-1-84520-193-7 (pbk.)
    ISBN-10: 1-84520-193-0 (pbk.)
  1. Globalization. I. Title.

  JZ1318.H67 2006
  303.48'2—dc22

                  2005037132

British Library Cataloguing-in-Publication Data
A catalogue record for this book is available from the British Library.

ISBN-13 978 1 84520 192 0 (Cloth)
         978 1 84520 193 7 (Paper)

ISBN-10 1 84520 192 2 (Cloth)
         1 84520 193 0 (Paper)

Typeset by JS Typesetting Ltd, Porthcawl, Mid Glamorgan
Printed in the United Kingdom by Biddles Ltd, King's Lynn

www.bergpublishers.com

For Emma, Anna and my family

Contents

Introduction: Globalization and Complexity

There is currently much debate about globalization. Some people stress the need to adapt to globalization, others to resist it. But what does it mean to be living with globalization? How do we experience and engage with its processes? And how are governments, societies and different social and cultural groups responding to and contributing to it? These are the concerns of this work. This is not to claim that globalization operates as a kind of autonomous all-powerful force sweeping all before it. Indeed, it will be shown that determining what globalization is and the form it is taking is a difficult task. In this regard, it will be argued that we should conceive of globalization emerging from the intersection and interaction of the global and the local. More specifically, when thinking about globalization we need to pay closer attention to how its numerous flows and processes are encountered and informed by different actors and agencies in a range of cultural, political and social contexts. The latter might be regional, national, local, religious, institutional, and so forth. As a result of this interplay between these different forces and groups within these different settings, we perhaps should not be surprised that complexity and heterogeneity are the recurring tendencies that emerge from living with globalization.

In addressing these themes, this work examines some of the key developments of the recent period, and seeks to determine the extent to which they are informed by globalizing processes. These include political transformations, important regional developments and socio-economic changes affecting particular countries as well as new forms of conflict. The 'third way', arguably the most significant political project of recent times, is examined in relation to globalization in Chapter 1. The resurgence of ethnic nationalism and far-right politics in Europe and the development of the European Union (EU) are investigated in Chapters 2 and 3, respectively. Chapter 4 looks at the emergence of Al-Qaeda and global terrorism. While Chapter 5 examines how aspects of globalization are contributing to the growth of China's power and the dramatic changes taking place within that country. Finally, Chapter 6 considers the United States of America's attainment of pre-eminence in international affairs, looking at how globalizing processes might have contributed to this development. By adopting this approach this book will provide an insight into the different dimensions of globalization and show how it is being interpreted by regional institutions, national governments, religious movements and so on. But rather than providing an exhaustive analysis and detailed case studies of the myriad of different ways in which globalization is operating in countries and regions throughout the world – and in a single book this would not be feasible – the primary intention is to emphasize the need for a differentiating and contextualist approach to the study of globalization. Readers therefore looking for connecting themes linking the chapters are likely to be disappointed. The concern is to identify what is going on in particular contexts in relation to the processes of globalization, rather than to make connections as part of an attempt to develop a grand narrative about the future direction of global affairs. Indeed, each chapter will have a different argument running through it, one that is specific to the subject being covered. All of which is an indication of the complex dynamics of contemporary globalization.

A further aim is to demonstrate the variable impact that globalization is having in the contemporary period. For example, in Chapter 2, it is argued that the multiple processes of globalization are unlikely to be contributing significantly to the rise of ethnic nationalism and racist violence in contemporary Europe. In contrast, it is claimed in Chapter 3 that globalization has provided much of the recent momentum behind the European project of political and economic integration, otherwise known as the EU. As will be demonstrated, the reason for this uneven impact is that globalization is a complex, contested and incomplete phenomenon. Moreover, any impact that globalizing processes are having is contingent upon local and particular conditions or circumstances. As a result it is unwise to make bold assertions and predictions about global trends, whether they be about the 'end of history' (Fukuyama, 1992), a 'clash of civilizations' (Huntington, 1997), the 'McDonaldization of society' (Ritzer, 1998) or 'jihads against McWorld' (Barber, 1996). Indeed, this work is in part a response to these and other writers who have to a varying extent, either implicitly or explicitly, viewed globalization as lending weight to their respective positions, though their claims will not be addressed in detail here. It will be argued that given its multiple forms and complex dynamics, globalization cannot be employed in such a manner.

What is Globalization?

Any study of globalization is immediately confronted with the considerable problem of the lack of agreement over what it *is*, with some commentators doubting its existence and others simply dismissing it altogether. Susan Strange, for example, has described globalization as 'a term used by a lot of woolly thinkers who lump together all sorts of superficially converging trends' (1995: 293). As will become evident during the course of this work, there are good reasons for this lack of consensus over the concept. Yet despite this there are already established debates and positions surrounding this subject, which form part of the discourse of globalization.[1] In particular, it is possible to identify three broad tendencies in relation to globalization. These schools of thought include writers who, while making their own particular contributions to the globalization debate, might be defined as *globalists, sceptics* and *transformationalists* (see Held et al., 1999). In the following outline of their respective positions the focus is essentially upon their conceptions of the economic dimension of globalization. They also have distinctive positions on its cultural, political, military and other dimensions, which are returned to during the course of this work.

Globalists consider that contemporary developments and processes constitute a new condition or phase within human history (see Greider, 1997; Guéhenno, 1995; Julius, 1990; Wriston, 1992). They write of the emergence of an integrated global economy with the emphasis upon open markets and the breaking down of national borders. Production is viewed as a global process evident, it is claimed, in the growing volume of international trade, the greater mobility of finance and capital, increased levels of foreign direct investment (FDI) and the heightened importance of multinational corporations (MNCs) and transnational corporations (TNCs). These developments are considered to pose a number of challenges to the nation-state, notably restricting the autonomy of national governments to pursue independent economic management. Indeed, some *globalists*, such as the Japanese business writer Kenichi Ohmae (1990), believe we are witnessing the passing of the nation-state.

As might be expected, *sceptics* challenge this position. For example, many on the political left consider globalization to be simply a further expansion of international capitalism and deny it constitutes a new epoch. They cite numerous instances of labour exploitation by MNCs and TNCs as examples of what it means for many people to live with global capitalism. Their conception of globalization has gained considerable popularity. Other sceptics like Paul Hirst and Grahame Thompson (1996, 2000) highlight the 'myths' that have become associated with globalization. They maintain that the world economy is far from being genuinely 'global'. Trade, investment and financial flows are concentrated in a triad of Europe, Japan and North America and look likely to remain so; these authors therefore contend it is more appropriate to talk of 'triadization' than globalization. Hirst and Thompson also argue that genuinely transnational companies are relatively rare; most companies are nationally based partly because it is costly to relocate. They acknowledge certain developments in the flows of trade, people, finance and capital investment across societies in the contemporary period but point to historical precedents such as the period 1870–1914 when, they claim, the world economy was even more internationalized than it is in our own time. Hirst and Thompson therefore conclude that contemporary trends can best be described as a process of economic internationalization, rather than fully developed globalization.

Transformationalists stress the unprecedented nature of current economic, political and cultural flows and levels of global interconnectedness (Held et al., 1999). According to David Held and his co-writers, leading advocates of this particular approach are Anthony Giddens (1990) and James Rosenau (1997). These writers consider the momentum behind globalization to be the combined forces of modernity. Globalization is therefore motored not just by capitalism, but by industrialization, technology, the Enlightenment, critical thinking, and so on. From this position, globalization is seen as a powerful and essentially indeterminate and open-ended transformative force or process responsible for massive change within societies and world order.

While these analyses of globalization are incorporated into the investigations undertaken here, the primary focus of this work is upon how globalizing processes are informing contemporary developments. In particular, this work examines how globalization is perceived at popular, local and governmental levels, and how individuals, groups and societies are contributing to and interacting with, and in turn shaping, its complex dynamics and multiple forms. Such an approach is based upon the following understanding of globalization.

Greater Interconnectedness – Not Simply Global Capitalism

First, globalization in our time entails, or is constituted by, more intensive and extensive forms of global interconnectedness than have previously existed, reflected in increased interdependency, the formation of global networks, transnationalism, deterritorialization, time–space compression and the speeding up of everyday life. These developments – though some parts of the world remain on their margins – stem from, or are facilitated by, advances in communications and information technologies improvements in travel and the growth of tourism, the expansion of global finance and trade and shifting patterns of migration. In essence, there are multiple globalizing processes and flows at work. And as will be shown they are having varied and ultimately unpredictable effects. Of all the general accounts of globalization, the approach pursued here comes closest to the transformationalist perspective, outlined by David Held and his co-writers (1999), in the sense that it concurs with their view of the indeterminate nature of globalization.

As was touched upon earlier, a popular conception of globalization is that it is global capitalism, and more specifically neo-liberal global capitalism. It is certainly the case that capitalism is providing much of the momentum behind contemporary globalization. Profit maximization is the primary reason that companies seek to expand and develop trade networks throughout the world. Moreover, capitalism is an important constitutive element of the transformationalist account. However, capitalism is not globalization. Put another way, globalization is more than simply global capitalism. People are moving across the globe and establishing global connections and networks for a variety of reasons, beyond the financial and economic. They are moving and connecting for a range of personal, cultural and sporting reasons, as well as the very human desire to travel and meet new peoples and enjoy new experiences. The multiple flows and processes that constitute globalization cannot therefore be reduced to economics, nor for that matter to technology or culture. Furthermore, with regards to the issue of the predominance of neo-liberal global capitalism, there is an increasing tendency within the literature to stress the plural nature of capitalism. There are Asian and Scandinavian versions or models of capitalism, for example, as well as national variants. This is evident in the existence of different business cultures. So-called 'Toyotism', for instance, provides an alternative to Fordist and post-Fordist managerial practices, and some Western companies incorporate Japanese business culture and modes of organization. Neo-liberal capitalism, though currently dominant and supported by powerful interests, is therefore not the only type of capitalism. Moreover, in reality neo-liberal capitalism is unlikely to exist in a pure form. Rather it is subject to local conditions and adaptations. Hence we encounter a blurring of neo-liberalism with national capitalist economies, in which particular societies and governments contribute to the form that capitalism takes within their respective countries. This is reflected in the dearth of a universal business culture. Companies in practice will employ a variety of methods and ideas, drawn from a range of sources, in order to enhance their business prospects.

Furthermore, the equating of globalization with global capitalism does not provide a full explanation of the history of the former. It neglects the forms of global interconnectedness that predate the advent of capitalism in the modern period. For example, Janet Abu-Lugod (1989) identifies the emergence of global processes as far back as the thirteenth century. In fact, there is considerable debate about when these processes began and the intensity and extent of forms of global interconnectedness in the pre-capitalist period. While between different regions of the world varied and was less intensive during this period than in our own time, it is possible to identify a range of different types of connection and interaction, from the cultural to the economic, during the pre-modern phase of globalization. These are evident in the spread of world religions, the forging of multicultural empires, such as the Roman and Islamic empires, the Silk Route that linked the Western Roman Empire and the Chinese Han Empire through to Europe's encounter with the New World from the late fifteenth century onwards. Indeed, it has been claimed that globalization is the human condition (Pieterse, 2004). From the first human beings emerging from Africa and spreading out across the globe, human history has been one of migration. Furthermore, long-distance trading activity and trade networks existed prior to the establishment of capitalism and even the emergence of Europe as a major economic centre, mostly centred upon vast cities, such as those in China and India. The long history of human interaction is also reflected in wars and the spread of diseases throughout the centuries. To repeat, all of these examples of human interaction predate the emergence of capitalism in the modern period. Furthermore, boundaries and borders were not as rigid prior to the establishment of the nation-state, itself another feature of modernity, enabling people to move freely and mix together.

In a sense therefore globalization is what human beings *do*. Interestingly, some of the different groups and movements examined during the course of this work display an awareness of the historical nature of globalization. For example, within many Muslim communities there is a sense that globalization is part of a long-term encroachment by Western powers into the Islamic world dating back many centuries (Chapter 4). Finally, a further danger with conceiving of globalization simply in relation to the history of capitalism is that of Eurocentrism. While the emergence of capitalism in Europe paved the way for its engagement with the rest of the world, notably through European imperial expansion, to focus only upon this would be to ignore the extent of interaction between other regions of the world. It would be to ignore important historical episodes, including the slave trade between Africa and America.

However, while we must acknowledge the long history of global interconnected-ness, the concern of this work is with globalization's contemporary form, which is marked by an intensification of multiple forms of global interconnectedness. It is therefore historically unprecedented. But, to repeat, whilst capitalism is an important dimension of contemporary globalization, it *is* not globalization. In this vein neo-liberal capitalism, with its emphasis upon free trade, has facilitated globalization in the recent period, but globalizing processes were in existence long before the advent of neo-liberalism in the 1980s and would have continued even if this ideology had never seen the light of day. The conception of globalization as global capitalism does not therefore provide us with a complete account. As will now be discussed, what globalization *is* emerges from the intersection of numerous forces within particular contexts.

A Differentiating and Contextualist Approach to Globalization

As well as mapping the different global flows and forms of interconnectedness that constitute globalization we need to investigate how people are experiencing and participating in these developments. In other words, if we are to gain an informed understanding of globalization it is necessary to employ a differentiating approach to the study of it, investigating the particular ways in which individuals, groups and societies engage with globalizing processes. The intention is to move beyond considering globalization in abstract, general and macro terms. The emphasis will be upon recognizing that globalization is a complex and multifaceted set of processes, which are understood and encountered in many different ways. This work therefore seeks to fill in some of the details which general theories and accounts of globalization – globalist, sceptical, Marxist and so on – inevitably overlook. Indeed, it seeks to contribute to the case for changing how we look at globalization, constituting a move from the general to the local and the specific (see also Hay and Marsh, 2001). General accounts of globalization often fail to comprehend its complex nature and effects, and the particular ways in which its processes are operating. Therefore, integral to a differentiating approach towards globalization must be an examination of how its multiple processes are experienced within specific contexts that are shaped by factors such as geography, history, culture, social conditions and the degree of economic development, to cite but a few. Of course, people contribute to and are part of these processes, they do not just passively experience them. Furthermore, there are structural (material) and ideational (agency) elements or dynamics at work (see Hay, 1999, 2002). For example, there is a material dimension to globalization entailing as it does the increased flows of products and peoples between different parts of the world and the globalization of production. This in turn can produce structural changes as some regions and societies become more fully integrated into the global economy, and others have to restructure their own economies in order to adjust to the new conditions – Western societies deindustrializing as companies increasingly outsource their manufacturing production to the newly industrializing economies of East Asia and Latin America, for example. The ideational dimension to globalization stems from how these processes and changes are perceived by different groups, societies and governments. As will become evident, perceptions of globalization can influence behaviour irrespective of how its processes are actually operating. Thus, ideas and ideologies about globalization are also an important part of the dynamic, and inform the interacting context. All of which ensures that globalization engenders different perceptions and responses.

For example, business people invariably view globalization as the expansion of the international economy and the prospect of new trading and financial opportunities. In contrast, for governmental leaders it entails greater economic competition from new regions and pressures from global financial markets. While ordinary citizens often consider the most notable aspect of globalization to be the emergence of a global culture, others are more specific and regard it is as simply a form of Americanization. For many religious people, and not just fundamentalists, globalization represents the ongoing spread of the forces of modernization, rationalism and secularism. Many conservatives and nationalists will tend to focus upon the ways in which globalization challenges their particular nation-state and national government. For those on the extreme right, it means more economic migrants and threats to perceived national 'ways of life', while many on the political left think of globalization primarily in terms of the spread of neo-liberal capitalism and/or American economic power. For many living in Arab and Muslim societies, globalization is experienced as the bombardment of Western ideas and images via global communications technologies. In short, it matters how globalization is conceived and who is making judgements about it. This in turn raises questions about power in relation to globalization, a theme that is returned to during the course of this work.

In line with the differentiating approach towards globalization advocated here, particular contexts or settings, such as a regional organization (Chapter 3) and specific countries in the shape of China and the US (Chapters 5 and 6), are examined in the case studies that constitute this work. Hence, while Chapter 1 considers the impact of globalization upon the third way project, the primary focus is upon the New Labour government in the UK. Similarly, Chapter 2 looks at Europe but the emphasis is upon the need to take account of regional and national diversity when considering the impact of globalization. Chapter 4 insists that the emergence of the Al-Qaeda phenomenon can only be understood in the context of the history of relations between Islam and the West and debates within the Islamic world. It is possible to detect the material, ideational, power and other aspects of globalization in these case studies, though the chapters are not overly preoccupied with identifying these themes. Instead, they are returned to in the Conclusion.

Globalization as a Contested Phenomenon

In considering the issue of power in relation to globalization, we need to be aware of how governments and other agencies will often seek to impose their own agenda upon its processes, constructing narratives to define what it entails, as well as seeking to shape its future course. This has been evident since the 1980s when the Reagan and Thatcher governments along with organizations like the World Bank and the International Monetary Fund (IMF) began to champion neo-liberalism. Furthermore, a truly differentiating approach requires that governments and other organizations be studied regularly so that changes in their thinking and policy approaches towards globalization can be detected. In particular, national governments in democracies are frequently replaced, and new governments will bring with them their own ideas and political agendas. What globalization is and entails is therefore often contested within countries. At an international level, the nature of globalizing processes, flows and forms of interconnectedness is similarly a source of dispute. In this regard, neo-liberal globalization is regularly challenged by anti-globalization protestors at summit meetings of the major global institutions, as well as by everyday grass-roots activity.

There are other developments afoot, which remind us that contemporary globalization is a contested phenomenon. Commentators detect the emergence of a global discourse surrounding issues such as international justice and law-making, and patterns of trade and economic development, in which civil society organizations, such as international non-governmental organizations (INGOs), pressure groups and social movements, are playing a growing role (see Ruggie, 2003). More significantly, in performing this role these organizations are increasingly viewed as helping to ensure that international policy-making is informed by and sensitive to a wider range of concerns and opinion (see Florini, 2000; Khagram et al., 2002). For example, civil society organizations and in particular human rights groups pushed for the establishment of the International Criminal Court. They actively campaigned for and helped to design the Ottawa Convention banning landmines (see Mekata, 2000; Thakur and Malley, 1999). They have also ensured that human rights, humanitarianism, global poverty and environmental issues are high up on the international agenda (see Keck and Sikkink, 1998; Thomas, 2002; Weber, 2002).

Likewise, INGOs and social movements have highlighted and often successfully campaigned for the need for humanitarian intervention in various places throughout the world.

In the economic sphere, civil society organizations have campaigned for the reform of international organizations, especially the Bretton Woods institutions and the World Trade Organization (WTO) (O'Brien et al., 2000). Similarly, although other factors were involved, civil society organizations played an important part in blocking the Multilateral Agreement on Investment (MAI) at the Organization for Economic Development (OECD), which would have entailed a reduction in the regulation of MNCs and TNCs (Goodman, 2000; Kobrin, 1998; Smythe, 1999; Walter, 2001).[2] They have also helped to ensure that other economic issues gain global prominence, notably the ongoing campaign for debt cancellation, promoted by groups like Jubilee 2000, among others. In a similar vein, the campaign for a Tobin tax on global financial speculation is receiving increasing attention.

More generally, civil society organizations continue to put pressure upon companies and governments to act in an ethical manner by highlighting and publicizing disreputable business associations, dubious financial dealings and poor labour practices. And there is evidence that this may be exerting some influence upon MNCs and TNCs in particular, if only because they do not like to receive bad publicity. All of which is leading a number of writers to debate the existence of an international or global civil society (see Colás, 2002; Kaldor, 2003; Keane, 2003; Scholte, 2002). The formation of new global networks is considered to be a visible manifestation of this development, while Mary Kaldor believes a genuine global politics is emerging from 'the interaction between the institutions of global governance (international institutions and states) and global civil society' (2003: 78). Morten Ougaard and Richard Higgott (2002) have taken this further and discuss the 'globalization of political life' and the emergence of a global polity.

Taken together these developments reinforce the notion that globalization is a contested and indeterminate phenomenon, and in doing so further challenge the view that there is one model of capitalism – usually the Anglo-American neo-liberal model – or one country – usually the US – driving or consistently shaping the different processes and dimensions of globalization, a theme expanded upon in Chapter 6.[3] In fact, neo-liberalism itself faces considerable opposition. This is evident in many of the arguments behind the campaign to cancel Africa's external debts as well as the growing call to address the international terms of trade. Indeed, in relation to the issue of development, some commentators detect the emergence of a post-Washington Consensus (see Higgott et al., 1999). For instance, global institutions such as the World Bank and the IMF are increasingly sensitive to and orientated towards poverty reduction. As might be anticipated, the success of the measures they have implemented, and their degree of commitment to them, are subject to debate (see Thomas, 2000; Weber, 2002).[4] Nevertheless, their reorientation towards issues to do with poverty and social inequality does appear to mark a considerable departure from the dominant approach pursued by these institutions during the 1980s and 1990s.

A possible response to the above point is to argue that while the future direction of global governance may be contested and uncertain, the actual experience of developing societies of globalization, both current and in the recent past, is one of exploitation. For millions of people in developing countries, globalization means discriminatory trade policies and being flooded by imported manufactured products from the developed world. However, we need to be clear about the terms we are employing here in order that globalization does not become an all-purpose concept devoid of any meaning. More specifically, we need to distinguish between globalization and international capitalism. As defined here, globalization means global interconnectedness constituted by numerous flows and processes, and not just the economic. Trade agreements, financial loans and external debts come under the heading international capitalism. Furthermore, when considering the plight of developing societies we need to take into account other non-globalization factors, such as decisions made by indigenous leaders, corrupt officials, socio-economic conditions, the nature of governance and natural resource endowment. Indeed, greater engagement with the rest of the international community can mean access to new markets and to resources that a developing society does not possess. In sum, we would need to examine a particular developing country in order to determine the relative importance that globalizing and non-globalizing factors are playing upon the course and nature of its development. Again we return to the importance of examining particular contexts.

Globalization Requires an Interdisciplinary Approach

Lastly, the underlying assumption of this book is that understanding the complex interaction of processes and perceptions which constitute globalization effectively takes us beyond any insight that can be offered by a single academic discipline. While an economic approach will provide us with important insights into some of the forces driving globalization as well as some of its organizational and institutional forms, it can never hope to provide a complete understanding of globalization. It will struggle to predict the prospects for the generation of a global consciousness, to account for forms of cultural hybridization, to explain the possible interrelationship between globalization and cosmopolitanism, to cite but a few examples. To rely upon this approach would be to neglect the cultural, political, social and other dimensions of globalization. In short, it would be to ignore the fact that globalization is multidimensional. Moreover, to repeat the central theme of this work, such an approach would struggle to account for the particular experiences and perceptions of those individuals, groups and societies subject to globalization's numerous processes. We will therefore have to move beyond existing disciplinary constraints in order to gain a more informed insight into what it means to be living with globalization. Ultimately, this will require synthesizing a range of disciplines in the pursuit of an interdisciplinary approach. This work acknowledges that the economic, the cultural, the political, the social and environmental dimensions of globalization overlap and are intertwined, and cannot be treated as independent entities, as they are in many globalization texts.

For the reasons outlined above this work will employ a differentiating and contextualist approach to the study of globalization. It will examine some of the general claims that are made in relation to globalization – notably that it engenders for example, cosmopolitanism, nationalist reactions, fundamentalism – but it will do so by looking at particular contexts. These claims have already received considerable critical attention, though again investigations have tended to remain at a macro level rather than considering specific case-studies.

The Structure of the Book

Having set out the approach of this work, it is now possible to outline in more detail the contemporary developments that will be examined in relation to globalization.

Chapter 1 examines the impact of globalization upon the third way, and specifically the New Labour government in the UK. It is claimed that the New Labour project is informed by a particular conception of globalization and how best to respond to it. Some critics argue that New Labour has uncritically accepted globalization as a new orthodoxy; others maintain that it has been politically expedient for New Labour to embrace globalization. This case study will therefore provide an insight into the structural and ideational dimensions to globalization within the context of the UK. Put simply, is New Labour responding to how globalization is actually operating? Or, to how it perceives it to be operating? In tackling these issues, the chapter will highlight the extent to which globalization is a contested phenomenon and provide an indication of what it means for many UK citizens to be living with globalization. The chapter concludes by considering whether New Labour's approach to globalization is evident elsewhere. More specifically, whether it is indicative of an emerging consensus among Western governments on how best to adapt to globalization.

Chapter 2 examines the impact that globalization is having upon patterns of conflict and identity-formation in contemporary Europe. More specifically, it considers the contention of some commentators that globalization and related processes are generating widespread insecurity which is encouraging a retreat into the familiar and the tribal in the form of national, ethnic and cultural identities (Bauman, 1996; Horsman and Marshall, 1995). Evidence of this phenomenon within Europe, it is maintained, can be seen in the resurgence of the extreme right in many countries, the recent rise of ethnic conflict and escalating levels of racial violence. It is also reflected in concerns expressed in some European states that aspects of globalization, such as higher levels of migration and American cultural imperialism, erode local cultures and national 'ways of life'. It is a national reaction that Benjamin Barber (1996) considers is part of the 'Jihad against McWorld'. However, the argument of this chapter is that globalization can only partly account for the reinvigoration of these identities within Europe. There have been other factors and developments contributing to this phenomenon, such as the end of the Cold War and the role of the mass media, which have little to do with globalization. Moreover, as is discussed in Chapter 3, there is also the prospect that globalizing processes will work to undermine the forces of particularism within Europe.

Chapter 3 looks at how globalization, as a result of the challenge it presents to the nation-state, is contributing to the growth of regionalism, focusing specifically upon the EU. It is argued that the EU and its member states have been pursuing an essentially defensive approach towards aspects of globalization, especially with regards to global migration. The appropriateness of this response is considered in relation to claims that globalizing processes are encouraging the spread of cosmopolitanism, which would seem to place the EU at odds with contemporary developments. Furthermore, cosmopolitanism, which entails being free from national prejudices and limitations, would seem to be a prerequisite for the development of a greater sense of Europeanness among the peoples of the region. However, it is argued that whether this means the EU should rethink its approach is ultimately dependent upon how accurate a portrayal of globalization this is. In this regard, as will be stressed throughout this work, the effects of globalizing processes are dependent upon how they are perceived by different cultural, social and national groups within particular societies, regions and localities. Just as it is unwise to assert that globalization produces national and parochial responses, it is equally problematic to claim that it leads to cosmopolitanism.

Chapter 4 explores the possible linkage between aspects of contemporary globalization and the rise of global terrorism, as embodied by Al-Qaeda. The chapter looks at the ways in which global flows and forms of interconnectedness are impacting upon the Islamic world. But integral to this investigation into the Al-Qaeda phenomenon is an examination of the broader context from which it has emerged, especially in relation to debates and developments within the Islamic community. The argument of the chapter is that to understand how globalizing processes might be contributing to the global terrorism pursued by Al-Qaeda it is necessary to examine this issue within the context of the history of relations between Islam and the West. In this regard, globalization is widely perceived as a form of Westernization and as part of an ongoing Western attack upon the Islamic world, dating back many centuries. Thus, it is when globalization is viewed as a continuation of Western exploitation and injustice that groups like Al-Qaeda benefit. The chapter concludes by considering these themes and issues in the light of the attacks of September 11, 2001.

Chapter 5 examines China's complex relationship with the processes of globalization. Given the diverse nature of Chinese society, in order to assess the primary effects of globalization the focus will be upon considering its different dimensions – economic, cultural, political and so forth – in relation to China's key institution, the party-state. The chapter will develop two arguments. First, that globalization is conceived of by the party-state as central to its modernization programme, a path that China began to take when Deng Xiaoping instituted the policy of 'reform and opening to the outside' in 1978. Second, that China has been pursuing multifarious strategies towards globalization with the party-state engaged to a varying extent and in distinct ways with its different dimensions. More specifically, China is economically interconnected and interdependent with the rest of the world, whereas militarily and strategically it is less so. As for the political and cultural dimensions of globalization, the party-state is seeking to manage any domestic effects that global forces and flows can have through such measures as promoting a nationalist discourse and monitoring the Internet usage of its citizens. The consistent theme underlying the Chinese Communist Party's multidimensional approach to the different aspects of globalization is simply its own survival.

Finally, Chapter 6 examines the ways in which the processes of globalization are impacting the world's existing superpower, the US. There is a fairly widespread perception that America is the prime beneficiary of many of the different forms of globalization, and that this is enabling it to assert its own agenda upon the rest of the international community. The merits of this view are assessed during the course of this chapter. The chapter considers counter-arguments suggesting the processes of globalization will either erode or restrict America's power, in certain respects. For instance, that they will contribute to America's relative economic decline as more and more countries and regions develop through participation in the international economy. Likewise, the greater interconnectedness that globalization represents will strengthen calls for global governance, as opposed to American hegemony. Consideration will also be given to those dimensions of globalization that are arguably shaping America. For example, the chapter will look at the extent to which global migration and ongoing immigration into the US are changing the ethno-cultural mix of the country and influencing electoral politics.

In the Conclusion, the arguments of the different chapters are drawn together as part of an attempt to ascertain what they tell us about the nature of contemporary globalization. It is stressed that, contrary to the claims of many leading writers, globalization is most appropriately viewed as encapsulating heterogeneity rather than homogeneity. In this vein, it is essential to recognize the particular ways in which its complex and multiple processes are experienced, perceived and informed by different social groups and formations, each with their own cultures and histories. The aim of this work is to demonstrate that this is an appropriate and productive way to think about and approach globalization.

Summarizing Points

- Globalization is a deeply contested phenomenon.
- Globalization is multidimensional.
- There are certain limitations with existing accounts of globalization, stemming from their rather generalized and abstract approach to the subject.
- While global capitalism is an important constitutive element of contemporary globalization, the latter is also made up of other processes and developments.
- There is a need for a differentiating and contextualist approach to the study of globalization.

–1–

Globalization and the Third Way

This chapter examines the impact of globalization upon the third way, which has arguably been one of the most significant political projects of recent years. In line with the differentiating and contextualist approach of this work, the main focus will be upon a specific instance of 'third-wayism': the New Labour government in the UK. New Labour under the leadership of Tony Blair has made a concerted attempt to implement the third way, as it views it. Of course, there are numerous reasons why the Labour Party embarked upon this approach. Notable among them are a desire to end a long period of Conservative rule, internal developments within the Labour Party, the role and influence of Tony Blair and a wish to reflect more accurately changes within British society (Hall and Jacques, 1989; Driver and Martell, 1998). In particular, there was a strong desire to modernize the Labour Party (Hay, 1994; Smith, 1994). The form that this took has been the subject of much debate, ranging from those writers who consider New Labour's approach to be essentially an updated version of Thatcherism (Hay, 1994, 1997; Heffernan, 2001) to those who maintain it remains within the Labour tradition (Rubinstein, 2000; Smith, 1994). Some writers – as well as those involved in the project – emphasize that New Labour is merely seeking to modernize social democracy in order to make it relevant to the contemporary period (see Gould, 1999). Mark Wickham-Jones (1995) maintains such modernizing has been carried out within a context shaped by Thatcherism, while Driver and Martell (2002) emphasize the 'novelty' of Blair's post-Thatcherite government.

The major features of the New Labour project will be outlined, but the primary concern is not to define New Labour, a task which would require more than a chapter. Indeed, what New Labour *is* and what it stands *for* are topics that have preoccupied many commentators (see for example Driver and Martell, 1998; Finlayson, 2003; Hay, 1999; Plant, 2001; White, 2001). It is also debatable whether New Labour can ever be completely pinned down in this way: it is a more complex and multifaceted project than perhaps many of its critics allow for. In this vein, Driver and Martell (2002) write of New Labours rather than New Labour. Instead, a recurring theme will be that the New Labour project is informed by a perception of how best to respond to globalization. In fact, globalization has come to serve as one of the central justifications for New Labour and the third way. In substantiating this position, a number of the primary claims made by advocates of the third way in relation to globalization are examined. These include the notion that globalization is the condition of our time, that it changes the role of government, that it necessitates a flexible workforce and, finally, that it leads to individualization.

As will be shown, these assertions are mutually reinforcing and have helped to establish globalization as a new orthodoxy that many critics believe has been politically expedient for New Labour. Many of these claims are linked with processes associated with globalization, notably post-industrialism and detraditionalization or 'reflexive modernization' (see Beck et al., 1994; Heelas et al., 1996). Massive and essentially unpredictable change on this scale accords with the transformationalist approach to globalization, of which Anthony Giddens, the leading theorist of the third way, is regarded as a key figure (see Held et al., 1999). Indeed, these developments have encouraged Giddens (1994) to pronounce the passing of traditional left-right politics. As a consequence, this investigation into the third way and New Labour will examine the contribution of Anthony Giddens, although it should be recognized that he and New Labour are not always as one. Certain differences can be detected in their respective positions, including in relation to how government should respond to globalization.

Lastly, while Blair's government has geared itself to dealing with globalization, critics maintain there is a lack of critical analysis and debate among New Labourites about its nature and direction, and a tendency to rely upon rhetoric in relation to this issue (see Hall, 2003). This is a further indication that globalization is a contested phenomenon. However, the aim here is not to determine whether the third way/New Labour conception of globalization is accurate or valid. Rather, it is to provide an indication of the ways in which globalization is being perceived and interpreted, and how in a very real sense it is coming to shape government policy within the UK. This first case study will therefore provide some insight into what it means for many British citizens to be living with globalization.

Following this analysis, in the second part of the chapter there is an attempt to broaden the discussion by considering whether New Labour's approach to globalization is evident elsewhere. Is it, for example, indicative of an emerging consensus among Western governments on how best to adapt to globalization? It is argued that while it is possible to detect common responses among mainstream political parties in many Western democracies, it is important to take account of – in line with the overall position of this work – particular contexts. More specifically, the national cultures, political systems, historical traditions and so forth of particular societies will have an important influence upon the nature of their respective governments' response to globalization and their attitude towards the third way more generally.

Globalization and New Labour

Globalization is the Condition of Our Time

An oft-heard criticism of the third way is that it lacks a coherent philosophical base, and for some commentators it is not even a discernible political philosophy (see, for example, Finlayson, 2002; Hattersley, 2000). This is reflected in its emphasis upon pragmatism: whatever works – whether the public or private sector (Private Finance Initiatives) or a combination of both (Public–Private Partnerships) – is the approach that should be employed. In this regard, Alan Finlayson considers that a major shortcoming of the New Labour project is that it is not based upon 'a substantial moral claim about the nature of society and the distribution of its resources' (1999: 271). Instead, it makes 'a sociological claim about the real nature of modern society' (Pratt, 2001: 18). More specifically, it claims to recognize and appreciate the degree of cultural, technological and economic change that has taken place in the recent period, and accepts policy must be adapted accordingly. It is for this reason that globalization is so integral to the third way. For exponents of the third way, globalization constitutes the 'real nature of modern society' and their project is largely a response to it. And in attempting to justify this position, third wayers seek to establish globalization either as a new phenomenon or as marking a new epoch. Tony Blair in his speeches and writings invariably refers to it in terms of the 'new global economy' or the 'new global market'. Meanwhile in the final chapter of his book *The Third Way and its Critics* (2000), Anthony Giddens urges us to 'take globalization seriously'.

However, critics have observed that there is scant evidence of this taking place within the third way. Indeed, there is little suggestion that globalization might be a contested concept or phenomenon, and barely an acknowledgement of any critical debates surrounding it. Some of these debates were outlined in the Introduction to this book. In particular, the work of Paul Hirst and Grahame Thompson (1996) has implications for the third way and New Labour. In essence, their study questions the newness or uniqueness of contemporary conditions, and in so doing presents a considerable challenge to the third way project. This would seem to necessitate exponents of the third way becoming fully immersed in the globalization debate. Yet even Anthony Giddens has only made a brief response to Hirst and Thompson's thesis. In his book *Runaway World: How Globalisation is Reshaping our Lives* (1999), he contrasts their work with the work of those he terms 'radicals', such as the Japanese business writer Kenichi Ohmae (1990), who are strong advocates of globalization, and asks 'who is right in this debate'? His response is simply: 'I think it is the radicals. The level of world trade today is much higher than it ever was before, and involves a much wider range of goods and services' (Giddens, 1999: 9).[1]

Reflecting this lack of meaningful engagement with the critical debates surrounding globalization, critics argue, there is little consideration within the third way that globalization might be an uneven or incomplete process. In particular, New Labour publications are permeated with unsubstantiated assertions in relation to this issue, evident in the dearth of supporting evidence, statistical data and academic references. Instead, globalization is regarded as self-evident and simply asserted as the condition of our time that we cannot resist or escape from. As Tony Blair declared in a speech he gave in Chicago in April 1999: 'we are all internationalists now, whether we like it or not. We cannot refuse to participate in global markets if we want to prosper' (Giddens, 2000: 23–4). In this vein, an oft-repeated theme of New Labour rhetoric is the danger of the UK being left behind if it does not participate in, or adapt to, the 'new global economy'. It will be left behind because globalization produces 'change' – another recurring New Labour word. But in New Labour-speak globalization is often portrayed as an 'opportunity' or a 'challenge' rather than a threat.

The New Labour project is often articulated in terms of having recognized these new realities. For critics, the attempt to establish globalization as the condition of our time has served certain political ends for New Labour. Globalization suggests a more neutral condition than global capitalism; it does not have the historical baggage associated with capitalism. Indeed, the word capitalism is almost completely absent from Tony Blair's speeches and writings. For example, in his *New Britain: My Vision of a Young Country* (1996), there is only one reference to 'capitalism', and that is in relation to the popular capitalism the Conservatives sought to introduce under Margaret Thatcher in the 1980s. Without capitalism there is no need to consider its main historical opponent: socialism. And this critics, would argue, is in line with New Labour's attempt to dispense with the Labour Party's socialist and labourist heritage (see, for example, Coates, 1999).[2] Establishing globalization as a new orthodoxy is therefore part of the process of excluding alternatives to New Labour and the third way, both inside and outside of the party. It is a theme Blair has pushed on numerous occasions, including at a meeting in Rome with Silvio Berlusconi (15 February 2002) after which he declared that: '[s]ome of the old distinctions between right and left are no longer as valid as they were 30 or 40 years ago' (Carroll, 2002). Giddens essentially concurs with this position, notably in his book *Beyond Left and Right* (1994), in which he lays the groundwork for his later writings on the third way.

The consequence of this rather uncritical approach to globalization is that its nature and form – to put it more bluntly what globalization actually *is* – are never properly investigated. Rather, globalization has simply come to inform many of the policies of the New Labour government, both at home and abroad. The domestic implications for British citizens will be discussed in the remaining sections of the first part of this chapter. As for the influence of globalization upon the New Labour government's foreign policy this has often been explicitly stated, especially in relation to international terrorism. It was also one of the justifications for British involvement in the Kosovan war. In his speeches at the time Tony Blair sought to place events in Kosovo, as he put it, 'in a wider context – economic, political, security – because I do not believe Kosovo can be seen in isolation' (Fairclough, 2000: 148). More specifically, he made a connection between globalization and global interdependence, between global economics and international security, as the basis for promoting his particular form of internationalism: 'twenty years ago we would not have been fighting in Kosovo. We would have turned our backs on it. The fact we are engaged is the result of … globalization' (Fairclough, 2000: 151).

Having sought to establish that globalization is the condition of our time, exponents of the third way naturally seek to demonstrate that their project is the most appropriate response to it. And there are two main claims to the case that they make. First, that the third way recognizes the implications of globalization for national governance and is able to adapt accordingly. And, second, that third way ideas and policies provide the best way for citizens and societies to survive and flourish in the new global conditions. These claims will now be considered.

The Changing Role of Government

The third way insists that globalization changes the role of national governments: unable to control global capital and financial flows, and therefore manage demand, governments are limited in the extent to which they can shape their economies. According to this logic, the primary role for national government is now to promote stability and incentives for capital investment. And this view has been fully embraced by New Labour. As Tony Blair declared in a speech given at the City University, London in May 1995: 'if companies are to invest they must have a relatively stable macroeconomic framework in which to plan' (1996: 79). In essence this means, as Gordon Brown, the British Chancellor, frequently states, overcoming the cycle of boom and bust. Hence his emphasis upon 'prudence' in all matters to do with the economy and upon ruling out any looseness with inflation, tax rises or public spending. Thus there has been a shift away from Keynesian demand management of the economy to an interest in supply-side reforms, discussed in the next sub-section. Keeping a tight rein on public spending also reflects a desire to avoid getting into the financial difficulties that plagued many previous Labour administrations. But it also explains, critics maintain, why at the end of New Labour's first term, the level of expenditure on public services continued to be lower in the UK than in much of Western Europe. Nevertheless there appears to have been something of a shift in emphasis during New Labour's second term in office, with a substantial increase in public spending announced by Gordon Brown in his 2002 budget. The proportion of national income allocated for public spending is due to rise from 39.8 per cent in 2002–3 to 41.8 per cent in 2005–6. More specifically, Tony Blair has promised to raise health expenditure to the EU average by 2006.

New Labour considers that a further way of attracting capital investment is by restraining government interventions in the economy. Blair's government therefore does not just accept globalization, but effectively seeks to extend it through its support of neo-liberal initiatives which, for example, expand free trade and encourage competitiveness. New Labour's commitment to free trade and open markets is evident in numerous speeches and policy pronouncements. As Tony Blair has put it: 'to compete in the new global market ... [a] country has to dismantle barriers to competition and accept the disciplines of the international economy' (1996: 118). This commitment has enabled New Labour to establish its business-friendly credentials, but it has also meant that MNCs and TNCs enjoy considerable freedom to operate in the UK. It provides an example of how globalization, once established as a new orthodoxy, becomes a self-fulfilling prophecy. New Labour considers capital to be highly mobile in the contemporary period and hence does little or nothing to control it thereby contributing to its very mobility. All of which has obvious implications for British citizens with regards to their job security, personal finances, ability to plan for the future and so forth.

However, as was mentioned in the Introduction, the notion that national governments are largely powerless to resist the forces of globalization has been challenged. To begin with national governments do retain considerable ability and power to shape the international economy. For example, the US and UK governments have done much to facilitate globalization through their promotion of neo-liberalism. Second, capital is not as mobile as is often claimed. As writers like Chris Harman (1996) have noted, relocating is expensive for firms because it entails building new factories and training new workforces. In this regard, Hirst and Thompson contend that most companies are still nationally based and do not detect the emergence of truly transnational corporations. As they put it: '[m]ost international companies still only operate in a small number of countries, or at most regionally' (Hirst and Thompson, 1996: 198). Lastly, the idea that national governments are largely powerless and unable to pursue independent economic management can be useful for governing parties and their leaders. For instance, economic recessions can simply be blamed upon the workings of the international economy thereby diverting attention away from their own handling of their respective economies.

Yet it is not the case that New Labour has completely embraced the neo-liberal notion of government refraining from involvement in economic and social life. In the case of the former, Andrew Gamble and Gavin Kelly (2001) contend New Labour has a notion of an 'active state', which distinguishes it from previous Conservative administrations. It therefore remains firmly within the Labour Party tradition of economic revisionism. The Treasury is looking at measures to improve productivity; the Department of Trade and Industry (DTI) is addressing the problem of the supply of capital and the need to finance research; and Regional Development Agencies have been set up to stimulate investment in the regions. Most notably, Gordon Brown has started to borrow in order to increase levels of investment. In relation to social policy, New Labour has pushed through the funding of free nursery places, upgraded child benefit and improved childcare provision. Moreover, Blair's government is not simply implementing an American model of welfare reform as has been claimed by some critics (see King and Wickham-Jones, 1999). In this regard, Claire Annesley (2003) believes New Labour's social policy, especially in relation to issues such as social exclusion, the New Deal and the treatment of lone parents, has been influenced by processes of Americanization and Europeanization.

In sum, the New Labour government regards a strong and stable economy that is internationally competitive in a globalizing era as the best means of funding public services and welfare provision. As well as providing the conditions for companies and investors to want to come to the UK, it seeks to promote competitiveness through such measures as the 1998 Competition Act. But perhaps one of the most novel features of the New Labour project is that it marks something of a change in the role of government and the state. Rather than there being a traditional social democratic interventionist state or the pursuit a neo-liberal notion of a limited state – as many on the left maintain – with New Labour we are seeing the emergence of the 'enabling state', which entails a change in the relationship between government and its citizens (Blair, 1998a). For example, New Labour has engaged in extensive public sector reform based upon the abandonment of the Old Labour notion that the state should deliver public services. It is here that New Labour's oft-mentioned pragmatism is most evident: whatever is the most effective way of providing services is the method that should be employed. In practical terms, this has meant utilizing and combining the talents and capacities of the public, private and voluntary sectors. This theme of the enabling state and the changing relationship between the British government and its citizens will be returned to later.

Globalization Entails the Need for a Flexible Workforce

A flexible workforce is another theme trumpeted by exponents of the third way in relation to globalization. They maintain that for individuals to cope in the new global age they must be adaptable or 'flexible'. Influencing the supply and quality of labour is therefore considered to be one of the few ways in which government can usefully intervene in the economy. New Labour prioritizes supply-side economics in the form of the provision of education and training, encapsulated in the phrase: 'Education, Education, Education'. This effectively entails a departure from traditional social democratic policies, and an acceptance of a changed and in many ways reduced role for government. In a speech to European socialists in Malmö (6 June 1997) Tony Blair stated that the role of government was now 'to give people the education, skills and technical know-how they need to let their own enterprise and talent flourish in the new market-place' (Blair, 1997).

Critics of this approach argue that it places British workers in a more vulnerable position than their European counterparts. The New Labour government's view of globalization entails them having effectively given up on managing demand in the economy, which in their opinion is dictated by the flows of global finance and capital. This means that British workers are especially affected by any downturn in the global economy because their government is less likely to intervene to influence levels of demand. It is in such ways that many UK citizens are experiencing globalization.

However, while this enthusiastic embracing of supply-side economics marks New Labour out from many other social democratic governments, it does not make New Labour Thatcherite. Indeed, New Labour's supply-side approach differs from that pursued by the previous Conservative administrations in the sense that it places greater emphasis upon the quality of what is being supplied. In essence, as well as seeking to get more people into the workplace through its welfare-to-work programme, New Labour seeks to encourage productivity through a more educated and skilled workforce. Moreover, New Labour has implemented 'social democratic' legislation in relation to employment and the workplace. In particular, it has introduced the minimum wage (albeit at quite a low level) and the working time directive and, with the 1999 Employment Relations Act, made it easier for workers to gain union representation. It signed the social chapter of the Maastricht Treaty, and has passed laws to facilitate maternity and paternity leave. Thus, it is still possible to detect a social democratic conscience within New Labour.

Nevertheless, the promotion of the flexible worker does have implications for the level of inequality in the UK. Under New Labour the emphasis upon universalizing access to opportunities has been accompanied by a reluctance to pursue more direct forms of income redistribution (Oppenheim, 2001). This means there is greater onus upon the individual, rather than government, to improve their own economic position through their education and skills. There are echoes here of attitudes of the late nineteenth century. Colin Crouch (1999) argues that New Labour's polices mark something of a revival of the new liberalism or social liberalism of that time and entail the government has effectively given up on the notion of protecting its citizens from market forces. In this regard, many critics of New Labour consider its welfare-to-work programme to be designed primarily to discourage welfare dependency, with the element of compulsion in many of its New Deal schemes especially concerning many on the liberal-left.

The approach just described would seemingly entail an acceptance by New Labour of the continuance of economic inequality, even though Britain remains a very unequal society in relation to the distribution of income and wealth. But again the picture is complex. Anthony Giddens, in an essay entitled 'The Question of Inequality', urges social democrats to develop a 'dynamic, life-chances approach to equality' geared to equality of opportunity, which would thereby more accurately reflect our increasingly pluralistic and diverse societies (2001: 178). Yet he believes equal opportunity necessitates addressing the issue of redistribution; otherwise unequal economic outcomes can preclude equality of opportunity. Tony Blair (1998b), however, attaches less significance to redistribution. He considers the notion of 'equal worth' and the principle of 'opportunity for all' to be part of New Labour's core values ('responsibility' and 'community' are the other two core values that he cites in his third-way pamphlet for the Fabian Society). Consequently, while some tax revenues have been redistributed to the public services and the low paid during Blair's second term, there has been no reduction in income inequalities under New Labour (Goodman, 2001). The Blairite philosophy is simply: 'that everyone should have some *minimum* opportunities or some basic fair chance in life and that no one should be excluded from this' (Driver and Martell, 2002: 75). It is for this reason that Blair's government attaches considerable importance to ensuring that the UK is a meritocracy, something which of course can also help to make the UK more globally competitive, a key New Labour concern.

Lastly, critics on the left maintain that for business and industry the flexible worker offers distinct advantages. Such a model worker is able to rely upon his or her own talents and abilities, and therefore has less need to belong to a trade union to ensure job advancement and better pay and working conditions. This has been reflected in the individualization of pay bargaining, notably the spread of performance-related pay schemes. Above all the notion of the flexible worker makes resistance by organized labour more difficult because it tries to create the impression that such resistance is unnecessary in a more competitive global age. This theme of individualization will now be considered in more detail.

Globalization Entails Individualization

The connection that many academic commentators make between globalization and individualization is along the following lines. Globalization both reinforces and is reinforced by a number of contemporary processes, such as post-Fordism or post-industrialism and detraditionalization (see Beck et al., 1994; Heelas et al., 1996; Hopper, 2003).[3] Cumulatively, these processes facilitate greater choice and thereby enhance individual freedom. However, they also introduce more insecurity, reflected in the passing of stable patterns of work and lasting personal relationships. We are no longer as able as we once were to rely upon our work colleagues, families, local communities and government for protection, reassurance and sources of stability. All of which, Giddens and other writers maintain, is fostering the development of more individualistic societies.

These themes are addressed in more detail in the next chapter. In relation to this particular discussion it is important to note the difference in emphasis between Giddens and Blair in their respective perceptions of the causes of individualization and greater individualism (Driver and Martell, 2002). In essence, Blair attaches more importance than Giddens to the role that the Thatcherite right played in generating individualism through its promotion of materialism and egoism. Nevertheless by concurring with the view that globalization is fostering insecurity, Blair does concede that there is also a structural/global dimension to this development. As he declared in a speech given in Tokyo in January 1996: 'with globalization comes its offspring – insecurity. People feel, and are, less economically secure than ever before' (Blair, 1996: 120). In a speech he gave in South Africa in January 1999, Tony Blair elaborated in more detail upon this point, arguing that globalization is producing profound economic and social change which is unsettling for people. Economic change assumes a range of forms. For instance, the greater interconnectedness of globalization creates unease because it reduces the control we have over our lives. It means, for example, that decisions taken in one part of the world can have a profound impact upon another part. For Tony Blair, this economic change can render 'all jobs in industry, sometimes even new jobs in new industries, redundant overnight' (Blair, 1999). Meanwhile social change is evident in the fragmentation of societies and changes 'to culture, to life-style, to the family, to established patterns of community life' (Blair, 1999).

In response to these processes, the New Labour position is that British citizens will have to become more self-reliant and entrepreneurial. Hence the New Labour emphasis upon the role of government as facilitator or enabler, allowing us to develop our own talents and abilities. More specifically, the government is to provide the education, training and skills for individuals to operate in the new global market. This enabling state is evident in a range of policy areas, and it marks a shift away from the philosophy of protecting citizens 'from the cradle to the grave' which defined previous Labour administrations. In an interview that he gave on 27 October 1997, Tony Blair spelt out this change: 'the role of government is to organize and secure provision rather than fund it all' (Michel and Bouvet, 1998: 140). He elaborated upon this by referring to the example of pension reform, declaring that 'people will have to provide more of their own financial independence' with government playing 'a role in organising that system' (Michel and Bovet, 1998: 140). The notion of the enabling state is a further reason why New Labour cannot simply be equated with neo-liberalism. Blair believes the Thatcher governments that promoted this philosophy were unable or unwilling to deal with some of the consequences of globalization, including the challenges it presents to community and family life. Enabling citizens to cope with these changes requires forms of government intervention, ranging from education and training to measures buttressing family life (Blair, 1999).

The many different aspects to the New Labour project make defining it a difficult task, though this has been attempted by some writers (see Driver and Martell, 2002; Smith, 2004b). But as has been shown here, globalization, or at least a perception of what globalization entails, is doing much to shape New Labour thinking. In this regard, critics contend that New Labour is taking a distinctly political (neo-liberal) approach to globalization, and that there is no necessary reason for any government to do this. There is not a single or uniform way that globalization is operating dictating how governments should function; rather national governments themselves can do much more to shape its nature and course if they so choose. Moreover, according to Colin Hay (2002) Britain has actually been deglobalizing or regionalizing over the past 40 years in the sense that its levels of trade with Europe have significantly increased as levels of trade with the rest of the world have declined. Thus, from Hay's perspective, it is ideas about globalization rather than globalization *per se* that have shaped New Labour thinking.

But it has also been shown here that New Labour is more complex than is often allowed for. It is not simply pursuing a neo-liberal agenda. Social democratic concerns and policies can still be detected within the project, notably in New Labour's desire to end child poverty in the UK within 20 years. This is reflected in the significant increase in child benefit and income support for children as well as the new children's tax credit introduced in 2001. Likewise, many of New Labour's fiscal reforms, such as the working families' tax credit, have been geared towards helping the low paid and poor. Another key aim is to tackle social exclusion through such measures as the 'Sure Start' programme for pre-school children. New Labour also seeks to help those people whose lives are blighted by crime and disorder on problem housing estates through the introduction of a neighbourhood renewal programme: the New Deal for Communities. Nor is New Labour simply pro-business as many of its critics on the left maintain. It has introduced regulation within the workplace, notably the minimum wage, while in April 2003 there was even the sign of a return to tax and spend, with a 1 per cent increase in the rate of National Insurance for employers and employees.

This complexity is further evidenced by the apparent contradictions within some New Labour policies. The New Labour government has been pursuing a globalist form of social democracy in its desire to build international and regional alliances, yet in the recent Iraq war it arguably chose to ignore international opinion and institutions. Similarly, while it has been actively seeking to reduce the debt burden of developing societies, it also believes they must fully participate in the international economy, which some would argue contributed to their debts in the first place. But again globalization may well be lurking in the background here. From a New Labour perspective, it is essential that a country can fully operate and compete in the new global economy as to be able to do so is the basis for domestic policy, dictating the amount that can be spent on social-welfare provision, for example. In political terms, this might be expressed as follows: 'economic neo-liberalism enables the implementation of forms of social democracy'. However, what New Labour is up to is actually more complicated than this equation, as within some policies both neo-liberal and social democratic elements can be detected. Colin Crouch (2001) contends this can be seen within the New Deal, which combines the neo-liberal desire to improve the workings of the labour market with a social democratic emphasis upon providing support for workers, in the form of training and childcare provision. Driver and Martell conclude that New Labour's third way is perhaps most accurately viewed as 'a mix of values and approaches' (2002: 86).

Thus, New Labour's conception of the third way is a response to changing contemporary conditions, shaped to a significant extent by globalization. The project insists that a range of approaches and methods will have to be employed if the values to which it adheres are to be sustained in a rapidly changing world. New Labour's maxim is therefore not just 'whatever works', but 'whatever works in a rapidly changing world'.

For critics, there are problems with this approach. To begin with much rests upon whether the world is changing in the way and to the extent that those behind the New Labour project insist upon, which again returns us to their reading of globalization. Moreover, the values that New Labour pragmatically seeks to pursue are themselves a reflection of its own ideological perspective (Plant, 2001). Put simply, it is the values and not just the approaches it pursues that define New Labour. And these values, as might be expected, are a source of dispute. Blair maintains they are a part of the centre-left tradition; his critics regard him and New Labour as merely continuing the Thatcherite tradition (Hall, 1994, 2003; Hall and Jacques, 1997; Hay, 1999). It also seems, critics note, that the New Labour philosophy is really 'whatever works as long as it involves an extension of market principles and the private sector' (see, for example, Callinicos, 2001). As yet there has been no notable attempt to expand public sector involvement in different sectors of government and society.

Leaving aside this debate between New Labour and its critics, the aim here has been to map the ways in which globalization is shaping the third way, as espoused by Blair's government. In this regard, in summary, it is clear that New Labour is very much orientated towards responding to contemporary globalizing processes. This motive is informing a range of policy approaches, from how New Labour manages the economy to its education and training programmes, with the latter geared to preparing British citizens for the new global economy. Nevertheless, a social democratic impulse or conscience remains within the New Labour project and can be detected in a number of its policies – although of course social welfare must be accompanied by economic productivity. This in short is the New Labour conception of the third way: a politics for a new and changing era, as Tony Blair might say.

Globalization and Governance: An Emerging Consensus?

So far this chapter has focused upon the third way in relation to the New Labour government in the UK. The investigation will now be expanded in order to consider whether a consensus is emerging among Western governments on how they should respond to globalization. To put it another way, is there any evidence that third-wayism and the New Labour approach to globalization are becoming widely accepted and imitated? And if this is what is happening, are we witnessing a degree of political convergence among Western democracies and are we indeed 'all third-wayers now'

(Reich, 1999)? This is a vast topic. In order to make it more manageable, the Western democracies that will be examined will be those of Western Europe.

Aspects of the Blairite approach to governance and globalization can certainly be detected outside of the UK, even within governments that do not identify with the third way. In particular, the recent shift to the centre right in Europe – notably in Italy, Denmark, Austria, France, Portugal, the Netherlands and until March 2004 Spain – has seen the election of governments broadly in tune with New Labour ideas. Broadly speaking, there is an acceptance by these governments that globalization and specifically the globalization of trade and capital require open markets, trade liberalization, flexible labour markets and minimal governmental interference or regulation. Early in 1999 Tony Blair and the former Spanish premier José Maria Aznar launched a Joint Declaration calling for a revision of the employment policies of the European Union with greater emphasis upon deregulation (Coates, 1999: 3). Similarly, the outcome of a meeting between Blair and Silvio Berlusconi in February 2002 was an Anglo-Italian agreement to promote economic liberalization within the European Union, with the focus upon overhauling its 'rigid' labour laws (Carroll, 2002).[4] The Barcelona summit of March 2002 saw the member states of the EU take further steps towards economic liberalization, especially with regards to establishing more flexible energy and labour markets.

However, while those on the centre right in Western Europe have pursued many Blairite policies, if we were to be able to talk plausibly about political convergence then those on the centre left would also need to be adhering to this approach. But as will be shown, what has been taking place within continental social democracy is actually a more mixed picture. There is little point in trying to discern whether New Labour third-wayism is spreading throughout Europe by examining the electoral fortunes of social democratic parties. Indeed, it is difficult to discern any clear political patterns within continental Europe at this moment in time. At the end of the 1990s there seemed to be a revival of fortunes for social democratic parties, but this has been followed in the early years of the twenty-first century with a number of gains by the centre right throughout Western Europe.

Lack of space precludes this subject from being examined in great detail. Nevertheless, it will be argued that while in a general sense it is possible to detect certain recurring themes among a number of parties of the centre left in Europe on how best to deal with globalization, their responses are shaped to a significant extent by their respective national settings. This reinforces the need to take into account particular contexts – national cultures, the nature of political systems, historical traditions and so forth – when discussing globalization.

So, to what extent are social democrats in Western Europe adhering to the New Labour approach to globalization and governance? In considering this question it is worth noting that even before New Labour came to power, some social democratic parties in Western Europe were implementing elements of Blairism. Aspects of what New Labour considers 'modernized' social democracy, notably the promotion of work-orientated welfare systems, were developed by the Dutch PvdA and the Swedish SAP before Blair entered the international political arena – although in the case of the Netherlands, the adoption of such an approach had perhaps less to do with responding to globalization than an urgent need to tackle the country's very high level of unemployment (Anker, 2001).

As for globalization, what is notable is that there is broad acceptance of its existence among European social democrats. Little credence is given to sceptical attitudes towards globalization. There is also no tangible sense, even among socialist governments, that globalization can be held back – whether or not it can be shaped is considered in a moment. From this starting point, one area where there is a growing consensus among the European centre left is on the need for sound public finances, with particular emphasis placed upon controlling inflation (Clift, 2004a, 2004b). This may in part stem from a sense that global financial markets and currency speculators are continually sitting in judgement on the condition of national economies. As a result, many social democratic parties are now devoting greater attention to wealth creation. They have become, if not pro-business, certainly more aware of the important wealth-producing and employment-generating functions of business. As Blair and Schroeder declared in a joint paper on the third way project: 'The development of prosperous small and medium-sized businesses has to be a top priority for modern social democrats' (Blair and Schroeder, 1999: 34). In this vein, some social democrats in Western Europe, such as the Austrian SPO, share New Labour's attachment to supply-side reforms.

As touched upon earlier, New Labour is not alone in having a welfare programme that is especially geared to encouraging citizens to return to work. Sweden has had a welfare state similarly orientated around employment and training since the 1950s – although in Sweden there is more state involvement in employment creation than there is in the UK where New Labour's emphasis is upon the private sector (Huber and Stephens, 2001). As for the rest of Western Europe, what can be said is that welfare reform is high on the political agenda of many European social democratic parties. And many of them are adopting, as Ben Clift has noted, an 'employment-centred social policy' (Clift, 2004a: 51). New Labour is in accord with this approach. Of course, there are likely to be a number of reasons why European social democracies are pursing such an approach, ranging from globalization to concerns about sustaining ageing populations, as well as particular domestic considerations.

There is also some evidence of European social democrats developing similar positions with regards to the role of government and the state. The notion of national management, in both an economic and political sense, has become less evident within social democratic thinking. Instead, there is greater emphasis upon both devolved and multi-level governance (Gamble and Wright, 1999: 5). Central bank independence, for example, can be found in countries other than the UK, such as in Germany and Sweden. Meanwhile collectivist approaches in the form of nationalization programmes have been abandoned across Europe. Moreover, because it is seen as a way of curbing public spending, there is now wider acceptance that the private sector can play a role in the running of public services. For example, the former French socialist prime minister Lionel Jospin, despite seemingly having little in common with New Labour, privatized more state companies than his centre-right predecessor. In particular, it is claimed that Jospin effectively supported the partial privatization of France Telecom and Air France (Michel and Bouvet, 1998). As a result of this new thinking Andrew Gamble and Tony Wright believe there has been a blurring of the lines between 'market and state, between public and private' (1999: 5).

The implications of such similarities in approach among the European centre-left are provoking considerable discussion (see Giddens, 1998; Sassoon, 1999b; Vandenbroucke, 2001). Driver and Martell note that 'since the 1980s, in the face of globalization, European social democratic parties have edged within the constraints of national traditions towards economic liberalization and welfare reform' (2002: 224). Donald Sassoon argues that globalization has brought about a convergence, especially in European politics, between left and right – 'and largely unavoidably on the terms set by the Right' (Sassoon, 1998: 95). This is because globalization has 'contributed significantly to a realignment of the European Left away from its traditional terrain: a "national" social democracy based on a welfare state and full employment' (Sassoon, 1998: 95). For example, debates about equality, Sassoon argues, are increasingly about attaining equality of opportunity rather than, as in the past, equality of outcome through forms of economic redistribution such as taxation: 'equality, though still appealing as a goal, may be tempered by the need to preserve incentives and competition' (Sassoon, 1998: 96). For Sassoon this is evidence that the 'new pan-European Left has accepted the constraints of the new global capitalism' (1998: 95). And in a comparative study of New Labour and other examples of social democracy in Europe, Sassoon contends that on many issues 'Blair's modernisers are part of the mainstream' (1999a: 30).

However, what is actually taking place among European social democratic parties is perhaps more complex than Sassoon allows for. Andrew Gamble and Tony Wright (1999) contend in relation to recent developments within European social democracy that it is more appropriate to think in terms of new social democracies than in terms of a single new type of social democracy. Similarly, Ben Clift (2004b) and Frank Vandenbroucke (2001) have examined the extent of social democratic convergence and, while acknowledging that significant similarities have emerged among social democrats over a number of public policy areas, they note important national differences, particularly in the case of the UK. In part, this is undoubtedly because in contrast to New Labour, many continental governments are coalitions which means that social democratic parties have to make compromises and therefore find it more difficult to implement their own agendas. Tony Blair has the advantage of confronting not only a weak opposition in the shape of the Conservative Party but an opposition that broadly concurs with his modernization approach for Britain. Moreover, despite introducing devolution, the UK remains a unitary political system with a strong centralized state and weak local government, making it relatively easy for the New Labour agenda to be pushed through. In contrast, Germany's decentralized federal Länder system of government made it more difficult for Gerhard Schroeder's SPD to implement its political programme (Busch and Manow, 2001).

Above all there are numerous examples of European governments taking a different line towards globalization and governance from New Labour. In particular, there are many centre-left European parties that do not passively accept globalization and the global capitalist economy, as is effectively the case with New Labour. French socialists (the PS) and the Swedish and German social democrats, the SAP and SPD respectively, are especially critical of globalization – even if they do not believe that it can be held back – and openly advocate controlling it through political means (Clift, 2002). Among the Belgian social democrats there is similarly a belief that national governments can do more to shape the global economy, especially in relation to its impact upon domestic employment (Vandenbroucke, 1998). Moreover, in general, continental social democrats are less inclined than New Labour to adhere to the notion that in an era of globalization the demands of international competitiveness largely dictate domestic economic and social policy. Consequently, the amount of redistributive taxation and regulation in their economies as well as minimum wage levels are generally higher in Sweden, Germany, France and Belgium, than in the UK.

Thus, within continental Europe there are alternate conceptions of globalization from that held by New Labour, which in turn are producing different responses to it. This is especially evident in the area of employment. In contrast to the UK's flexible workforce approach, elsewhere in Europe, notably in Germany and Sweden, social democratic parties seek to ensure there is greater employment protection and rights for workers, including casual workers (Clift, 2004a). And, contrary to Sassoon's claim, while New Labour and many centre-left parties in Europe concur on the need for full employment, there are significant differences between them as to how this should be attained. The latter place greater stress upon the state as provider of employment – with some still attracted to Keynesian demand-side solutions – than does New Labour, which is more private sector and market orientated. The PS in France in particular is geared to generating employment via public spending as well as regulating the market in order to protect jobs. Furthermore, in countries like Sweden, levels of unemployment benefit are higher than they are in Britain – 80 per cent of previous income in the case of Sweden (Vartiainen, 1998).

Many of New Labour's continental counterparts also have a different understanding of equality. The Swedish SAP, for example, has not given up on egalitarianism in its traditional social democratic sense of entailing 'a fair redistribution of wealth' (Persson, 2001). The SAP's notion of equality therefore entails something more than New Labour's desire that everyone has a minimum of opportunities or life-chances, discussed earlier. Similarly, the PS in France has a conception of equality that goes beyond equality of opportunity and entails the French state playing a key role in ensuring this outcome (see Jospin, 2002). The Netherlands has a more open economy than France and is therefore more in line with the UK, but it nevertheless pursues more redistributive policies than the UK because it has a tradition of collaboration and consensus-building politics, discussed below. Overall, therefore, many centre-left parties on the continent do not share New Labour's approach to globalization and believe in a more interventionist role for the state in the running of their respective national economies and societies.

The existence of national variants of social democracy suggests that there are 'third ways' rather than a 'third way'. This is a point made by a number of commentators (see Driver and Martell, 2002; Kelly, 1999; Merkel, 2001; White, 1998). Stuart White (1998), for example, writes of 'not one third way, but many'. Similarly, Wolfgang Merkel (2001) identifies various third ways of social democracy, ranging from the market-oriented way of New Labour to the statist way of the French socialists.

How can we account for the different types of third-wayism or social democracy being pursued by parties of the centre left in Europe? The answer lies with the numerous historical, political, cultural and social factors and influences that exist in the societies from which these parties have emerged. In this vein, Charles Lees (2001), in his analysis of Germany and Britain, has sketched out the ways in which institutions and structures of governance can influence the nature and form of social democratic projects. It is also the case that political parties possess their own intellectual heritage and political traditions, which shape their goals and approaches to policy-making. Some centre-left parties in Western Europe will have been influenced by their encounters with Marxism, which were often manifested as struggles with communist parties. In contrast, New Labour was clearly shaped by the legacy of Thatcherism, rather than Marxism. As a result, the governments of Germany, Sweden, France and the Netherlands work much more closely with the unions in policy-formulation than New Labour because their corporatist cultures have not been diminished to the same extent. New Labour's Thatcherite inheritance has entailed that in the UK there is a greater emphasis upon privatization, competition, individualism and neo-liberalism than can be found elsewhere in Europe where more statist and co-operative traditions persist. The Dutch have what is known as the 'Poldermodel', which is a more social democratic consensual approach to politics involving government in constructive negotiations with interested and relevant non-state organizations and interests groups in particular areas of policy-making (see Anker, 2001). Similarly, the approach of the PS mentioned above, which in some ways stands at odds with the modernization of social democracy, reflects France's public-sector and statist tradition. Indeed, the nature of French political culture was evident in the regional elections held at the end of March 2004, in which Jacques Chirac's centre-right governing UMP party suffered a crushing defeat. Commentators believe this was largely because the French voters did not like the implementation of the UMP's public sector reforms, which were perceived as Blairite and a threat to the French way of life.

There are also economic influences that condition the form that social democracy takes within countries. Some parties will be confronted with particular economic problems, such as budget deficits, which may well determine the version of social democracy that they pursue, notably in relation to the amount of money that can be committed to public spending. In its first term, New Labour was especially concerned to reduce the UK's budget deficit, as well as adhere to the previous Conservative government's spending plans during its first two years in office, and this had considerable implications for the type of policies it pursued. At a more general level, the economic cultures of particular countries will do much to shape their respective policies. New Labour is greatly influenced by the Anglo-Saxon or Anglo-American model of capitalism, which is laissez-faire and market-orientated in comparison with the more collaborative social market approach – sometimes termed the 'Rheinland' model of capitalism – prevalent on the continent (Driver and Martell, 2002). In addition the demands of EU convergence and membership of the euro also exert a pressure upon the fiscal policies pursued by European governments, notably in the form of the Growth and Stability Pact. And as will be argued in Chapter 3, EU integration is itself in part a response to globalization.

In sum, it is possible to detect certain similarities in approach among social democratic parties within Europe, and globalization is contributing to this development. However, 'certain similarities' is not the same as 'convergence', and significant differences in philosophy and approach remain. In essence, national conditions and factors will continue to hinder such convergence. This means that Donald Sassoon's claim about the 'unifying force of globalization' needs to be balanced by recognition of how particular contexts shape responses to globalization as well as the political programmes of social democratic parties, in general. As is claimed throughout this work, the 'effects' of globalization emerge from particular interacting contexts. We should therefore not be surprised by the existence of different social democratic perspectives on the nature and significance of globalization, as well as on appropriate responses to it.

On a related issue, despite national variations, the extent of the similarities over policies and the lack of ideological debate between major political parties within countries may in part explain why growing numbers of citizens in Western democracies are becoming disengaged from mainstream politics. Political disputes are increasingly about technical competence and leadership abilities rather than ideological principles, often focussing upon image and personality politics. Most citizens are unlikely to be aware of the particular details and nuances of the debates between supply-siders and Keynesian demand-managers. Rather, they are confronted with mainstream political parties on both the left and the right developing policies for a more globalized era that combine a mixture of state and market strategies, and private and public sectors.

Geoffrey Garrett (1998) contests the notion that globalization has eroded partisan politics, claiming that when powerful left-of-centre parties are allied with strong and centralized trade union movements, social democracy continues to be a distinctive force. But Garrett's work has itself been challenged. For example, Colin Hay believes that while globalization may not yet have 'laid waste the social democratic welfare state, it may well still be the case that this is precisely the view to which social democrat politicians have increasingly been converted' (2000: 150–1). Hay concludes 'that social democratic corporatism may not have been undermined by globalization *per se*; but it may very well have been undermined by ideas about globalization – ideas about its corrosive effects on welfare states and encompassing labour market institutions' (2000: 151).

Conclusions

The main purpose of this examination of the third way has been to provide an example of the ways in which globalization is informing everyday life within a particular society, in this case, the UK. New Labour has a particular conception of globalization and how best to respond to it. It therefore formulates policy accordingly, which in turn impacts upon the lives of British citizens. This is one, albeit very important, way in which British people experience globalization. And Tony Blair has been quite explicit about the role that globalization has played in the development of the third way. As he declared in a speech that he gave in South Africa in January 1999: 'The driving force behind the ideas associated with the third way is globalization because no country is immune from the massive change that globalization brings' (Blair, 1999).

But the aim here has not been to determine the accuracy or appropriateness of the New Labour conception of globalization. While many critics of New Labour's approach to globalization have been cited during the course of this discussion, this has been in order to highlight the way in which New Labour is dealing with this phenomenon. These critics will of course have their own conceptions of globalization, which in part will be shaped by their political views and agendas. All of which merely reinforces the point made earlier: that globalization is a contested phenomenon. Ultimately, whether New Labour or its critics have a better understanding of, or approach to, globalization is not significant in relation to the central concerns of this work. Rather the focus here is upon identifying the ways in which globalization is being perceived, interpreted and experienced, and how these in turn are shaping attitudes and behaviour. This approach will hopefully provide new insight into the nature of globalization and the impact it is having in the contemporary period.

The danger in focusing upon the role globalization has played in shaping New Labour's third way is that other factors and influences are neglected. Subsequent analyses of New Labour's political programme would therefore need to balance this approach with more detailed consideration of non-globalizing influences.[5] Indeed, New Labour's approach to globalization has almost certainly been conditioned by factors such as the legacy of Thatcherism and changes within British society.[6] Nevertheless, it has hopefully been shown that there is considerable merit in viewing the New Labour project as constituting a fairly concerted response to the realities of globalization, as perceived by its leading figures.

Finally, in relation to the debate about an emerging consensus on governance and globalization among mainstream political parties in Western Europe, we may be witnessing an unwelcome reaction to this development. More specifically, some writers consider that the emergence of the radical or extreme right is in part a response to the convergence of the political left and right in European societies (see for example Delanty and O'Mahony, 2002). The third way and the coming together of left and right that it entails – the so-called 'politics of the new centre' (Hombach, 2000) – have enabled the radical right to position itself as an ideological and political alternative. In the context of the dissipation of traditional left–right positions and debates, the radical right is now able to present itself as offering something distinct from the political consensus. The rise of the extreme right in Europe, and the ways in which the processes of contemporary globalization may have contributed to this development are the concern of the next chapter.

Summarizing Points

- Globalization has been the central justification for the third way.
- Opponents of New Labour and other new social democratic parties argue that New Labour has uncritically accepted a neo-liberal conception of globalization.
- Globalization is encouraging many political parties to rethink the role of government and the state, especially in relation to the citizenry.
- Globalization is associated with wider socio-economic processes, such as post-industrialism and detraditionalization.
- While it is possible to detect common responses to globalization among social democracies, national variations remain.

−2−

Globalization and Conflict in Contemporary Europe

This chapter examines the ways in which globalizing processes are impacting upon patterns of conflict and identity-formation within contemporary Europe. More specifically, the focus will be upon an increasingly heard argument that globalization and related processes are creating uncertainty and generating insecurity which is encouraging a retreat into the familiar and the tribal in the form of national, ethnic and cultural identities (Barber, 1996; Bauman, 1996; Horsman and Marshall, 1995). Within Europe evidence of this phenomenon, it is maintained, can be seen in the resurgence of the extreme right in many countries, the recent rise of ethnic conflict and escalating levels of racial violence.[1] It is also reflected in concerns expressed in some European states that aspects of globalization, such as higher levels of migration and American cultural imperialism, erode local cultures and national 'ways of life'.

Mathew Horsman and Andrew Marshall argue this retreat by individuals into communities defined by 'similarities of religion, culture, ethnicity, or some other shared experience' (1995: x) constitutes a form of tribalism and is happening throughout the world. The focus of this chapter, however, will be upon ethnic, national and racial identities within Europe.[2] While 'tribalism' is an imprecise term, it will be employed here as a convenient catch-all concept to describe the patterns of behaviour that have been outlined above. This chapter will begin by outlining in more detail what has been taking place in Europe during the recent period, before going on to consider the arguments that have been raised suggesting 'tribal' attitudes and identities are being provoked or stimulated by globalization.

It will be argued that globalization can only partly account for the reinvigoration of 'tribal' identities within Europe. There have been other factors contributing to this phenomenon, such as the end of the Cold War and the role played by the media in some countries, which have little or nothing to do with globalization. Most importantly, if we are to determine the influence that globalization is having upon these developments, we need to take into account the way its processes are working within particular regions and areas within Europe, which are in turn informed by historical, cultural and other influences.

Forms of Tribalism within Europe

A number of discernible forms of tribalist behaviour have emerged within Europe in the recent period. For instance, there has been an increase in racist violence in many parts of Europe since the 1980s (Björgo and Witte, 1993). Attacks have been directed against groups such as immigrants and refugees, as well as minorities who have lived in Europe for generations, such as Jews and Roma people, while ethnic Hungarians have faced difficulties and hostility in Slovakia, Romania and the former Yugoslavia. Some violent racist incidents have attracted international attention, such as the desecration of Jewish graves in Carpentras in France (1990) and the violence against African street vendors in Florence (1990). Racist attacks against asylum seekers in Germany – specifically in Hoyerswerda (1991) and Rostock (1992) and the racist murder of three Turkish women in Mölln (1992) – attracted external criticism and deep unease within the country. A few years later, in January 1996, ten migrant workers were killed in an arson attack in Lübeck.

There has also been a notable growth in support for extreme nationalist parties and far-right groups since the late 1980s (see Ford, 1992).[3] In France, the Front National (FN) is a significant political force, especially in the south of the country, and this is despite suffering a recent and major internal split within the party. Indeed, in April 2002, 17 per cent of the French electorate voted for Le Pen in the first round of the presidential elections enabling him to stand in the second round (see Neocleous and Startin, 2003). In Austria, Joerg Haider's Freedom Party (FPÖ), an extreme nationalist, anti-immigrant party, gained enough votes to form a coalition government following the election of February 2000. Similarly, in Italy, the Lega Nord (Northern League) – a strongly anti-immigrant party – has been involved in power-sharing with the Berlusconi government. In Belgium, the far-right Vlaams Blok party became the largest political grouping in Antwerp in October 2001, and wants to repatriate all non-European foreigners. In Denmark, a centre-right coalition underpinned by the ultra-right Danish People's Party swept to power in the November 2001 election and has drafted tough new asylum policies and cut aid to the developing world. In Portugal, a right-wing coalition which includes the fiercely anti-immigration Popular Party won power in March 2001. While in the Netherlands, Lijst Pim Fortuyn (LPF), the party formerly led by the flamboyant anti-immigration politician Pim Fortuyn, emerged from political obscurity to become the second largest party in the 2002 general election – although commentators consider this result was influenced by the assassination of Pim Fortuyn a week before the polls opened (Bruff, 2003). In Norway, an administration propped up by the far-right Progress Party took office in October 2001. The Progress Party wants to cap immigration to 1,000 people per year. Of equal concern is that in some European countries mainstream political parties appear to be adapting their political programme to woo voters of the extreme right. Finally, in Switzerland, the anti-immigrant far-right People's Party, the SVP, has become a major political force in

Swiss politics. In the general elections of October 2003, the SVP secured 27.7 per cent of the vote – more than any other party (Harding, 2003).

The examples cited thus far are all confined to Western Europe. However, an increase in racist violence, far-right activity (see Szayna, 1997), extreme nationalism and xenophobia is also evident in many former communist countries in Central and Eastern Europe. There is, for instance, a growing skinhead culture in Poland, Hungary, East Germany, the Czech Republic and Slovakia (Hockenos, 1993). In the Czech Republic, for example, it is estimated that there are many thousands of skinheads and there is considerable evidence that Czech skinhead groups have contacts with other far-right organizations in Europe, such as Combat 18 in Britain. There are also persistent violent attacks upon the Roma population within the Czech Republic, especially in parts of Bohemia.

In Poland, since the fall of communism a Christian nationalist right has gained increasing prominence and claims of anti-Semitism have been raised against it and Solidarity, the leading independence movement (see Hockenos, 1993). In Russia, nationalist extremism is doing much to destabilize the nascent liberal democracy, which undoubtedly reflects the profound changes Russian society has undergone in the recent period (see Cox and Shearman, 2000). There are numerous radical-right and ultranationalist groups in Russia, and they are attracting an increasing amount of support from young people (Tolz, 1997). In this regard, the Liberal Democratic Party – an extreme Russian nationalist party led by Vladimir Zhirinovsky – captured 23.4 per cent of the vote in the elections to the Russian parliament (Duma) of December 1993.

There is also considerable recent evidence of the vigour of nationalist forces in this part of Europe. It was nationalism, as well as a desire for freedom, that brought communism to an end in the region. The movement or force that swept across Central and Eastern Europe in 1989 rejected the influence of Moscow and sought national independence. Since then we have witnessed the emergence of a destructive and bloody ethnic nationalism in the Balkans to the extent that 'ethnic cleansing' has become part of our vocabulary. And still nationalist tensions simmer in Serbia, Montenegro, Macedonia, Kosovo and Albania.

It is sometimes suggested that we should not be surprised about current patterns of ethnic nationalism, virulent racism and far-right activity in Europe as such practices have been evident for generations, notably in the pogroms of Eastern Europe and the period of Nazi rule in Germany. Indeed, many cultural critics – such as the late Edward Said and A. Sivanandan – have argued that Europe is constructed upon ideologies associated with race, such as nationalism, imperialism and anti-Semitism, evident in the colonial past of many European countries.

Europe's dark past cannot and should not be denied. Yet it was widely assumed – or perhaps just naïvely hoped – that the Second World War (and specifically the Nazi death camps) was a defining moment in European history, never to be repeated. And it is of course important not to exaggerate or overestimate recent events. What has been going on since the early 1990s is nowhere near on the scale of what took place in the 1940s. Nonetheless we do appear to be witnessing something of a revival of such forces in our own time. The task of this chapter is to try to determine whether aspects of globalization might be contributing to this revival.

Globalization and the Retreat into Tribalism

In this section, the arguments and claims suggesting that globalizing processes are contributing to a 'retreat into tribalism' will be examined. This will entail looking at the possible linkage between globalization and insecurity; the issue of cultural separatism in age of migration; the notion or reality of the retreating state; and, lastly, the impact of global communications. These will now be considered in turn.

Globalization and Insecurity

Writers like Anthony Giddens (1999) and Ulrich Beck (2000a, 2000b) believe globalization cannot be viewed in isolation. Rather they view it as inextricably linked to processes such as post-industrialism and detraditionalization (or 'reflexive modernization') that define our late modern age. For example, one of the main connections between post-industrialism and globalization is the developments in communications and information technologies. These developments have facilitated the establishment of post-industrial working practices. They have also made it easier for companies to relocate abroad and in so doing have contributed to globalization. From the perspective of those living in European societies, especially in Western Europe, these developments have often meant seeing their jobs being transferred to low-wage economies in the developing world (see Brewer, 1990; Harris, 1990). Hence for many people, as will be discussed further in a moment, their personal experience of globalization can be one of economic upheaval and social dislocation.

Similarly, some aspects of globalization are considered to be disruptive of tradition. For instance, the emergence of a global culture may erode national traditions and cultures. The spread of market principles and mechanisms via (the Anglo-American model of) globalization is also widely viewed as operating in this way: traditional institutions and forms of authority become simply within the market place and their aura and authority are undermined. In the UK, for example, political parties, schools, government and even the royal family have all undergone this process in recent years, and this may in part account for their decline in public esteem. And once these traditions and traditional institutions have been challenged their former authority cannot be regained. Thus, as will be shown in Chapter 3, we enter a late modern age: a period of reflexive modernization in which we are freer from the traditions and customs of the past and more able to forge our own life paths.

However, these developments are also perceived to be contributing to an 'age of uncertainty', in which the fixed identities, structures and certainties of the past are increasingly absent in everyday life. We have greater individual freedom and choice, including in our personal relationships, but this can foster insecurity: we are less able to rely upon others and build permanent relationships based upon a high degree of trust. And as mentioned above, globalization and its related processes can create considerable job insecurity. Under the new conditions, not only is there the ongoing prospect that a company will relocate to another region or country, but the employment offered by companies – as a result of the globalization of markets and the spread of communications and information technologies – is increasingly of the freelance or subcontracted variety. Meanwhile the flexibility and geographical mobility which are required in, as Beck (2000b) has termed it, 'the brave new world of work', have contributed to the break-up of traditional work-based communities and put pressure upon personal relationships.

Many people have responded to living in an 'age of uncertainty' by resorting to individualistic strategies and focusing upon the private realm (Beck and Beck-Gernsheim, 2002; Hopper, 2003). However, some commentators contend that these conditions encourage tribalist patterns of behaviour. In particular, it is argued that the search for security and stability has led some people to try to rediscover old certainties and commonalities in the form of ethnic, racial and national identities. This tendency is encapsulated in Zygmunt Bauman's declaration that: '[t]he dissipation of the social rebounds in the consolidation of the tribal. As identities go, privatization means tribalization' (1996: 57).

Horsman and Marshall essentially concur with this view. They consider the retreat into tribalism to be 'driven by fear and confusion, and fed by the reassuring "sameness" of others in the group' (Horsman and Marshall, 1995: x). The human need for a sense of belonging is widely recognized. In this respect, Anthony Giddens (1990) stresses the psychological appeal of nationalism and its ability to satisfy our need for a sense of identity, considering it to be especially necessary under modern conditions in which processes like globalization have led to the 'disembedding' of experience of a specific time and space. Benjamin Barber (1996) goes further declaring the resurgence of ethnic nationalism to be part of a wider reaction against globalization that constitutes a 'Jihad against McWorld'. As he puts it: 'the forces I identify with Jihad are impetuously demanding to know whether there will ever be a Serbia again, a Flanders again ... or Catalonia again' (Barber, 1996: 164). Likewise, Manuel Castells (1997) argues that contemporary forms of nationalism constitute 'resistance identities' in the sense that adherents feel threatened by globalization and associated developments. This type of national reaction is therefore defensive, but one which is 'always affirmed against the alien' (Castells, 1997: 27). This point will be returned to later.

Further support for this position can be identified in the work of Alberto Melucci (1989). He contends that as the bases for group membership, such as class, erode in increasingly complex, individualistic and differentiated societies, ethnic identity has considerable appeal. Above all it offers forms of solidarity that are 'based on a language, a culture and an ancient history' (Melucci, 1989: 92). Likewise, Ulrich Beck and Elizabeth Beck-Gernsheim (1996) see a retreat into ethnic identity stemming from the 'precarious freedoms' we are confronted with as a result of the process of individualization. They raise the question of what is 'to integrate highly individualized societies?' (Beck and Beck-Gernsheim, 1996: 43). And they consider that the rebirth of nationalism and ethnic conflicts in Europe has been a response to this dilemma. Nationalism and ethnic conflicts constitute a tried and trusted means of dealing with challenges and difficult conditions: turning inwards for protection – and the reassurance of sameness – while turning against those perceived as 'outsiders' (Beck and Beck-Gernsheim, 1996: 43).

Another writer supportive of this position is Michel Wieviorka (1994). He has sought to identify the reasons for the recent rise of racist activity in Europe, and especially in France. The particular aspect of the 'age of uncertainty' that Wieviorka concentrates upon is post-industrialism or post-Fordism, which he views as a major socio-economic transformation, or as he puts it, 'une grande mutation' (1994: 178). For Wieviorka, this new epoch is defined by a shift away from collective action – with the individual becoming increasingly isolated from his or her work colleagues – and the marginalization or permanent exclusion of some people from mainstream society. As Wieviorka notes: '[t]hose who are "out", or fear to be, have a feeling of injustice and loss of previous social identity' (1994: 179). The individual is able, Wieviorka contends, to find new forms of collective behaviour and group identity by turning to race and ethnicity; thus he or she is able once again to feel part of a group. Ethnic revival and even forms of racist activity therefore permit a degree of reorganization of society and an escape from isolated individualism.

Wilhelm Heitmeyer (1993) takes a similar line with regards to the rise of racism and racial violence in Germany, a phenomenon mainly linked to young people. He considers this to be a result of the process of individualization that modern societies like Germany have undergone. The concomitant decline in social and communal life means social status and social identity are no longer 'givens', but have to be achieved through personal effort with a great risk of failure. In response, some young Germans are defining their identity in terms of race and nationality; they find some sense of belonging in close-knit racial groups. And for some such membership requires involvement in racist violence as a way of proving and demonstrating their identity. As Heitmeyer puts it: '[w]hen natural social membership and acceptance disintegrate to such an extent that only the certainty of being German remains, then violence is given a direction' (1993: 27). The fact that the growth of the extreme right and the increased incidents of racial violence have been mainly in the former GDR would seem to reinforce Heitmeyer's claim about the influence of individualization. This region has undergone massive economic restructuring in the transformation to a market society. The collective security and protection once provided by the GDR

– notably in the form of jobs and public housing – have come to an end. And in adapting to the new conditions, the GDR's former citizens have had to become more self-reliant and independent.

Cultural Separatism in an Age of Migration

Globalization entails that we are confronted with 'the Other' upon almost a daily basis – and as Stuart Hall (1996) has observed, identity is forged in the relationship between us and 'the Other'. The greater movement of peoples across the globe for all sorts of business, cultural and other reasons means we encounter more frequently than in the past those of other societies and different cultures. Some people, however, will try to resist these developments and hold on to old certainties in the form of national identities, traditions and 'ways of life'. In a sense this is a reaction against contemporary life, described by Eric Hobsbawm in the following way: 'Wherever we live in an urbanized society, we encounter strangers: uprooted men and women who remind us of the fragility or the drying up of our own families' roots' (1992: 173).

This type of reaction can be seen within many European countries. It is reflected in debates about the impact of globalization and patterns of migration upon national cultures. In particular, asylum seekers and economic migrants, and how to deal with them, have become a key political issue in most states within the EU. In response, many national governments have sought to assuage any fears their citizens may have over the security of their jobs and access to welfare states. They have largely done this, in conjunction with the EU, by tightening immigration controls, restricting the movement of 'non-Europeans' within Europe and building what has been termed 'Fortress Europe' – an issue that is dealt with in more detail in the next chapter.

The extreme right in Europe has sought to exploit concerns about the potential erosion of national cultures, arguing that aspects of globalization are leading to a blurring of cultures and the loss of national distinctiveness. For example, the Republican Party in Germany and the National Front in France have emphasized cultural separatism and the right of people to their own national identity and culture within their own country, which, they argue, can only be attained by limiting immigration.[4] While in Austria, the spectacular growth in support for Joerg Haider's Freedom Party (FPÖ) in the late 1990s was to a significant extent based upon its anti-immigration agenda. Austria is one of the richest countries in the world per capita and its level of unemployment is among the lowest in Europe. However, the Freedom Party tapped into a long-standing fear of mass immigration, which was heightened at the time by the prospect of eastern countries joining the European Union (Batha, 2000). Indeed, in a 1997 poll, 42 per cent of Austrians admitted to some degree of racism and xenophobia, compared with an EU average of 33 per cent (Batha, 2000).

Similar forms of resistance to globalization are evident in the endeavours of many national governments and political parties to protect aspects of national life, such as their language, customs and culture. Often the cultural threat is perceived to come from America and to constitute a form of Americanization.[5] The National Front in France, for instance, has often raised concerns about US cultural hegemony, even expressing hostility towards Euro-Disney.[6] Mainstream French politicians have declared that American fast-food restaurants are changing the country's gastronomic habits and thereby eroding French culture (Ritzer, 1998: 73), while in recent years French governments have attempted to preserve the French language and endeavoured to limit the number of American films that can be shown in France in order to protect its indigenous film industry.[7] One French citizen, José Bové, has become a kind of folk hero for his stand against globalization, which has involved wrecking a McDonald's restaurant.

The concerns expressed within Europe about Americanization and US cultural hegemony are often articulated in terms of 'cultural imperialism'. However, as John Tomlinson (1999) notes, the cultural imperialism thesis has been subject to considerable criticism largely because it is unable to encompass the complex and multidimensional nature of globalization.[8] As Joseph Nye observes in his book on American power: 'Globalization is more than just Americanization' (2002: 81). Similarly, Anthony Giddens is right when he contends that globalization 'affects the United States as it does other countries' (1999: 4). Indeed, it is not even the case that globalization is ushering in a global monoculture, American or otherwise. Far from producing cultural uniformity, the processes of globalization are allowing people to become more aware of fashions, music and lifestyles from across the globe, with many choosing to 'mix and match', incorporating aspects of other cultures into their everyday life. Nor does globalization mark the end of local traditions. If anything, global communications – notably the Internet – have allowed for local customs and products (such as foodstuffs and crafts) to gain a much wider audience and thereby help to ensure their continuation.

However, in a sense it does not matter that the notion of cultural imperialism has lost some credibility among academics. Crucially, to return to a stated theme of this work, within Europe and beyond globalization is widely perceived and interpreted in this way. Tomlinson rightly notes that globalization has become part of the general cultural vocabulary of modern societies' (1999: 80). And rightly or wrongly, many people within Europe believe that globalization has entailed the further encroachment of American culture into European societies.[9] A survey undertaken in the mid 1990s revealed that many European – including 61 per cent of French citizens, 45 per cent of Germans, and 32 per cent of Italians – perceived American culture as threat to their own culture (Nye, 2002: 70–1). Reflecting such concerns, the EU unsuccessfully attempted in 1997 to enact legislation ensuring that at least half of all television programmes shown in Europe were domestic products (Hertsgaard, 2002: 178).

The Retreating State

Another way in which globalization may be contributing to 'tribalist' patterns of behaviour relates to the challenge it poses to the nation-state. Commentators such as Guéhenno (1995), Ohmae (1990) and Wriston (1992) argue that the processes that constitute globalization are eroding the ability of national governments to manage their own economies, including performing a social welfare role. Moreover, substantive economic and political decision-making is increasingly the preserve of non-state institutions and organizations. As a result, it means ordinary citizens have little or no input into governmental processes. This is perhaps reflected in declining voter turnout across Europe. No longer as able to rely upon their national government or state for support, some people are turning their back on national politics and political parties and taking matters into their own hands by seeking local solutions (Miles, 1994; Starr, 2000). Rather than simply accepting and identifying with a particular nation-state, people are redefining *their* communities.

These changing attitudes are, it is claimed, reflected in the growth of identity politics. They are also evident in the difficulties some nation-states are having in containing ethnic nationalist demands for autonomy and separatism. Since the early 1990s there has been a trend within Europe towards the formation of more ethnically homogeneous and exclusive states, evident in the break-up of the former Soviet Union and Yugoslavia, and in the division of Czechoslovakia in 1993 into separate Czech and Slovak states. Russians living in Estonia and Latvia have faced pressure from indigenous nationalist movements to restrict their civic rights; a move which runs counter to the Enlightenment principle of universal citizenship upon which the nation-state has generally been constructed within Western Europe. It is a development that George Schöpflin (1996) believes can be identified elsewhere in Eastern Europe, where some post-communist governments, such as the Slovak and Romanian governments, have favoured forms of political representation that are more geared to ethnic and national coherence than inclusiveness.

It is not just in Central and Eastern Europe where this phenomenon can be detected. Separatist or independence movements have become a significant factor in the domestic politics of countries like Belgium, Italy and Spain; and within the UK, Scotland and Wales now enjoy greater autonomy as a result of devolution. John Newhouse contends that Europe's rising regionalism rather than the European Union constitutes 'the larger threat to the authority of the nation-state' (1998: 36).

Taken together these developments lead Horsman and Marshall (1995) to question the future viability of the nation-state in its present form. Likewise, Benjamin Barber notes contemporary '"nationalists" boast about their deconstructive potential and revel in hostility to the state and other constituencies that make up the state' (1996: 165). 'Exit the nation-state, enter the tribes' is Zygmunt Bauman's succinct description of this state of affairs (1993: 141).

It is the economic dimensions of globalization that are especially viewed as challenging the nation-state and reinforcing national or tribal positions. In this regard, it is interesting to note that some extreme-right parties in Europe, such as the FN in France and the FPÖ in Austria, consider free trade to pose a threat to their country's economic and national interests.[10] The former described global free trade as a 'war without pity' in one of its programmes (Front National, 1993: 244). Indeed, the FN favours a form of economic protectionism as part of its 'national preference' programme. It also sought the suspension of France's participation in the General Agreement on Tariffs and Trade (GATT) negotiations on world trade. These policies stem directly from the belief that France as a result of globalization is facing greater economic competition, not just from traditional rivals and their multinationals, but also from newly industrializing countries (NICs).

In short, 'globalization' is perceived as a threat to national ways of life by numerous radical right-wing populist parties, especially in Western Europe, and presented as such to their respective electorates. It does not matter whether globalization actually constitutes such a threat; these parties and their supporters seemingly care little about academic debates concerning such matters. Instead, they choose to interpret globalization in a particular sense, ranging from the claim that it is undermining the authority of national governments to the contention that it dilutes national cultures. In this regard, aspects of globalization are also considered to erode national frontiers. This is reflected in the fact that the FN started to campaign for the reintroduction of customs controls at the borders during the 1990s (Betz, 1994: 129). Similarly, an important feature of the Freedom Party's vision of European integration is a customs union, as well as a common security pact (Haider, 1993: 283).

Global Communications

Many commentators insist that there is another aspect of our post-industrial global age contributing to ethnic mobilization. That is the developments in electronic media and communications technology, which facilitate the work of informal or non-state networks and organizations. These developments are enabling ethnic communities and nationalist groups to disseminate their message, paving the way for the establishment of world-wide support networks, especially among emigrant and diaspora populations who are able to maintain contacts with their 'homeland' (Richmond, 1984; Schlesinger, 1991). At the same time far-right groups are increasingly using the Internet to spread their message. For example, an annual report by Germany's intelligence agency on extremist threats, published in April 2000, warned that far-right German groups had set up some 300 web sites (BBC World Service, 4 April 2000).

These developments are a reflection of greater interconnectedness, which, as was suggested in the Introduction, is one of the defining features of globalization. The cases highlighted here can be viewed as evidence of time–space compression, the greater velocity of global flows and the extensiveness of global networks (Giddens, 1990; Harvey, 1989; Held et al., 1999). They may also reflect deterritorialization, providing examples of the ways in which our cultural practices, experiences and identities are becoming separated from the places we inhabit (Tomlinson, 1999). Many of the groups and organizations mentioned above, however, are reacting against deterritorialization and seeking to promote the importance of attachment to their respective territories. In this sense they are an indication of the persistence of territoriality.

Globalization and Tribalism: Some Doubts

To recap, the argument of this chapter is that globalization is at best only a partial answer to the increased significance of ethnic, national and racial identities within Europe in the recent period.[11] And that the actual ways in which globalizing processes are operating within and impacting upon Europe are much more complex than this correlation allows for, dependent as they are upon particular contexts, local conditions, and so forth. In justifying this contention it will now be shown that some of the linkages between globalization and tribalist patterns of behaviour made in the previous section are far from proven. The discussion will focus upon four areas: first, the issue of the retreating state in relation to globalization; second, an examination of the European context; third, the role of the mass media in stirring-up tribalist patterns of behaviour; and, fourth, whether globalization might generate cosmopolitanism rather than tribalism.

From the outset, however, it should be noted that a major difficulty in considering the impact of globalization upon identity-formation and forms of conflict in Europe lies in the lack of consensus over what globalization actually is. Indeed, as was outlined in the Introduction, it is possible to identify three broad approaches to globalization. To remind the reader, writers who adhere to these approaches have been labelled *globalizers*, *sceptics* and *transformationalists* (see Held et al., 1999). And in terms of this particular discussion, if there are such divergent views on globalization – and one of these schools of thought even questions its existence – it makes it difficult to talk about its effects. Put simply, how can we be sure that globalization provokes 'tribal' identities and attitudes when we are unclear about what we mean by globalization? Following on from this, how can we be certain that globalization is fostering insecurity? Moreover, to make such a claim risks overlooking the fact that some people are flourishing under contemporary conditions, notably enjoying the increased opportunities to travel and experience different cultures, and are benefiting from global communications technologies and the greater access to information they afford.

Is the State Really Retreating?

A number of commentators have questioned the idea that globalization undermines the nation-state and the ability of national governments to act independently. Hirst and Thompson (2000) consider this to be one of the 'myths of globalization', enabling politicians to play down their responsibility for the management of their respective national economies. In reality, European governments have much more influence upon our lives now, and perform many more functions, compared with, say, 50 years ago. Writers like Rosenau (1997) believe that, rather than simply being in decline or retreat, the role and authority of national government are merely being redefined in response to the growing complexity of processes of governance in a more interconnected world.

Hirst and Thompson contend that the major economic nations in the world retain the capacity, especially if they co-ordinate policy, to exert governance over financial markets and other economic tendencies. Global markets are therefore not beyond regulation and control. Indeed, as mentioned in the Introduction, an obvious example of how national governments shape the global agenda is the fact that the neo-liberal policies facilitating globalization have been actively promoted by successive administrations in the US and the UK.

Moreover, even if the arguments for the retreating state are accepted, this does not necessarily pave the way for tribalism. More specifically, the claim that the individualization fostered by globalization and related processes has led to the search for forms of collective identity and security in the shape of ethnic and national groups requires closer scrutiny. As mentioned above, for many people the new conditions, far from producing feelings of insecurity, allow for greater autonomy and provide new opportunities. Breaking from the structures, practices, codes and traditions of the past can be viewed as a liberating experience, and many people will therefore have no need to turn to their particular tribe or group. Thus, for a variety of reasons there must be some doubt as to whether tribalism, in the form described by Horsman and Marshall and others, has emerged because of the challenges that nation-states face from globalization.

However, to return to a point made in the previous section, it has to be conceded that many groups and parties of the extreme right in Europe are seeking to exploit, as well as promote, the view that globalization challenges national cultures and ways of life. This reinforces the need to examine how globalization is perceived and provides a further indication that it is a contested phenomenon.

The Importance of the European Context

The primary reason the linkage between globalization and tribalism should be questioned is that as an explanation it operates at the level of broad trends and does not allow for the importance of local conditions. These conditions constitute the context in which globalization is interpreted and experienced by the peoples and societies of Europe, and which will largely come to determine any effects that its processes will have. Moreover, by adopting this approach to globalization it soon becomes apparent that there have been other important developments within Europe contributing to the resurgence of national and ethnic identities.

For example, the collapse of the communist or state socialist regimes in Eastern Europe not only brought to an end the Cold War but arguably enabled forms of ethnic and cultural nationalism to flourish. In particular, many of the recently independent nations, such as the Baltic States, have been actively promoting their national culture and history as way of consolidating their independence. This point will be returned to later.

Meanwhile within Western Europe the resurgence of the far right and the rise in racist violence have been linked to the severe economic recession experienced by many countries in the region during the first half of the 1990s. Some commentators have considered the recession as a by-product of German reunification in which Germany's economic difficulties, notably growing unemployment, spread to the rest of Europe. Such conditions, it has been claimed, widened the appeal of the simplistic racist solutions of the extreme right, especially among the economically insecure low- and un-skilled groups in European societies who often perceive immigrants as competitors in the job market.[12]

These two examples highlight the need to take into account regional differences when considering the heightened importance of ethnic, national and racial identities and politics in Europe. In this regard, a distinction is often made between Western and Eastern Europe in terms of their respective histories, socio-economic development and political systems. For example, some academics delineate different conceptions of nationalism. Hans Kohn (1945) in his classic study on nationalism distinguished between a 'western' and an 'eastern' forms of nationalism: the former was based upon the rational association of individuals within a given territory, while the latter was more organic and authoritarian in nature. Kohn's thesis has provoked much critical debate. Yet irrespective of the validity of this particular distinction, being aware of regional differences is essential when seeking to determine the influence that globalizing processes may be having in Europe, a point returned to towards the end of this sub-section.

In looking at the European context it is essential to consider the continent's history. For example, Seamus Dunn and T.G. Fraser (1996) believe the ethnic tensions that have been on display in many parts of Europe during the recent period can be traced to decisions taken during the First World War and at Versailles. However, many commentators consider that the recent upsurge of tribalist behaviour has even deeper historical roots. Misha Glenny (1993), for instance, argues that Europe's history has 'returned' following the revolutions of 1989. More specifically, he views the Cold War as a temporary phase in European history in which ethnic rivalries were generally suppressed and contends that Europe – especially Eastern Europe – has now returned to its traditional preoccupation with borders, territory, nationalism, ethnicity and race. It is possible to point to particular instances of ethnic conflict that were suppressed during the Cold War. For example, ethnic divisions and tensions in the former Yugoslavia were suppressed during Tito's regime, only to resurface again in a brutal fashion in the 1990s. Indeed, there was much discussion during the Bosnian war of 1991–95 of there being an element of revenge for past atrocities and perceived injustices, in some cases dating back many centuries, in the ethnic cleansing inflicted upon the different communities.

This 'rebirth of history' or 'return of history' thesis has been criticized on a number of grounds. In particular, the historical accuracy of this interpretation is challenged. It is pointed out that Eastern Europe and specifically the Balkans have not always been plagued by ethnic conflict. Indeed, the 'return of history' perspective is viewed as playing down the periods of relative calm, co-operation and even prosperity in the region. In this respect, Sarajevo is often cited as having been a model cosmopolitan city for half a millennium, only dividing into ethnic enclaves in the 1990s. More importantly, Shari Cohen (1999) and other commentators maintain that the recent troubles in the Balkans evolved into an ethnic conflict, but certainly did not start out as such a dispute. Other factors such as the role of regional leaders provide more accurate explanations.

Interestingly, Shari Cohen's book was written prior to the Kosovan war of 2000. This war, certainly for Serb nationalists, was about their history, culture and identity. From their perspective, Kosovo is the cradle of the Serb nation and it was lost to Ottoman Turk forces on 28 June 1389 at the Battle of Kosovo Polje ('The Field of Blackbirds'), in which the Serbs were led by their legendary hero, Prince Lazar. This episode is etched deep into their historical memory and consciousness. The defeat marked the beginning of a period of Ottoman Turk rule that lasted until the late nineteenth century. Serbia only became a fully independent state again in 1878, and the Serbs did not regain Kosovo from the Ottoman Turks until 1912 during the First Balkan War. In the late twentieth century therefore Serb nationalists refused to countenance giving up this territory to the Kosovo Albanians.

However, this view of the history of the region is disputed, and not only by ethnic Albanians. Noel Malcolm (1998) contends that Serb historians have distorted this period of their history. The Battle of Kosovo Polje, for example, was hardly a straightforward confrontation between Orthodox Serbs and the advancing Ottoman Turks. Prince Lazar's side contained mercenaries from across Europe, including, among others, Albanians, Bosnians, Hungarians and Germans, while the Ottoman forces of Sultan Murad were assisted by Serb noblemen. For the Serbs this glorious defeat and the desire to 'avenge Kosovo' formed the basis of Serbian nationalism in the nineteenth century. Malcolm therefore highlights many of the myths upon which Serbian history has been based.

But this perhaps misses the point in relation to recent developments. This historical episode clearly resonates among a significant section of the Serb population. In a sense therefore it does not matter whether or not this version of history is accurate. Nationalists have been confusing history and myth for hundreds of years, and not just in Serbia. The significance of this history lies in the influence it is able to exert upon current generations. And there is little doubt that it did shape the thinking of both the government and citizens of Serbia in the build-up to the recent war. Indeed, the loss of Kosovo almost certainly was a contributory factor in the subsequent fall from power of President Milosevic. History and culture cannot therefore be ignored when trying to determine the reasons for the retreat into tribalist patterns of behaviour in Europe.

In considering the European context it is also necessary to examine how political structures and processes, both existing and of the recent past, have come to shape ethnic and national identities. Rogers Brubaker (1996, 1998) believes this is especially evident in the former Soviet Union. He contends that, contrary to the widespread perception that all aspects of nationhood were suppressed during the Soviet era, the different nationalisms in the region actually took shape around the institutional framework established by the authorities. The Soviet Union was built upon more than fifty national territories, each organized as the homeland for a particular ethnonational group. The regime also divided and classified the citizenry into over a hundred different ethnic nationalities. Brubaker therefore challenges the 'rebirth of history' or, as he puts it, 'return of the repressed' perspective, placing greater emphasis upon the political interventions made during the communist period than on pre-existing or pre-communist cultural and ethnic groups in accounting for post-communist nationalism.[13]

There are other ways in which the legacy of communism may have contributed to current patterns of racism and extreme nationalism in Central and Eastern Europe. At a general level, the systems established by the communist regimes may have helped to produce the strain of authoritarianism which is evident in many of the nationalisms that have emerged since the fall of the Berlin Wall. Communism strengthened a tradition of submission to authority and wariness of individualism in countries that had lived almost entirely under absolutist monarchies or fascist dictatorships. More specifically, many of the communist regimes lacking genuine popular legitimacy sought to gain support by stirring up nationalist and racist sentiments. For example, the communist authorities in Czechoslovakia played on divisions between the Czechs and the Slovaks. Similarly, in Poland anti-Semitism was a feature of communist propaganda in the 1960s. Some of the communist regimes resorted to methods identical to those in fascist regimes. For example, Bulgaria engaged in its own form of ethnic cleansing by trying to force its Turkish minority either to change their names or to leave the country. Likewise, Ceauşescu's attempt to achieve ideological and national homogeneity in Romania involved the suppression of all forms of diversity.

It is also possible to detect the influence of political structures and processes upon tribalist patterns of behaviour within Western Europe. The radical right has taken advantage of democratic electoral systems to promote its agenda. As Hans-Georg Betz has noted, the parties and movements of the new radical right have been 'careful to stress their commitment to representative democracy and constitutional order' (Betz, 1998: 3). In so doing they have been able to participate in elections and promote their ideas and policies through the democratic process. Moreover, issues such as immigration – especially when discussed in relation to the welfare provision received by economic migrants – and law and order are high on the political agenda in many Western European countries. For example, Andersen and Bjørklund (2000) in their study of radical-right populism in Scandinavia found that immigration became a key issue during the 1990s. This was evident in the Danish 1998 election in which 'immigration was the most salient issue next to welfare policies' (Andersen and Bjørklund, 2000: 210).

Support the extreme right is often viewed as a form of anti-party politics and as a protest vote, a way of electorates registering their unhappiness with the established parties (Lane and Ersson, 1994), while the people who vote for the extreme right are frequently those who are the most disillusioned with mainstream politics, often to the point of cynicism. Nevertheless, such has been its recent share of the electoral vote that the radical right has become institutionalized in many European countries. For example, returning to the Scandinavian case study, Andersen and Bjørklund (2000) believe that radical right-wing populist parties in countries like Denmark and Norway are now an established presence on the political scene and therefore unlikely to disappear. It should also not be overlooked that in many instances when people vote for radical-right parties they are actually voting *for* something in the sense that they wish to see the polices of these policies implemented (Eatwell, 1998). Moreover, the fact that people are voting in this way is perhaps a reflection of the profound structural developments affecting Western European societies discussed earlier, notably the shift from class-based to identity-based and issue-based politics (Inglehart, 1990).

A further example of the influence of political structures and processes upon European affairs can be seen in the transition to democracy that the countries of Central and Eastern Europe have undertaken following the collapse of the communist regimes. The democratization process has given nationalists the freedom to organize and campaign, with many doing so along ethnic and cultural lines. For democracy to function effectively it requires certain prerequisites to be in place, such as a tradition of pluralism, compromise and toleration, as well as a vibrant civil society. Such democratic foundations take time to become embedded within societies where they have hitherto been largely absent. And when a democratic state is not firmly established and considered to be unable to distribute resources on an equitable basis, there is a greater likelihood of people resorting to groups in order to protect their own interests and gain access to these resources (Offe, 1996).

A number of writers contend that whenever democracy is inchoate nationalism will often step in to fill the void (see for example Denitch, 1996). In a certain sense this is understandable as nationalism and ethnicity can serve, as Ulrich Preuss (1993) has argued, an 'integrative function'. This includes constructing and appealing to a national past as part of the process of national consolidation for newly independent states. Yet ultimately such a process is divisive and dangerous. In Romania, for example, some nationalists look to a pre-communist past, which was a period of fascist rule. On 1 June 1991, the National Assembly observed a minute's silence on the fiftieth anniversary of the execution of Marshal Ion Antonescu, the country's fascist military dictator in the early part of the Second World War.

For the countries of Eastern Europe democratic transition has been all the more traumatic because it has been accompanied by an economic transformation as they seek to become market-orientated economies and move away from centralized models. There is also disquiet that the anticipated improved standards of living have largely failed to materialize. And if anything the real beneficiaries of the revolutions of Eastern Europe have been Western companies able to take advantage of the new economic opportunities they have presented. It is in such circumstances that nationalist voices are more likely to gain an audience.

However, there are limitations to the 'transition to democracy' thesis as an account of tribalist patterns of behaviour. To begin with many of the countries of Eastern and Central Europe have undergone a relatively peaceful transition to democracy. There are countries and regions where this is not the case, such as in the Balkans, but this may be due to particular local conditions rather than the transition process itself. Furthermore, the transition to democracy cannot of course explain the resurgence of the extreme right in the established democracies of Western Europe (Delanty and O'Mahony, 2002). Again this highlights the need to take into account regional differences within Europe when seeking to explain these developments.

This rather broad sweep across Europe has revealed a number of factors that are contributing to the recent rise in tribalist patterns of behaviour, but are not directly related to globalization. They include historical and cultural influences, as well as political transformations and processes, and economic developments. But if we are to determine the influence that globalizing processes are exerting we need to take account of the European context, and to be sensitive to diverse regional and national conditions within Europe. It is these different conditions that shape the nature of the engagement with global flows and forms of interconnectedness, and it is only by considering them that we can properly ascertain whether or not globalization is contributing to tribalism in Europe. This can be illustrated at the regional level, and specifically by an examination of Western Europe and Eastern Europe. The following discussion will reveal the distinctive aspects of the two regions which condition the nature of the interaction with globalizing processes. Furthermore, it will reveal the unevenness of these processes.

Western Europe has almost certainly been more directly engaged with globalizing processes than Eastern Europe. This is largely as a result of Western Europe's history, including the legacy of colonialism and its ties with countries like the US and Japan during the twentieth century, as well as its degree of social and economic development. It is confronted with high levels of migration and is deeply interconnected with other parts of the globe through trade, financial and capital movements. In addition, many countries in the region have undergone a post-industrial transformation with the establishment of service, hi-tech and information-based economies, which are export-orientated. Consequently, many of the peoples of Western Europe will have regular experiences of aspects of globalization. Indeed, globalization will be part of their everyday lives. The nature and significance of their encounters with globalizing processes must form part of our investigations into patterns of conflict and identity-formation in the region.

In contrast, Eastern Europe is arguably less integrated into the processes of globalization. This is due to factors such as its lack of a colonial past, the Cold War period effectively sealing off the region from much of the rest of the international community, and the fact that many countries within Eastern Europe are still developing economically. Moreover, many of the companies and businesses in the region were state-owned during the communist period and/or artificially protected by the state, and had little need to be globally competitive. All of which means, for example, that economic migrants are generally not heading towards Eastern Europe in search of work – indeed, some indigenous workers of the region are moving to Western Europe. Similarly, many of the economies in the region have fewer connections and ties with the international economy than their counterparts in Western Europe. And while the countries of Eastern Europe are now confronted with the demands of global competitiveness and many of them are restructuring their economies accordingly, they have not gone through the same processes as countries in Western Europe. This especially applies to the process of post-industrialism, as many states in Eastern Europe have not yet reached this stage or level of economic development. Globalization and related processes would seem therefore to be an insufficient explanation for the increased significance of ethnicity and nationalism in parts of Eastern Europe. To understand this phenomenon, it would perhaps be more productive to focus upon regional influences and developments, such as those outlined above.

If we move beyond the regional level and examine national contexts, we are likely to find an equally complex picture.[14] But we need to undertake such analyses if, for example, we are to explain how the far right has become more of an electoral force in, say, France than in, say, the UK. The respective histories, cultures and polities of these countries have contributed to this difference. Furthermore they have ensured that the two countries have engaged with globalizing processes in different ways. For example, the UK has been associated with neo-liberal globalization, has sought to spread the Anglo-American model of capitalism and has generally welcomed American cultural products. In contrast, France has striven to maintain its own capitalist formation, has been more protective of its culture, and has generally been wary about the extension of American influence via global flows and increased global interconnectedness. There are therefore differences in the way globalizing processes are encountered within the two countries, which may or may not have had an impact upon the electoral fortunes of their respective extreme-right parties, but determining this must form part of our investigations.

The Role of the Media in Fostering Tribalism

One consequence of the passing of the Cold War has been that certain political figures and movements have taken advantage of the political vacuum and sought to establish power bases dependent upon the promotion of aggressive forms of ethnic nationalism. This form of elite manipulation was especially evident in the Balkans during the 1990s. Figures such as Slobodan Milošević and Radovan Karadžić exacerbated nationalist tensions for their own political advantage and sought to create a climate in which ethnic conflict was central to political life. They were aided by another relatively recent development which must also be considered to have contributed to ethnic, racial and nationalist tensions within Europe: the mass media.

Akbar Ahmed (1995) notes that we are now able to see on our television screens the aftermath of many ethnic killings and other atrocities. He believes that seeing such events happening to one's kith and kin encourages retaliation, and serves to perpetuate ethnic violence. More specifically, Ahmed believes that the state-controlled television in Belgrade played an important role in shaping Serb opinion and thereby paved the way for the conflict of the early 1990s.

Within Western Europe, Tore Björgo has discussed how media coverage of racist violence has encouraged 'copycatting' and conferred 'status and prestige on those who commit such acts' (1993: 111). He notes that attacks against immigrants and asylum-seekers in, for example, Scandinavia and Germany during the 1990s tended to come in waves or clusters. More generally there is often a tension between accurate, informed and impartial reporting and the need to secure high viewing figures. In order to achieve the latter, media organizations will be faced with the temptation to present sensationalist, and inevitably simplistic, coverage of what are frequently complex ethnic and cultural disputes (Sadkovich, 1996: 138). Thus, the nature and format of the media coverage of such conflicts often obscure understanding and can potentially be used to exacerbate tensions.

Cosmopolitanism and the Global Citizen

It is possible that globalization may encourage cosmopolitanism rather than simply reinforcing existing ethnic and national identities. We possess multiple identities and increased flows of information, products, services and, above all, people in a global era can potentially foster attitudes and outlooks that transcend national boundaries. Greater geographical mobility ensures increased contact with different cultures, and greater familiarity might develop understanding, insight and even tolerance (Featherstone, 1990, 1995). It is also the case that aspects of globalization, such as greater cultural interaction and shifting patterns of global migration, can contribute to cultural hybridization and multiculturalism and the fragmentation of existing or established identities (see Werbner and Modood, 1997). Of course, by challenging national cultures and traditions these cosmopolitan tendencies will provoke a range of reactions. Indeed, Mary Kaldor (1996) considers the contest between cosmopolitanism and nationalism will do much to shape the twenty-first century.

These points and the theme of cosmopolitanism will be developed in more detail in the next chapter. For now it is sufficient to observe that our global era will not necessarily provide fertile ground for the forces of ethnic nationalism and racism.

Conclusion

In this chapter a number of different phenomena have been bracketed together and discussed under the heading of 'tribalism' in order to allow consideration of the work of writers such as Benjamin Barber, Horsman and Marshall and others. It has been shown that globalization and its related processes can only be considered a partial explanation – at best perhaps a background factor – for the resurgence of ethnic nationalism and racism in many parts of Europe. There have been other factors at work. Furthermore globalization is an uneven, complex and contested set of processes, and thus we experience it in different ways. It provokes varied responses and reactions, ranging from resistance to engagement with and contribution to its multiple global flows and forms of interconnectedness. This means that its processes should not be viewed as simply threatening and displacing local and national cultures; they may complement or coexist with cultures and traditions. Globalizing processes, as we will see in the next chapter, may also stimulate new identities. Moreover, as has been indicated, some of the developments associated with globalization hold out the prospect of the diminution of 'tribalist' forces in the future and the fostering of cosmopolitan attitudes. Above all, if we are to determine the impact that globalization is having upon patterns of identity-formation and conflict in contemporary Europe, it is necessary both to acknowledge this complexity and to focus upon the European context. More specifically, to take into account the regional, national and local diversity that exists within Europe, which has been forged through specific historical, cultural, political and other circumstances and which informs the ways in which globalizing processes are experienced. All of which means it is unwise to assert that globalization leads to tribalism.

Summarizing Points

- There are claims that the insecurity and cultural mixing generated by globalization and related processes are encouraging a retreat into the familiar and the tribal in the form of national, ethnic and cultural identities.
- The media and communications technologies facilitate both globalization and ethnic mobilization.
- The issue of whether the state is retreating under conditions of contemporary globalization is unresolved.
- Globalization is unlikely to be the primary factor behind the increased significance of ethnic, national and racial identities within Europe in the recent period.

–3–

Globalization, Cosmopolitanism and the European Union

This chapter examines some of the ways in which the European Union and its member states are adapting to globalization. It is argued that the EU is essentially pursuing a defensive response towards globalization, and some of its policies, notably in relation to global migration, can best be described as 'anti-cosmopolitan'. This runs counter to the widely held view of the EU as an 'actually existing' cosmopolitan democracy, and has implications for the future development of Europe, including the prospects of generating a European consciousness or identity. Cosmopolitanism is receiving increasing critical attention within globalization studies, and its sociological and cultural, as opposed to philosophical, dimensions will be considered here in relation to Europe and the EU (see also Amin, 2001; Bellamy, 2000; Bellamy and Castiglione, 1998).[1]

The chapter begins by sketching out how the EU and its member states have been responding to the different aspects of globalization.[2] In the second section, the EU's approach to global migration is considered and it is argued that for a range of reasons it is an inappropriate response. In the third section there is a discussion of the ways in which globalization can potentially facilitate the development of cosmopolitan attitudes within Europe. This section seeks to counterbalance the link that is often made between globalization and tribalist patterns of behaviour, discussed in Chapter 2. The fourth section looks at how those with a cosmopolitan disposition are likely to regard the EU in its current form. It is here that what it means to be a cosmopolitan is explored, and where it is claimed that cosmopolitans are likely to find many aspects of the EU unappealing. Some consideration is also given to the type of European project that cosmopolitans would identify and ally themselves with. The chapter concludes by considering the impact that the processes of globalization and cosmopolitanism are likely to have upon the future development of the European project and the fostering of a sense of Europeanness.

Globalization and the European Union

There is a fairly widespread view within the EU that globalization necessitates ever-closer economic and political integration. First, globalization, it is believed, is ensuring that European countries are operating in an increasingly competitive world market, facing growing competition from areas such as East Asia. Furthermore, developments in communications and information technology mean that it is easier for firms to relocate to developing countries where labour costs are cheaper. Integration is seen as helping the development of the European economy. Moreover, when the EU achieves its proposed expansion to twenty-eight members its total population will rise to roughly 550 million, thereby helping it to get closer to the numerical advantages enjoyed by China and India.

Second, there is a perception within Europe that globalization is contributing to American power and dominance. It is considered to be enabling America to spread its cultural influence and flex its economic muscle. This is perhaps reflected in the difficulties and tensions over trade agreements between the US and Europe, most recently in the form of the dispute over the steel quotas imposed by the Bush administration. Consequently, for some within Europe, the further development of the EU marks an attempt to counterbalance the American monolith. Such attitudes could be detected in the build-up to the Iraq war of 2003, in which Germany and France in particular appeared to be offering an alternative vision for the conduct of international politics to that being pursued by Washington. The attempt by the French, German and other governments to develop a European defence force and common European defence policy may in part be motivated by similar concerns.

Third, for reasons that have been outlined earlier in this work, globalization is frequently perceived as undermining the nation-state. This has led many within Europe to view the EU as a way of regaining some of the powers that national governments have lost to globalizing processes (Hutton, 1996: 315–16). The EU therefore constitutes on the part of member states a pooling of their national sovereignty in order to have greater influence on the international stage and within the institutions of global governance (Milward et al., 1993).

Finally, there is a further sense in which European countries are seeking to resist or at the very least restrict an aspect of globalization, and this is in relation to migration. Contemporary patterns of global migration, especially economic migration, are considered by many European governments to be generating economic and social problems within their respective societies. This is despite the fact that many of these societies are facing labour shortages as a result of ageing populations (see Harris, 2002). The particular ways in which the EU and its member states are standing against global migration are outlined in the next section.

In response to these perceived challenges and difficulties, European governments have been pushing ahead with the development of the EU. More specifically, the European project – as it will often be termed here – evolved from the 1980s onwards from forms of economic and political co-operation to the push for integration (Davis and Rootes, 1994; Delanty, 1998). The project has included implementing or seeking to implement measures such as the European single market, a common currency and the European constitution.[3] Many would like to see the emergence of a pan-European identity as a way of consolidating and strengthening the European project. Above all it has entailed the expansion of the EU. At the end of 2002, the EU grew to twenty-five member states with the admission of ten more countries: Poland, the Czech Republic, Hungary, Slovakia, Slovenia, Cyprus, Estonia, Latvia, Lithuania and Malta. These countries officially joined the EU on 1 May 2004 raising its population to approximately 450 million. And there are plans to expand the EU still further. At a summit held in Copenhagen in December 2002, EU leaders underlined their support for the next expansion by backing the ambition of Romania and Bulgaria to join the union in 2007 as well as announcing that Turkey's application to join would be reviewed in December 2004.

Globalization is considered to be an important contributory factor in the spread of regionalism, and the EU is often regarded as a notable example of this tendency. Of course, individual member states have their own agendas and ideas about the development of Europe and their role within it (which will often change with different governments). Nevertheless, broadly speaking, globalization has given the European project additional momentum by providing further incentives for economic and political integration (see Rhodes et al., 1997).[4]

Globalization and 'Fortress Europe'

The most controversial of the EU's responses to globalization is in relation to migration and more specifically immigration and asylum. This goes to the heart of the debate about who is a 'European'. However, contemporary patterns of migration are a source of considerable debate. Paul Hirst and Grahame Thompson (1996) consider that levels of international cross-border migration were as high if not higher in earlier periods of history. In particular, they regard the century after 1815 to be the 'greatest era for recorded voluntary mass migration' (1996: 23); recent levels are therefore not unprecedented. On the other hand, Stephen Castles and Mark Miller (1998) describe how migration became a global phenomenon during the late twentieth century, with many more countries being affected by it. For instance, nearly all parts of the world are now importing or exporting labour.

It is difficult to determine exactly what is happening with regards to this sensitive and contested issue. Yet even Hirst and Thompson acknowledge that a lack of economic development in Africa and elsewhere is creating strong incentives for economic migration to Europe (1996: 159). And there certainly has been a rise in the number of people seeking asylum within the EU in the recent period. Almost 400,000 people lodged asylum applications within the then fifteen EU countries in 2000, leading to suspicions in some quarters that many of those claiming to be asylum seekers are economic migrants (Dunkerley et al., 2002: 89).

There are multiple reasons for economic migrants and asylum seekers entering the EU in such numbers, many of which have little to do with globalization. For example, wars and other forms of conflict invariably lead to an increase in those seeking political refuge. Recent wars in Afghanistan and Iraq, as well as conflicts within Europe – such as the disintegration of Yugoslavia and the ethnic violence in Bosnia and Kosovo – will therefore have contributed to this pattern. Likewise, the break-up of the Soviet Union in the early 1990s led to an increase in internal migration within Europe, especially involving ethnic migrants returning to their 'homelands'.

However, there are aspects of globalization that have contributed to this pattern. In particular, improvements in the various forms of travel have led to the emergence of what is sometimes termed 'jet-age asylum seeking'. Meanwhile, as a result of global communications technology people in the developing world are increasingly aware of the higher standards of living within Europe. Globalization has helped to break down the information barriers and in so doing intensified the desire of those frustrated by a lack of opportunities within their own societies to come to Europe (Elliott, 2002). Such attitudes will be all the stronger whenever they are accompanied by a desire to join extended family members who have already settled in what in many cases are former colonial powers. Of course, colonialism itself was arguably an early phase in the history of globalization (Harper, 2002).

In response to shifting patterns of global migration, member governments of the EU have been taking a harder line on immigration and asylum. Many EU countries are increasingly less willing to distinguish between economic migrants and genuine victims of repression, and instead are now setting annual deportation targets (Doyle, 1996). In this vein, some EU leaders are seeking revisions to Article 1 of the 1951 Geneva Convention, which establishes the principle of the right to asylum for those fleeing persecution, arguing that it was drawn up before movements of refugees reached current levels. The Schengen Agreement, while removing border controls between signatory states, has significantly strengthened their external borders. Enforcing this approach has led to the setting-up of Europol (the European police agency) and the Schengen Information System to, among other things, monitor immigration. By 1999 the signatory states included the following EU members: Italy, Spain, Greece, Portugal, Austria, Sweden, Finland, France, Germany, the Benelux countries and Denmark. And the following non-EU states: Norway and Iceland. The signatory come to be termed 'Schengenland'.[5]

Cumulatively, these policies have led to a significant rise in the number of deportations from EU states. In 1995 Germany deported 60,000 immigrants by air alone; whilst France sets itself a target of deporting 20,000 per annum (Doyle, 1996). Being seen to take a tough stance on immigration and asylum may in part be motivated by concerns that the extreme right does not attract further support, but it has institutionalized forms of discrimination and exclusion within the EU. This approach is reinforced by the EU's conception of citizenship, which was established as a legal principle in the Maastricht Treaty of 1992 and is widely viewed as discriminating against third country (or non-EU) nationals. In particular, the right to freedom of movement within the EU – arguably the defining feature of EU citizenship – only applies to those individuals who are nationals of a member state. Moreover, the single market, which came into being with the Single European Act (1 January 1993), introduced greater restrictions upon the freedom of movement of non-Europeans within Europe. It also established stricter entry requirements for third-country nationals wanting to enter Europe, as well as enhancing the security measures preventing them from doing so. There is therefore considerable merit to the claim that EU member states are engaged in building 'Fortress Europe'.

Such has been the determination to hold back global migration that the EU has gone against its own founding principles. Article 6 of the Treaty on European Union declares: 'The union is founded on the principles of liberty, democracy, respect for human rights and fundamental freedoms, and the rule of law, principles which are common to the Member States' (Lacroix, 2002: 946). Certain EU practices and policies, especially in the areas of citizenship and immigration, are at odds with these stated universal principles. This is evident in the democratic processes established by the EU, with voting rights extended only to member state nationals. Third country nationals are disenfranchised and effectively second-class citizens.

The EU and its member states are therefore engaged in promoting the idea of Europe and a pan-European identity in contradistinction to an 'Other'. Asylum seekers have become the 'Other' against whom to define the 'true' European. As well as marginalizing existing immigrant communities, European integration in this form simply lends credence to the arguments of the extreme right. It also means that there are contradictory processes at work at the heart of the EU. While the EU has actively sought to identify and combat racism (see Ford, 1992), its efforts have been undermined by its approach to non-European nationals in other policy areas.

Constructing Europe upon forms of exclusion and discrimination is likely to offend those of a cosmopolitan disposition. Given Europe's history of nationalist wars, ethnic tensions and racism it might be thought that cosmopolitans are an insignificant minority group. However, there are grounds for believing that cosmopolitanism may become more widely disseminated and that aspects of globalization can contribute to this process (see Beck, 2002; Hopper, forthcoming; Tomlinson, 1999). This possibility will now be explored before a judgement is a reached upon its likelihood in the conclusion to this chapter.

Globalization and Cosmopolitanism

Before outlining the ways in which globalization might help to generate cosmopolitanism, it should be made clear that this connection is far from universally accepted. Many writers stress the anti-cosmopolitan effects of globalization. Richard Falk (1996) maintains that the interests and agendas of TNCs, major banks, currency dealers, media organizations and so forth define the nature of globalization. For

Falk, we are confronted with a market-driven globalism, which 'has almost no affinity' with cosmopolitanism (1996: 57). Similarly, Alain Touraine maintains that 'globalization is crushing cultural diversity and personal experiences' and turning the 'citizen into the consumer' (1997: 68). But this view of globalization is particular and rather narrow. As we have seen thus far, different groups and individuals experience globalization in a multiplicity of ways. And for many people, globalizing processes are enabling them, contrary to Touraine, to *consume* a range of cultural experiences.

Greater Intercultural Contact and the Fostering of New Allegiances

As was suggested in Chapter 2, aspects of globalization, notably the increased flows of information, ideas, images and people and the greater interconnectedness that it entails, afford us all more opportunities to experience and encounter other cultures, traditions and societies. There is the possibility that understanding and even empathy can develop from increased contact and greater familiarity with different cultures. More intensive global cultural flows and interaction can lead to cultural hybridization and the formation of new identities, such as hyphenated identities. The multiple processes of globalization also provide us with an opportunity to think beyond our particular environments and societies, which in turn can foster new allegiances and challenge established loyalties. An inherent feature of globalization is therefore the potential for the generation of more cosmopolitan attitudes and lifestyles. This does not mean that national identities will disappear. Yet it is widely believed that multiple identities, allegiances and citizenships will increasingly define our global age, leading to the blurring or overlapping of identities. In the European context, the cosmopolitanism that globalization can help to generate can serve to challenge national cultures, the primary obstacle to the development of a pan-European identity, while hyphenated identities might take the form of 'Italian-European', 'Polish-European', 'French-European' and so forth. And such cosmopolitanism is arguably already evident within Europe. Living in increasingly multicultural societies, many Europeans are taking advantage of the chance to experience different cultures, ranging from trying new foods and cuisines to learning about different religious faiths. Others have engaged in forms of cultural hybridization, fusing or blending different cultures together especially in the areas of music, dance, fashion and theatre. Yet finding it easier to think beyond the confines of their national borders and cultures will not necessarily lead citizens of the EU to consider themselves more 'European'. For this to happen, the European project must have wide appeal, a point that will be returned to later.

Of course, there is no guarantee that cosmopolitanism will spread to all sections of society. In the past cosmopolitanism was the preserve of a wealthy elite and some writers maintain this continues to be the case (see Sklair, 1998). However, in at least two respects aspects of contemporary globalization can contribute to the wider dissemination of cosmopolitanism. First, some of the poorest groups within European societies are immigrant and diaspora communities, but many members are bi- or multi-lingual, possess hyphenated identities and have a range of allegiances and loyalties beyond identification with their 'host' country (Appadurai, 1996; Cheah and Robbins, 1998). Many of them are therefore in a very real sense exposed to other cultures and influences and live in a cosmopolitan manner. Second, some of the forces driving contemporary globalization can help to ensure that cosmopolitanism can be found at the popular level. The cheapness of foreign travel, and access to global media and communications technology mean that a greater cross-section of society is able to experience and draw upon a range of cultures and influences. Young people and students in particular, while generally among the least wealthy in society, are also among the most cosmopolitan.

Having more 'cosmopolitan opportunities' will not necessarily lead people to become more cosmopolitan. James Davison Hunter and Joshua Yates (2002) identify what they term 'parochial cosmopolitans': people who travel widely but remain within the 'protective bubble' of their own culture, which prevents them from properly experiencing indigenous cultures. Similarly, as we also saw in Chapter 2, more intensive and extensive forms of global interconnectedness might serve to reinvigorate national identities and local cultures because of perceived threats to national traditions and ways of life. However, as will now be shown, there are reasons to believe that national and parochial reactions to globalization will not necessarily be the dominant and permanent response. This view is based upon the ways in which national education policies are being developed in many countries, which globalization is also helping to shape.

The Rise of the 'New Cosmopolitans'

There is an emerging consensus among European governments about the necessity of providing well-funded education systems which attain high standards. Education is increasingly regarded as a necessary prerequisite to full participation in our global age. Such attitudes can be detected among 'third-wayers' who, as we saw in Chapter 1, consider that globalization necessitates government playing a key role in influencing the supply and quality of labour. Tony Blair has been quite explicit about this declaring that: 'the increasing globalization of the world economy means that the required levels of education and skills are now being set by international standards' (1996: 78–9). In particular, if established industrial societies are to survive and prosper their citizens must be able to play a full part in increasingly knowledge-based economies. The strength of attachment to this view was evident in the UK debate on tuition fees, which Blair considered to be a defining policy for his government. Other political parties throughout Europe, and not just social democratic parties but parties across the political spectrum, are adopting a similar approach towards education, which means in this area of policy-making there is very little dividing the political left and right (see Kelly, 1999).

The consensus over the importance of education for citizens and societies is reflected in the expansion of higher education in both European and non-European countries, with one recent survey suggesting there will more than 2 billion graduates in the world by 2025 (Norton-Taylor, 2001). Crucially, in relation to the discussion here, education – especially higher education – has the potential to engender critical, liberal and enlightened attitudes among its recipients and thus the basis of a cosmopolitan outlook. Educated citizens are more likely than uneducated ones to question the claims of nationalists and national leaders, to challenge racial and cultural stereotypes, and to resist the essentializing of other peoples. They are also more likely to be aware of the constructed nature of many national traditions and aspects of national culture within their respective countries. No longer as constrained by a sense of national loyalty, these people are able to develop a broader perspective and to think beyond their national boundaries. These developments are reflected in the recruitment crises faced by the national armies of many European countries. Numerous studies also indicate that citizens are becoming more critical of their governments, with many commentators noting a diminution in trust in government and politicians, which may in part account for declining voter turn-out and membership of political parties, and a general sense of disengagement with national politics. Likewise, more and more pressure groups are scrutinizing the external ethical dealings of national governments, especially in relation to the environment, foreign policy, arms contracts and trade with the developing world. All of which is another indication that people are becoming more interested in matters beyond their national borders, and perhaps a further sign of an emerging cosmopolitanism.

Of course, not every national education system within Europe is set up in the way described here. Moreover, within EU countries not everyone will participate in the expansion of higher education: many citizens will still not go to university. Nevertheless the developments described facilitate the emergence of a more educated and informed 'transnational' citizenry within Europe, increasingly willing and able to relocate to other countries for reasons both professional and personal. It is education that provides individuals with the knowledge, skills and professional qualifications required to ensure they enjoy greater autonomy and are in turn less dependent upon their respective states.

Reflexive Modernization

A further development likely to be contributing to cosmopolitanism is 'reflexive modernization'. As was touched upon in Chapter 2, Ulrich Beck and fellow writers (Beck et al., 1994) consider our late modern age – which globalization has helped to shape and define – to be characterized by the loss of authority of traditional institutions, structures and forms, ranging from the family to the church. This entails greater individuation in that we are more able to forge our own life paths. We increasingly choose our own labels, identities, values and cultural associations rather than simply adopting those of our parents and the communities in which we are raised. Self-constitution and self-identity are therefore an integral part of reflexive modernization (Beck et al., 1994). This has implications for cosmopolitanism. As Samuel Scheffler has argued, cosmopolitanism entails 'that individuals have the capacity to flourish by forging idiosyncratic identities from heterogeneous cultural sources, and are not to be thought of as constituted or defined by ascriptive ties to a particular culture, community or tradition' (1999: 258). Thus, the cosmopolitan is a reflexive self-constituting subject, formed from numerous cultural experiences and allegiances. The cosmopolitan should not therefore be thought of as an autonomous agent free from attachments to particular places or cultures, allying only with world institutions, such as the UN. At the same time, globalizing processes further contribute to cosmopolitanism by affording us the opportunity to experience a greater range of cultural influences and traditions, to mix and match, in the process of self-constitution.

Thus, improved levels of education for greater numbers of people, as well as the prospect of the emergence of the reflexive self in the late modern age, can help to lessen our allegiance to particular countries and national cultures. Therefore, far from stimulating the forces of nationalism and racism, aspects of globalization may well be helping to produce cosmopolitan citizens. In short, reflexive modernization and the greater individuation that it entails are a necessary prerequisite for cosmopolitanism. This serves as a further counter to the arguments examined in Chapter 2 claiming that reflexive modernization is contributing to a retreat into forms of tribalism. Again the importance of studying the interacting contexts, of looking at how globalization and related processes are experienced and perceived by different groups, individuals and societies, is emphasized. For some, globalizing processes will be viewed as a threat, for others, an opportunity.

As might be anticipated, reflexive modernization is a condition or description of our age that is not universally accepted. In particular, whether people actually make such active choices is debatable: people are born with identities or into communities and cultures that shape their outlook and behaviour. For this reason, some commentators believe a post-national European identity is never likely to provoke the same strength of allegiance and commitment as national identities (see Hutchinson, 2005). Even if the European project comes to be viewed as providing improved standards of living this does not mean that it will entail a weakening of national loyalties. To claim this would be the case, John Hutchinson argues, is to ignore the extent to which shared myths and memories bind people to a particular nation, and to assume that people simply act in instrumental terms.

However, if the Hutchinson thesis is correct, in a certain sense the more conditional nature of people's attachment to Europe – compared with their more 'natural' and deeply held national allegiances – might be more suited to our global era. This is because globalization, for reasons ranging from the opportunities it can provide to the insecurity it can foster, is often considered to be generating greater individualism within modern societies.[6] It is in this sense that the weaker hold a European identity may exert over us would have considerable appeal. A European community based upon values like democracy and freedom, yet making few demands of us in terms of taxation and emotional commitment, would in many ways suit global citizens. They would have the political and economic freedoms they require enabling them to pursue their own lives, with little meaningful reference to collective groups other than those of their choice, such as family and friends. As D.M. Green has noted, contrary to Hutchinson, our political identities are becoming increasingly viewed in instrumental terms, a matter of preference rather than psychological necessity (Green, 2000: 85). In a similar vein, Delanty considers that '[p]ost-national Europeans do not see themselves as bearers of the whole, be it the totality of the nation or Europe, but as citizens whose identity is formed by their interests' (1995: 10).

Globalization and the Limitations of the Nation-State

A further connection that can be made between globalization and cosmopolitanism is along the following lines. The processes and developments that constitute globalization are eroding national sovereignty and the role and functions of the nation-state, forcing people to become self-reliant. This in turn is weakening their attachment to their own nation-state and leading them to search for new forms of security, allegiance and meaning.

However, in at least two respects this is not an entirely satisfactory thesis. First, as we saw in Chapter 2, the issue of whether globalization is undermining the nation-state is deeply contested, with some commentators pointing to the steady increase in provision and functions the state provides for its citizens in Western societies during the post-war period (Dunn, 1995; Holton, 1998; Mann, 1997). While some governments are seeking to introduce an element of privatization into their welfare states, notably in relation to health and pensions, levels of public spending have not in general declined – although again public perception of what is happening is perhaps what really counts with regards to this issue. Second, rather than the nation-state, some people are looking towards their particular national groups for forms of security and identification. This marks a further challenge to the nation-state, but it is also the antithesis of cosmopolitanism. It is a development that presents a significant challenge to any claim that we are witnessing an emerging cosmopolitanism in our globalizing era, a point returned to at the end of this chapter.

Nevertheless, there is another sense in which the nation-state is struggling to come to terms with contemporary global conditions. This concerns what might be termed 'global problems', such as issues to do with the environment, development, trade policies, global diseases and health scares, population growth, nuclear weapons proliferation, international crime and terrorism. These require cosmopolitan thinking and international solutions, and specifically the further development of institutions of global governance, such as the UN and the EU, and transnational conceptions of justice, such as human rights regimes. David Held and many other writers believe this necessitates individuals being cosmopolitan because they will have to mediate between the local, the national and the global (Archibugi and Held, 1995). Moreover, the international media and global communications, coupled with the higher levels of education discussed earlier, ensure not only a wider awareness of these problems but arguably a greater proclivity to take an active interest in such matters and a desire to resolve them.

Certain globalizing processes and developments may therefore be encouraging individuals to adopt a wider perspective and transcend national boundaries. That is, to act in a cosmopolitan manner. For instance, environmentalists are increasingly challenging their respective governments because they believe their policies are harming the environment. While these policies may be in the national interest and of benefit to their own country, environmentalists will frequently take the global view, and many will be prepared to break national laws to make their point (Falk, 1995). This can perhaps be viewed as evidence of the emergence of a global consciousness (see Robertson, 1992). Such an outlook may also be reflected in the growth of fair trade food in European societies. In the UK, fair trade sales have now reached £100 million per annum (Vidal, 2004). In addition, there is evidence that ethical considerations are influencing other areas of consumption, ranging from cars to pensions. This is a further indication that reflexive modernization can help to generate critical awareness and cosmopolitan outlooks rather than simply a preoccupation with the self.

In sum, if it is not yet retreating, the nation-state is clearly facing difficulties in the contemporary period, while the incorporation by national governments of international laws, especially in the area of human rights, is entailing that citizenship is increasingly divorced from nationhood (Soysal, 1994). As Delanty has noted: '[u]niversal personhood is coming to replace nationhood' (2000: 79). It would therefore be wise, as Habermas maintains, to consider citizens rather than collective bodies or institutions as sovereign in our global era. Indeed, the numerous challenges that globalization presents to the nation-state raise difficulties for Kantian cosmopolitanism, which is centred upon a system of states regulated by international law (Anderson-Gold, 2001; Heater, 2002).

Connected Cosmopolitans

The cumulative effect of increasing intercultural contacts, greater emphasis upon education, reflexive modernization and individuation, and the problems confronting nation-states is that different types of demands and pressures are being placed upon individuals. New skills and coping strategies are now required: we are all having to become more independent, entrepreneurial and geographically mobile. There is also greater emphasis upon interpersonal communication skills and developing networks of contacts and associates. While not everyone is living and operating according to these changes, it is possible to detect the emergence of what might be termed 'connected cosmopolitans', and not just among the young. They are well travelled, *au fait* with modern communication technologies (notably the Internet) and used to networking. Many have developed extensive contacts both domestically and abroad. In short, they are well adjusted to operating within knowledge-based societies or economies.

Ideas and information are key sources of wealth generation and societal development within knowledge-based economies. The development of such economies requires regular communication between and across societies, which in turn can lead to individuals forming new acquaintanceships and friendships in different countries. While this exchange of ideas and information has gone on in the past, it is the current intensity and extent of such exchanges that make our own era different from earlier periods of history. In particular, universities are primary sites of cultural interaction and exchange, and becoming increasingly so. As well as lecturers attending international conferences and students studying for degrees abroad, the formation of transnational information/policy networks and 'disciplinary communities' via the Internet has been an especially notable recent development (Stone, 2002). For governments, allowing their citizens to exchange ideas and best practice is a productive way of improving material conditions within their respective societies. Indeed, even governments participate in exchange, sending delegations abroad to learn from other countries. This makes it difficult for governments to control the activities of global policy networks, and to prevent their citizens from acting in this way. Moreover, for a government to try to prevent such activity would be to harm its own economy and society. There is an abundance of evidence of societies isolated from the international community – notably North Korea, apartheid South Africa and Saddam Hussein's Iraq – falling behind comparable societies. Thus, while the motives behind these forms of global exchange might be selfish or nationalistic such exchange is nevertheless facilitating cross-cultural and cross-societal dialogue and interaction, which in turn are further prerequisites of cosmopolitanism.

Global policy networks and the exchange of information are not just confined to academia and governments. Non-governmental organizations, even groups opposed to globalization, organize in this way. For Manuel Castells (1996) this is all part of the 'network society' that defines our age, characterized by the global diffusion of information: information flows are multidirectional and largely ignore national borders. Above all the openness and non-hierarchical nature of global networks encourages the formation of transnational public spaces and even virtual communities and hence facilitates sociality beyond the nation-state (Axford and Huggins, 1999). The network society is therefore a cosmopolitan place. It has led Ulrich Beck (2000a), among others, to write of the emergence of a 'world society'.

With these developments facilitating cosmopolitanism, the question of what can be done to ensure 'connected cosmopolitans' identify with Europe as well as world society is raised. As will be returned to later, to avoid identification with Europe seeming a parochial almost regressive step will require the EU being run along universal principles. But there is also a sense in which the EU, by not being a formal state and by having greater emphasis – because it facilitates transnationalism – upon policy networks than national governments, functions as a form of 'governance without government' (Rosenau and Czempiel, 1992). In this sense the EU is in tune with contemporary 'network society' (Castells, 1997; Keohane and Hoffman, 1991), with the potential to be a network polity (Axford and Huggins, 1999).[7]

Finally, while this section has sought to describe contemporary lifestyles and the demands increasingly being placed upon individuals, as well as some of the implications of globalizing processes, we need to reflect upon whether these factors will actually change attitudes. Put simply, does travelling to and trading with more countries necessarily lead to a greater appreciation of other cultures? Such activity will certainly have an influence upon the individuals operating in this manner, but whether this always leads to cosmopolitan outlooks is more debatable.

The Contested Nation

The processes that constitute globalization are also contributing to greater cultural diversity within nation-states, leading to them becoming more fragmented, a development that has cosmopolitan implications. Recent research on nationalism has stressed the extent to which 'the nation' is increasingly contested by ethnic minorities, cultural groups, women, former colonial peoples and immigrants (Bhabha, 1990; Özkirimli, 2000). Much more so than in the past, competing narratives seek to shape and define nations and national cultures. Consequently, national cultures are less stable and homogeneous, and arguably less distinctive. It is now less possible for a single conception or narrative of the nation to predominate, and to marginalize or exclude other narratives in the process. The uncertainty this engenders ensures that the nation is less able to exert a hold upon the imaginations of its citizens.[8] But this again provides citizens with the opportunity to think and look beyond the boundaries or confines of their respective countries. It thereby facilitates cosmopolitanism or at the very least makes it more of a possibility.

The challenge to the national is in Gerard Delanty and Patrick O'Mahony's (2002) view reflected in the decoupling of nation and state, or as mentioned earlier, nationality and citizenship. They argue that while nationalism emerged from the merging of the political project of modernity (e.g., state formation) and the cultural project of modernity (e.g., the forging of new identities), the connection between the two is increasingly challenged in our global era. There are now numerous ways in which citizenship is no longer exclusively defined by nationality. For example, with globalization there has been greater emphasis upon group or cultural rights within societies that are increasingly pluralistic and multicultural. This manifests itself in many forms, ranging from affirmative action policies to religious groups, migrants and ethnic minorities becoming more assertive about their rights, as well as better organized to articulate their demands (Soysal, 1994). In the US, the strength of the forces championing multiculturalism has led some commentators to wonder whether American culture and society are unravelling, a point returned to in Chapter 6. Meanwhile the French government has passed new laws to ensure religious minorities assimilate into the country's secular culture and the British government has introduced citizenship ceremonies to inform new citizens about British culture. These are essentially defensive measures designed to preserve national cultures facing fragmentation as a result of cultural pluralism and contestation.

There are numerous instances of the de-linking between citizenship and nationality, especially in regards to the diminution of patriotism and the sense of duty to one's country. In other words, the maxim 'my country right or wrong' is being challenged, for example in the increasing number of citizens prepared to question the legitimacy of their country going to war and when civil servants leak classified documents and former government ministers reveal state secrets. What motivates them is an ethical framework that extends beyond the confines of their particular nation-states. It is a consideration for the fate of other nationals, which translates as a concern for the fate of humankind. In this sense therefore they are acting as world citizens rather than as national citizens.

National cultures face other challenges, ranging from being permeated by diverse cultural influences as a result of global communications technologies to the spread of the culture of global capitalism. Similarly, global cities, such as London or Paris, are offering alternatives to the nation-state and national cultures both in terms of sources of authority and everyday experiences for their inhabitants. They are an important element of the trend towards multilevel governance, which is itself a reflection of the erosion of national sovereignty (Delanty, 2000). But arguably they are also more tied into the processes of globalization than the nation-state as a whole, something which is reflected in the cosmopolitan nature of city life.

In sum, the nation is increasingly an arena where the forces of pluralism and solidarity encounter each other, and frequently compete. This is not to suggest that national cultures are disappearing, merely that their internal form is changing at an unprecedented rate. The nation is increasingly a site of cultural contestation, constituted by numerous influences, and therefore difficult to pin down and imagine. All of which reduces its significance, and entails a loss of status and authority. Any notion that our national identity is our primary or defining identity is no longer sustainable: it must increasingly compete with a plethora of identities for our attention. This in turn makes it more possible to become a cosmopolite.

If what has been described is indeed what is happening then it would appear that the high point of the nation-state and relatively homogeneous national cultures is passing or has passed. In the case of Europe this development would mark something of a return to its past as its pre-nation-state history was dominated by polyethnic societies (see McNeill, 1986). Polyethnicity, with the lack of a distinct and unitary conception of the nation that it entails, is an especially suitable condition and environment for cosmopolitanism.[9] Although we should bear in mind that the extent of the changes the nation-state is undergoing remains contested.

Cosmopolitanism is Good for Us

A final reason why we might witness the spread of cosmopolitanism is that, quite simply, it is good for us. A cosmopolitan outlook enables us to experience and learn about different cultures and societies, and therefore to expand our knowledge and widen our horizons. To be opposed to cosmopolitanism is therefore to impose limits upon our lives. Martha Nussbaum (1996) believes that cosmopolitanism facilitates self-knowledge because the more we know about others, the better able are we to know ourselves. Cosmopolitanism is also good for societies or countries, facilitating their development. It enables them to incorporate new ideas and cultural influences and prevents them from stagnating and decaying.

This particular claim is not directly related to globalization. Although as has been shown, aspects of globalization, such as global communications and increased travel and interconnectedness, can facilitate cosmopolitan experiences. Indeed, to resist cosmopolitan pressures would entail individuals and societies trying to seal themselves off from the processes of globalization. Of course, some people seek to do just this by sticking with their own kith and kin. In this vein, it might be argued that there is little tangible evidence of the emergence of cosmopolitanism and 'new cosmopolitans'. Within Europe, this impression is reinforced by the recent growth in support for far-right parties and groups. However, electoral fortunes are a notoriously unreliable indicator of public trends. Arguably, as has been suggested here, of more significance is that a number of lasting processes and developments associated with globalization – such as advances in communications and information technologies, increased travel, reflexive modernization, challenges to the nation-state and greater emphasis upon higher education – have the potential to generate forms of cosmopolitanism.[10] While we must not downplay or underestimate the dangers of the extreme right, it is possible that historical trends are working against them.

Indeed, the extreme right's recent revival may in part be a defensive reaction to these developments. There is also a sense in which, in a globalizing era, all Europeans will have to change their attitudes and outlooks if they are not to become anachronistic. For Europeans to refuse to adapt would be to place themselves at odds with the different forms of interconnectedness which define our age. The individuals who will flourish in our global era are likely to be those who are open to other cultures and traditions and able to learn from and draw upon them.

However, becoming cosmopolitan does not mean giving up on our national cultures. Our national identities and national cultures need not preclude the development of a cosmopolitan perspective – and given the prevalence of nationalism and the nation-state it is unlikely that anyone can ever be completely free from national attachments. One can still be British or French, for example, and a cosmopolite. Becoming a cosmopolitan, and thereby open to other cultures and cultural experiences, requires simply being free from national limitations or prejudices. As long as we are not defined by our national culture – or any culture, community or tradition – there is the prospect of us developing a cosmopolitan disposition. Globalization can contribute to this development. Globalization is not leading to the demise of national cultures and identities, but its processes do present numerous challenges, making it more possible for individuals to think and act beyond these confines. As we have seen, globalization it enables individuals to experience a plurality of cultural influences and to gather and develop multiple allegiances and attachments. Becoming a cosmopolitan is therefore an eclectic process; we are not born cosmopolitans. Rarely, if ever, is cosmopolitanism an absolute condition.

Cosmopolitans and Europe

Having shown how certain globalizing processes can potentially facilitate the spread of cosmopolitanism, this will now suggest that cosmopolitans are likely to be put off by many aspects of the EU, as it is currently functioning. Consequently, they will have little reason to add a sense of Europeanness to their collection of allegiances and identities.

To begin with, much of Europe's recent history, including the rise of the far right, an increase in racist violence and virulent ethnic nationalisms, will appal cosmopolitans. These forms of anti-cosmopolitanism have largely been perpetrated at a popular level. But the dearth of a cosmopolitan outlook can also be detected within European governments as well as the EU itself. It is evident in the attempt by the French government to ban the wearing of Muslim headscarves and other religious symbols in French schools, a policy that at the time of writing was also being discussed in Belgium. Cosmopolitans will especially wish to distance themselves from the construction of 'Fortress Europe'. Almost certainly they will feel uneasy about current European policies towards economic migrants and asylum seekers. As we have seen, the EU's much discussed 'democratic deficit' is especially applicable to these groups. Cosmopolitans will also feel alienated by the language being employed by political parties and member governments of the EU in relation to immigration and asylum. Terms such as 'illegal', 'criminal', 'clandestine', 'swamp' and 'flood' are regularly used when discussing these issues.

In short, it is difficult to view the EU as a properly functioning cosmopolitan democracy. It is cosmopolitan only in the sense that it is constituted by democratically elected member states. But the EU is far from cosmopolitan in the sense of welcoming and accommodating other peoples and cultures. At best the EU is pursuing cosmopolitanism partially or incompletely. It is therefore not cosmopolitan in the true sense of the word.

For cosmopolitans to identify with Europe, the EU will have to undertake significant reform. The obvious areas that will need to be addressed, such as its democratic deficit, the treatment and status of economic migrants and asylum seekers by member states and the economically orientated EU conception of citizenship, have already attracted much comment (see Føllesdal, 1999; Grundmann, 1999; Shore, 2000).[11] However, it will also be necessary for the EU and its member states to display a 'cosmopolitan sensibility' in areas such as foreign policy, aid to the developing world and decisions to go to war, if a number of its citizens are not to distance themselves from the whole project. Likewise, the EU's agricultural policies will have to be reformed so that they no longer harm many farmers, and by extension economies, in the developing world.

Further, it follows that many existing and proposed approaches to generating a pan-European consciousness and identity need to be rethought. Cosmopolitans are unlikely to be attracted by attempts to build the European project upon the language and concepts of nationalism, especially given Europe's past (see Billig, 1995). These attempts include trying to identify or construct shared myths of origin and historical memories as a basis for identity-formation (see Guibernau, 1996). They would not want to ally themselves with any project that appeals to a Romantic conception of nationalism based upon history, cultural uniqueness and exclusivity. Likewise, any attempt to foster a European identity in contradistinction to an 'Other', and hence make the project one founded upon exclusivity, would find little support from those with a cosmopolitan disposition. Many cosmopolitans would also be uncomfortable with the EU positioning itself as the embodiment or protector of 'European civilization'. With Europe expanding ever eastwards and a Muslim-dominated state in the form of Turkey likely to join in the near future, the notion of a European civilization and the question of who determines what it is become even more problematic (see Delanty, 1995; Eisenstadt, 2003). Finally, if it is to be accepted by cosmopolitans the EU cannot be an elite-led project.

In sum, the European project would have to be based upon a more inclusive and generous notion of what it means to be a 'European' if it is to appeal to cosmopolitans. Quite simply, the EU would have to become more cosmopolitan.

How this might be achieved is more complicated. Jürgen Habermas (1992, 1999) believes the development of Europe must be founded upon a 'constitutional patriotism' (see also Lacroix, 2002). More specifically, the European project must be built upon political principles of democracy and the constitutional state. Habermas acknowledges that a constitution by itself will not be able to achieve a pan-European solidarity, but considers that it can make an important contribution to this end. Thus, given that in many of its official documents and declarations the EU makes claims to adhere to such principles, it is necessary to ensure that they are actually put into practice. In a similar fashion, Gerard Delanty maintains that if the concept of Europe is to be inclusive in nature, we must 'separate the ethno-cultural idea from citizenship' (1995: 159). More specifically, we must move away from basing citizenship upon nationality, which currently entails that 'exclusion is an intrinsic feature of contemporary ideas of Europe and Europeanness' (Guerrina, 2002: 188). With a post-national conception of citizenship forming the basis of membership of the EU, a 'European citizen' would be 'determined neither by birth nor nationality but by residence' (Delanty, 1995: 162).

In terms of generating a European identity or at least identification with the European project, there would be at least three advantages of ensuring the EU is run along truly democratic and inclusive lines. First, such a model would have wide appeal for EU citizens, and be especially valued by cosmopolitans. In particular, the universal principles or values of democracy and inclusion would provide a reason or purpose for being 'European', and a project for the EU's citizens to aspire to and believe in. This is all the more significant given that the EU, in contrast to the US, was not forged out of adversity or struggle and therefore lacks an important unifying element. Of course, this point should not be overplayed as member states are already democracies – indeed being a democracy is a precondition for membership to the EU. Nevertheless, the EU can play a role whenever member governments err from these standards or principles, and thereby pose as their guardian. Second, as Habermas himself has noted, the emphasis upon political principles and political citizenship is appropriate for the increasingly pluralist and multicultural societies that are a feature of our global age, and which cannot be held together by traditional nationalism (1998: 408). Furthermore, basing the European project upon political principles would make it more likely that a single sense or notion of Europeanness would develop; without this, given the regional diversity within Europe, it is likely that many conceptions of Europe would evolve. Third, particularly appealing to cosmopolitans is that the sense of Europeanness emerging from a project run along these lines would provide people with the space to hold other allegiances and retain other identities. Unlike national identities, it would not demand that the individual either belong to the national community or risk exclusion. It would allow for cultural autonomy and pluralism, which in turn would be reassuring to existing ethnic minorities within European societies.

Conclusion

This chapter has explored some of the ways in which the EU and it's member states have been responding to aspects of globalization. It has also addressed one of the academic debates surrounding globalization, namely its relationship to cosmopolitanism. As we have seen, there are certain long-term processes associated with globalization that are potentially able to facilitate cosmopolitanism, which the EU has thus far chosen to ignore. This is significant for the European project because cosmopolitanism – which entails being free from national prejudices and limitations – is a necessary prerequisite for the attainment of allegiances and identities beyond the nation-state, such as a sense of Europeanness. Thus, given that it can serve as the basis for generating transnational identities, it is in the interest of the EU to encourage the spread of cosmopolitan attitudes across Europe. This might entail the EU portraying immigration in a more positive light: challenging some of the myths that have become associated with it and highlighting the potential benefits it can bring, such as reinvigorating national economies and ensuring the age of retirement is not raised. It would also necessitate nurturing the idea of Europe as a settler continent, in the way that Australians have been raised with the idea of Australia being a settler society. For this to happen, member states of the EU would have to educate their respective populations about such matters. This would mean demonstrating to them not only that immigration is in their own interests, but that there are important humanitarian and moral reasons for treating economic migrants and asylum seekers in a fair and just manner.

Yet it has to be conceded that a combination of constitutional patriotism and cosmopolitanism alone will be unable to generate a European consciousness or identity, especially given how the proposed EU constitution fared during 2005. Additional approaches, such as the use of the education system and promotional campaigns, the development of a European public sphere as well as demonstration of the tangible benefits that closer integration can bring to the peoples of Europe, will be required (see Grundmann, 1999; Leonard, 1998). This is because European identity-formation faces considerable obstacles, notably the lack of consensus over Europe's geography and history (Davies, 1997; Duroselle, 1990), nation-states continuing to pursue national agendas, the emergence of 'Euroregions' (Newhouse, 1998), the revival of ethno-cultural nationalisms and the lack of popularity of the EU (Leonard, 1998). Such obstacles, along with the shortcomings of existing approaches to generating a sense of Europeanness, suggest it would be wise for the EU to look for additional strategies for generating a sense of Europeanness, including perhaps nurturing cosmopolitanism. But this in turn will require the EU re-examining how it is responding to aspects of globalization.

However, the case that has been developed here is ultimately dependent upon the accuracy of its understanding of how globalization is working. As we saw in Chapter 2, there are claims that the processes of globalization are encouraging national and parochial reactions. It is possible therefore that in adopting anti-cosmopolitan measures, especially in relation to global migration, the member states of the EU are accurately reflecting the concerns of many of their citizens. Hence, any claims about globalizing processes helping to generate cosmopolitanism must be counterbalanced by consideration of these expressions of anti-cosmopolitanism. More broadly, the fact that Chapters 2 and 3 have indicated starkly contrasting responses towards aspects of globalization within the same continent reinforces the point that it is unwise to suggest that globalization is working in certain ways and producing particular effects. Whether aspects of globalization provoke cosmopolitan or tribal reactions will be dependent upon how individuals and groups are experiencing and interpreting its different processes within particular societies and localities. Therefore, whether understanding and even empathy develop from increased contact and greater familiarity with different cultures will be largely dependent upon the 'baggage' individuals and groups take with them into the encounter. Such baggage will be shaped by factors such as the particular histories, life experiences and social and educational backgrounds of the groups and individuals involved. These factors will influence whether or not people wish to experience different cultures, regard migrants as a threat, are willing to do business with foreign companies and so on. It is for these reasons that the nature and influence of globalizing processes are both complex and uneven. These themes will be returned to in the Conclusion.

Summarizing Points

- Globalization has given added momentum to European economic and political integration.
- The EU is essentially pursuing a defensive 'anti-cosmopolitan' response towards globalization, especially in relation to global migration.
- Aspects of globalization are compatible with the spread of cosmopolitanism; whether this happens or not within Europe will be dependent upon particular contexts and the actors and agencies involved.

–4–

Globalization, Al-Qaeda and Global Terror

The emergence of global terrorism is one of the most significant developments of recent times. This chapter considers the ways in which aspects of globalization may be contributing to the global terrorism pursued by Al-Qaeda. There is no attempt to suggest that globalization is the direct cause of the increase in global terror, even though one commentator, John Gray, contends that Al-Qaeda is a 'by-product of globalization' (2003: 1). The aim is merely to assess the extent to which its processes are a contributory factor. This will entail an examination of Muslim perspectives and experiences of globalization. It is argued that to understand the general perception within the Islamic world of globalization as a form of Westernization and an extension of Western economic power and cultural influence, and hence a largely hostile development, it is necessary to take into account Islam's historical encounter with the West. From the perspective of Osama bin Laden and Al-Qaeda, and the tradition of radical Islamic militancy from which they have emerged, globalization provides an additional reason for confronting the West at this important juncture in the history of Islam. In substantiating this position, the Al-Qaeda phenomenon is explored, especially in relation to debates and developments within the Islamic community. There are obviously many different traditions and schools of thought within 'Islam'; indeed some commentators prefer to discuss it in plural terms. However, given the nature of the current investigation, and the fact that Al-Qaeda is a global phenomenon or network cross-cutting many Muslim regions and societies, and drawing support from different sections of the Muslim community, Islam will largely be considered in a generic sense. Following on from this the second section considers how contemporary globalization is impacting upon the Islamic world and Al-Qaeda and includes an outline of the ways in which some of its processes and manifestations are being utilized by the terrorist network. The third section focuses upon the historical, cultural and political context that has both shaped Muslim perceptions of globalization and contributed to the emergence of extremist groups like Al-Qaeda. In the final section, the themes of this chapter are examined in relation to the attacks of September 11, 2001.

What is Al-Qaeda?

One of the many difficulties in writing about Al-Qaeda, which emerged in 1991, is that in a sense it does not actually exist (Burke, 2003). The term 'Al-Qaeda' refers to a global database of supporters and operatives. But with the leadership of Al-Qaeda on the run, and its key base in Afghanistan dismantled, Al-Qaeda's form has inevitably changed form. Indeed, Al-Qaeda is an ideology or worldview as much as it is an organization, and it has effectively become a cover name for disparate terrorist groups. For this reason, the focus here will be not upon key figures and organizational structures but upon the factors leading to Al-Qaeda's emergence and the philosophy that lies behind it. This will include, in the next section, looking at the ways in which the processes of globalization may have contributed to its development.[1]

A further difficulty is that we lack an agreed or common vocabulary to describe the ideas of Osama bin Laden and his associates. Jason Burke writes of 'modern Islamic extremists' (2002: 38); another commentator, Bassam Tibi, believes it is more accurate to write about 'Islamic fundamentalism' and urges us not to use the terms 'extremism' and 'fundamentalism' interchangeably (2003: xxv). However, the origins of the term 'fundamentalism' lie with Protestantism, and many Muslims consider it to be a Western construct (Schweitzer and Shay, 2003). Moreover, associating Al-Qaeda with Islam is problematic as in numerous respects it distorts the religion. For instance, bin Laden has been issuing fatwas when only religious leaders can legitimately do so. Furthermore, Al-Qaeda has been acting without reference to Islamic law on the waging of a just war (Ruthven, 2002). This is especially significant given that legalism is an important theme within Islam. There are, for example, strict decrees that retaliation must be proportionate and not inflicted upon innocent civilians. While there are occasional references to periods of terror in the Koran, it does not sanction terrorism; nor are there any words that are akin to 'terrorism' within it (Schwartz, 2002).

Some writers employ the term 'political Islam' or 'Islamism' in relation to Al-Qaeda (Kepel, 2002; Ruthven, 2002). But as will discussed in a moment, whether Al-Qaeda actually has a coherent political agenda is a point of contention. Moreover, just as there are multiple Islams, there are multiple Islamisms, and not all Islamist groups resort to terrorism.[2] Those Islamist groups that do engage in forms of terrorism often have a specific national agenda, as is the case, for instance, with Hamas. Al-Qaeda's terror agenda, in contrast, is globally orientated.

In short, Al-Qaeda resists neat definitions and categorization. This is succinctly encapsulated by Jason Burke who argues that bin Laden and Al-Qaeda 'are Millenarian, fundamentalist, reformist, revivalist, Wahhabi/Salafi and, at least in their rootedness in modernity if not their programme, Islamist' (2003: 39). And there is a danger of becoming too preoccupied with concepts and terms that are in any case deeply contested and arguably unable to encompass the extent of the diversity within the Islamic world. Consequently, there will not be a great deal of emphasis here upon defining and classifying Al-Qaeda. To repeat, the concern is with mapping the broader historical and political developments leading to its emergence (as well as of course identifying the role that globalizing processes might have played). Such an approach is especially appropriate with regards to Al-Qaeda because it is a profoundly historical movement. This is evident in bin Laden's reference to 'Crusaders' and the 'Muslim Holy Places'. History also formed part of his justification for the September 11 attacks: 'Our nation has been tasting humiliation and contempt for more than 80 years' (bin Laden, 2001). The '80 years' is believed to be a reference to either the fall of the Ottoman Empire – the last Muslim empire – at the end of the First World War, the British takeover of Palestine or both of these events. Moreover, as will be shown, there are certain historical events and political developments, especially in relation to 'the West', which in conjunction with social and economic conditions in the Islamic world and debates and tensions within the Islamic community have contributed to the emergence of Al-Qaeda. It is only by taking these factors into account that we will be able to determine any influence globalization might have had upon its philosophy and development.

However, to understand why particular militant groups develop connections with Al-Qaeda and others do not, it is necessary to examine the particular contexts from which they have emerged as well as their specific aims and objectives (Esposito, 2002). In Indonesia there are several Muslim militant groups, notably Jemaah Islamiah (JI), the Islamic Defenders' Front (FPI), Darul Islam and Laskar Jihad, but they are essentially the products of Indonesian society, have domestic agendas and were set up prior to the emergence of Al-Qaeda. Even JI, which is believed to be behind the October 2002 Bali bombings and probably has the closet links with Al-Qaeda, wants a pan-Islamic state for the region rather than the return of the Islamic caliphate that bin Laden desires. It therefore has a different agenda, one that is shaped by local conditions. Likewise, it would be impossible to understand why a number of Islamic militant groups, such as Jaish-e-Mohammad and Lashkar-e-Toiba, have recently emerged in Kashmir, without awareness of factors such as the history of the region, the role of the Indian security forces and the encouragement given by Islamabad. Indeed, this point about the importance of examining local or particular contexts applies to the emergence and development of Islamist and fundamentalist groups and movements in general. Such groups and movements pave the way for Al-Qaeda. Al-Qaeda did not emerge from nowhere, but from wider developments and debates within the Islamic world. While these different groups and movements, as well as their particular situations and environments, will be referred to during the course of this chapter, Al-Qaeda is considered primarily as a general phenomenon. Although inevitably the approaches of these groups and movements will to varying degrees be similarly informed by the broader context sketched out here.

Another challenge presented by Al-Qaeda is that it is quite unlike any previous terror organization. In the past, terrorist actions were invariably geared to the achievement of definite political ends, such as national liberation. Al-Qaeda, in contrast, is more global in its scope, organization and ambition, and inevitably its objectives are less specific and focused. Even where it is possible to detect an 'Al-Qaeda position' on certain issues – such as its support for Palestinian self-determination and opposition to America's military presence in the Arabian Peninsula – a change in policy in these areas will not necessarily cause Al-Qaeda to cease its activities. For example, it was actually during the 1990s, when the US under the Clinton administration sought to play a constructive role in bringing about a peaceful resolution to the Israeli–Palestinian dispute, that Al-Qaeda began its attacks upon America. In this period the US government applied considerable diplomatic pressure upon the Israeli government to enter and persist with peace discussions, which helped pave the way for the Oslo peace process (McDowall, 1995). Yet during this time Al-Qaeda was either involved in or directly behind attacks on US troops in Yemen and Somalia in 1992, the bombing of the World Trade Center in 1993 and the bombing of the US Air Force complex at Khobar in Saudi Arabia in 1996. Al-Qaeda is also widely believed to have been responsible for the attacks on the US embassies in Tanzania and Kenya in 1998. Bin Laden himself issued a declaration of jihad against the US on 23 August 1996, entitled *Declaration of Jihad against the Americans occupying the Land of the Two Holy Places*. This was followed on 23 February 1998 by a further statement of intent, known in English as the *World Islamic Front Statement Urging Jihad against Jews and Crusaders*. This stipulated that 'every Muslim who is capable of doing so has the personal duty to kill Americans and their allies, whether civilian or military personnel, in every country where this is possible' (Kepel, 2002: 320).

In a similar vein, when the Bush administration announced at the end of April 2003 the withdrawal of virtually all US military personnel from Saudi Arabia this did not lead to a change in Al-Qaeda's strategy, even though the US presence in Saudi Arabia was a primary cause of bin Laden's anger against America. A few days after the announcement the US government had to issue a warning about another possible Al-Qaeda suicide mission. Intelligence information indicated an attack using an aircraft packed with explosives was being planned on the US consulate in Karachi. It suggested that as far as Al-Qaeda and related organizations were concerned: the war continues. This was confirmed in the following weeks with the terrorist attacks in Riyadh and Casablanca in May 2003.

All of which has led many to conclude that Al-Qaeda and its supporters and operatives are simply fanatics and little will be gained from negotiating with them, especially as it is Western culture that offends their sensibilities as much as the policies of Western governments. There is therefore no coherent Al-Qaeda agenda to which the West could respond, even if it were inclined to do so. Moreover, it is difficult to engage in meaningful dialogue with those who consider they have a mandate from God to kill their foes and believe that death in God's cause brings its own reward. The leadership of Al-Qaeda claims to base its actions upon divine guidance, which includes reading the Koran to determine possible targets for terrorist attacks. As Mark Juergensmeyer (2001) has noted, in the minds of terrorists and their supporters, religion can provide moral justification for terrorist acts, as well as framing the world in terms of a cosmic war. Indeed, even the vocabulary of Al-Qaeda, with its talk of 'martyrs', 'martyrdom missions', 'infidels' and 'holy warriors' and its division of the world into good and evil, with the US invariably described as the 'great Satan', belongs to an earlier age. However, given that Al-Qaeda and the threat of global terror affect all our lives, and are likely to continue to do so in the future, it is important to try to understand this phenomenon.

Globalization, Islam and Al-Qaeda

Many Muslims, and not just radicals and militants, associate globalization with Western, or more specifically American, economic penetration, which in turn is cited as a primary cause of the wretched economic condition of their societies. From this perspective, globalization has allowed the US and its allies to exert their economic power in the Middle East and elsewhere, and in so doing has further enhanced this power (Falk, 1999). There is also a cultural dimension to globalization that many Muslims regard as a threat to their own religious culture. Often it is perceived as a form of Westernization or Americanization. More specifically, there is a concern that globalization has entailed the spread of consumerism, materialism and individualism, which are viewed as undermining the Islamic way of life and values. Some Muslims are more ambivalent towards the US: they reject its values and lifestyles, but are fascinated by it and would like to migrate there, a point returned to in a moment. With the fundamentalists or Islamists, however, there is no ambivalence. The West and the US must simply be resisted. During his lifetime, Ayatollah Khomeini warned of a 'black and dreadful future' for Islam and the Muslim people, a statement that was widely interpreted as a reference to the global domination of America's economic power and culture (Juergensmeyer, 2001: 181). In a similar vein, Osama bin Laden has spoken of an American world order: *Pax Americana* (Tibi, 2002: xiii). And the September 11 attacks deliberately targeted the key centres and symbols of US economic and military power (Rogers, 2002), the power viewed as driving globalization and benefiting most from it (Talbott and Chanda, 2001).

Malise Ruthven (1995) believes the spread of global communications technologies has enabled the West to impose its own cultural hegemony upon the rest of the world. It entails that Islamic societies are bombarded daily with images of Western lifestyles, advertisements and alternative sources of news and information. Western culture and values are omnipresent via television, music and films. From the perspective of many Muslims, such a presence makes it difficult to preserve their own cultural distinctiveness and identity. Moreover, the nature of modern communications technology – notably the Internet – makes it extremely difficult, if not impossible, for Islamic regimes to control the flow of information. Thus, they can do nothing more than fight a rearguard action, as their citizens are presented with contrasting accounts of political reality.[3] At the same time, global media organizations and technology ensure that Muslims are more aware than they were of their poorer standards of living in comparison with people in the West, which for some will be a further source of resentment. Muslim migration to Western societies – another feature of globalization – demonstrates an awareness of this disparity and a desire for self-improvement. The attempts to keep Muslims out of these societies and, from the perspective of those Muslims who do settle in the West, an increasing tendency in the context of the 'war on terror' to view them as 'the enemy within' foster further resentment. For example, a March 2004 survey of British Muslims found that their desire to integrate into mainstream British culture is waning because of what they consider is a 'war on Islam' (Travis, 2004).

The existence of more and more Muslim communities in the West also presents a challenge to Islam. Since the 1960s there have been growing numbers of Muslims migrating to the West. For example, there are around 6 million Muslims now living in the US, while in the UK the figure is approaching 2 million and in Europe as a whole roughly 16 million. The fear of many Muslim leaders is that those living in the West are adapting their faith to Western conditions (see Roy, 2002), and more specifically that Muslims are attending mosques less frequently and that the original Islamic teachings are being watered down and modified to suit their new environment and lifestyles. From the perspective of the fundamentalists, Muslims within Western societies are living in *jahiliyyah*, the condition of ignorance and unbelief. Of course, globalization also entails the influence of *jahiliyyah* is spreading to Islamic societies, hence the need, from fundamentalist perspective, for jihad.

Akbar S. Ahmed (2003) believes the sense of being under siege from globalization is not only felt within Islam, but experienced by many faiths. As he puts it: 'Over the last decades the pace and scale of political, cultural, and technological changes coming from the West have unsettled people living in traditional societies' (Ahmed, 2003: 47). Mahathir Mohammad, the former prime minister of Malaysia, is more specific about the challenge that globalization presents Muslims. He considers that Muslims and Muslim countries are faced with a tremendous and frightening challenge. Globalization in the form that it takes now is a threat against us and our religion' (Mohammad, 2001: 24). Globalization facilitates the infiltration of Western norms and codes of behaviour, notably the West's sexual mores, into the Islamic world, making it harder to maintain Muslim cultural distinctiveness. Likewise, many Muslims consider the institutions of global governance – such as the UN, the World Bank and the IMF – are Western-dominated and a means by which the West can impose its values and practices upon them. In this regard, many Western governments use these forums to condemn Islamic regimes for their lack of human rights and democracy.[4]

So far globalization has been presented as a set of forces that are permeating and disrupting Islamic societies and communities. However, there is a sense that the Middle East and Central Asia are disconnected from economic globalization. For example, in the case of the Middle East, apart from 'some tourism, minerals, or garment/toy assembly' the economies of the region are not properly integrated into global markets (Langman and Morris, 2003: 62). Many MNCs prefer to go elsewhere where labour is as cheap or cheaper, and where above all societies are more stable. Of course, the Al-Qaeda network by targeting Western workers and businesses – as in the bombings in Saudi Arabia and Turkey in 2003 and 2004, respectively – will ensure that Western companies think even harder about setting up in the region. Likewise, the rumours that Al-Qaeda and/or associated groups are seeking to target Western commercial interests, especially those connected with oil extraction, in Kazakhstan and Uzbekistan will have a similar consequence in Central Asia.

The marginalization of regions like the Middle East and Central Asia within the global economy reinforces and contributes to the economic inequality that exists between the nations of the world. In the case of the Middle East, it is having a number of internal effects for Arab and Muslim societies. In particular, domestic populations are confronted with limited opportunities, with many people having to become economic migrants. Many Palestinians, for example, are working in the Gulf States and Israel because there are simply not enough jobs available to them in the Palestinian territories. Others in the region are seeking to migrate to wealthier Western societies. In the oil-producing states, such as Saudi Arabia, oil has enabled elites who are tied into global financial and trading networks to become wealthier thereby increasing inequality within these countries. Unsurprisingly, poverty, unemployment and inequality are breeding disenchantment and radicalism, making it easier for the extremist networks to recruit new members. The situation is exacerbated by the considerable demographic problems confronting the Middle East. Many commentators have discussed the population explosion in the region, although Gilles Kepel (2002) detects a slight falling-off of the Muslim birth rate at the end of the 1990s, which he contends was due to the difficulties of sustaining large families in what are increasingly urban societies. His view is confirmed by the World Bank, which says the population growth rate is slowing in the region from 2.5 to 2.0 per cent per annum, but this is still much higher than the world average of 0.5 per cent (BBC, 2003b). What it is also clear about the demography of the region is that there has been significant rural–urban migration in the recent period and that two-thirds of the population in some of the Gulf States are under the age of thirty (Beaumont, 2001). This means there is a generation of disgruntled young people with few opportunities, and whose numbers look set to swell. According to a 2003 World Bank report, the countries of the Middle East and North Africa, which already have an average unemployment rate of 15 per cent, must create more than 100 million new jobs over the next 20 years or face growing social unrest (BBC, 2003b).

Al-Qaeda draws much of its support from this 'demographic bulge' of young people living in urban areas and with limited prospects (Rogers, 2002). This support is not confined to the poorer sections of society. Many of the leading figures within Al-Qaeda, including the suicide bombers of September 11, are university-educated, middle class and technically literate. Their involvement in radical groups like Al-Qaeda is in part a result of frustration at not being able to use their education and skills within their own economies (Bruce, 2003). Extremist groups provide a channel for their energies and their anger. And as will be discussed later, this combination of economic and demographic problems is similarly affecting Central Asia and South-West Asia, and has also enabled radical Islamist groups to gain support in these areas.

Of course, the reason for the economic plight of many Muslim and Arab societies is not simply that they have been excluded from certain globalizing processes and the workings of the international economy. Many governments in the post-colonial period have been incompetent and/or corrupt, a condition facilitated by the lack of democratic accountability and generally weak civil institutions. In many Arab countries the economy is dominated by the state, with little diversification and over-reliance upon oil revenues, which are declining in real terms. Traditionally, Arab economies have been highly restricted and not open to either foreign investors or global trade (BBC, 2003a). Furthermore, in Arab countries education systems are geared more towards ideological than practical and technical training and so young people are often ill-equipped to participate in the global economy (BBC, 2003a). There are therefore important internal factors for the marginalization of many Arab and Muslim countries within the processes of economic globalization. Yet some leaders in the region have been happy to blame the West as a way of distracting attention from their own mismanagement. Ayatollah Khomeini, for instance, declared during his reign that all of Iran's problems were the fault of 'foreign colonialists' (Juergensmeyer, 2001).

Some Muslim scholars, and in particular liberal Muslims, articulate a sense of the Middle East being left behind by the tide of history. All the great power shifts and economic developments are happening elsewhere. This perception is heightened by the fact that a number of Asian countries (the so-called 'Asian Tigers') have surpassed countries of the Middle East in terms of economic growth and development. According to the World Bank, between 1980 and 2001, the Middle East and North Africa region grew at an annual average of 3.1 per cent compared with 6.4 per cent for South-East Asia. The annual average for developing countries as a whole is 3.4 per cent (BBC, 2003b). Indeed, the Middle East's growth rate of 1 per cent per capita, when population increase is taken into account, was the worst of any region except sub-Saharan Africa (BBC, 2003b). Liberal Muslims often express concern that their respective countries are not fully participating in the global economy and the institutions of global governance. Some regimes, such as the former Taliban regime in Afghanistan and the theocrats in Iran, have ensured that their countries have been effectively isolated from the rest of the international community. This point, however, needs to be balanced by the fact that beyond the Middle East there are Muslim-dominated societies, such as Malaysia, which are integrated into the processes of globalization and are prospering. Again this highlights the importance of examining particular contexts.

Thus, in a variety of ways, many Muslims perceive globalization as a challenge or a threat to their faith. To repeat, a number of commentators articulate the notion of Islam being under siege, with globalization being a contributory factor (Ahmed, 2003; Esposito, 2002). This is of obvious benefit to extremist groups like Al-Qaeda. They are able to present globalization as a Western project, one which Muslim societies are variously excluded from or exploited by, and in turn present themselves as the means of resisting it. It has been suggested that globalization 'does not present clear targets to oppose' (Langman and Morris, 2003: 66). As we have seen, globalization is a complex and uneven process, and in many respects difficult to pin down. But in targeting the World Trade Center, Al-Qaeda certainly struck at one of the symbols of globalization. And globalization itself has been viewed as one of Al-Qaeda's targets (Talbott and Chanda, 2001).

However, globalization should not be thought of as simply at odds with and alien to Islam. Islam is a global religion and Muslims are part of a truly global community (the *ummah*). To an extent therefore national distinctions probably hold less significance for Muslims than they do for many non-Muslims. Indeed, Islam has a history of empires and sultanates that only came to an end with the collapse of the Ottoman Empire. Moreover, many radical Islamists, including Al-Qaeda and its associates, desire the return of the caliphate and the continued global spread of Islam.

There is also a sense in which globalization serves a useful purpose for Islam and has contributed to what John Esposito and François Burgat (2003) have termed the 're-Islamization' of Islam during the last three decades. The plethora of different forms of global interconnectedness, such as travel and modern communications, serves to bring Muslims closer together and reinforces their collective identity. The creation of international Muslim and Arab newspapers and media, such as the television station al-Jazeera, has played an important role in this respect. While some of these sources have been accused of presenting partisan accounts and fermenting radicalism, they do mean that Muslims no longer have to rely upon Western sources, such as CNN and the BBC, for information. They are also likely to be very aware of the different parts of the world where fellow Muslims are suffering. Media images of atrocities committed against Muslims whether in Chechnya, Palestine, Iraq, Kashmir, Bosnia or elsewhere foster a sense of solidarity. Of course, this is also of considerable benefit to extremist groups, like Al-Qaeda. Indeed, radical Islamists use such film footage for the purposes of recruiting new members to the global jihad.

Al-Qaeda, in particular, has embraced many aspects of globalization. As a global network it is held together by a combination of modern global communications, including satellite communications, and old-style messengers. John Gray (2003) considers that Al-Qaeda is a modern phenomenon and this is evident in its organizational form, use of communication technologies and media awareness. It is certainly the case that Al-Qaeda utilizes the products of global modernity, such as the Internet, laptop computers, satellite phones, as well as, of course, aeroplanes. Internet web sites have been used by a number of Islamists groups for recruitment and organizational purposes, but Al-Qaeda is believed to have made use of encrypted web sites. And Gray is correct in his assessment of the Al-Qaeda leadership's media awareness. From its perspective, the attraction of committing atrocities like those of September 11 is that spectacular images in an era of global communications will instantly receive a global audience. Indeed, the global media has aided Al-Qaeda's cause, albeit unintentionally, by allowing video and audio messages from bin Laden and other members of the Al-Qaeda leadership to be relayed across the world.

Another feature of global communications technologies is that it is leading to the formation of information societies. Such societies are, however, extremely vulnerable to cyber-terrorism. Walter Laqueur (1996), a leading writer on terrorism, believes that given the nature of advanced industrial societies, if terrorists directed their energies toward information warfare this would have an even greater impact than a biological or chemical attack. Concerted sabotage of vital areas of a country's computer systems, especially its power supply systems, could render it unable to function. Alarmingly, there have been claims that the Al-Qaeda network is endeavouring to pursue this form of cyber-terrorism (Gray, 2003).

A further dimension to globalization that has contributed to international terrorism concerns the use of global finance. The US and its allies are having considerable difficulty in tracking down the financing of international terrorism. This is due to the fluid nature of international financial markets and the sheer volume of financial transactions: at the end of twentieth century 'the flow of foreign exchange across national boundaries exceeded $1.3 trillion per day' (Biersteker, 2002: 74). Al-Qaeda and related organizations have established an elaborate global financial network for raising and moving funds. They receive and generate money from a variety of sources, such as wealthy benefactors, and use Islamic foundations and charitable organizations as well as banks and companies to act as 'fronts' to finance their operations. For example, the CIA estimated in the mid 1990s that fifty Islamic charities 'support terrorist groups or employ individuals who are suspected of having terrorist connections' (Gunaratna, 2002: 62). In this vein, the US Senator Carl Levin commented in evidence given to a Senate Committee set up to investigate the financial aspects of the September 11 attacks that it was 'clear that terrorist organizations are using our own financial institutions against us' (Navias, 2002: 60). Bin Laden also has considerable experience of and expertise in money transfer techniques in support of terrorist attacks. Equally worrying, as Brian Jenkins has noted, is that: '[t]errorism is not costly. A few hundred thousand dollars would have sufficed to cover the September 11 operation' (2001: 13).

This section has outlined in broad terms the ways in which the different aspects of globalization are impacting upon the Islamic world in general. It has also looked at how they may be contributing to the phenomenon of Islamist extremism, as embodied by Al-Qaeda. However, in order to understand how the different aspects of globalization are being received and interpreted, and in turn influencing behaviour, it is necessary to look at the historical, cultural and political context from which Al-Qaeda has emerged. This will now be examined.

Al-Qaeda: The Context

Al-Qaeda is symptomatic of the struggle going on within the Islamic community over the future direction of Islam. Many people in the West only became aware that something was stirring within the Islamic world with the Khomeini revolution in Iran in 1979. However, the struggle dates back further than this episode. John Esposito (2002) rightly notes that Islam has a tradition of reform movements. But according to Bernard Lewis (2002, 2003) and other writers, the struggle really started when Muslim societies began to be overtaken by the West as a result of Europe undergoing the Enlightenment and the Industrial Revolution. Prior to that time, the Islamic world led the way in areas such as military organization, scientific and technological development and the arts. Armed with their modern ideas and approaches, Europeans were able to shape much of the Islamic world in their own image and in terms of their own interests through colonialism. In particular, the division of the Middle East into states by the European colonial powers after the First World War did much to shape the subsequent development of the region, especially in relation to politics and religion. This reversal of fortunes provoked considerable debate within the Islamic community, which has continued to the present day. It has ranged, broadly speaking, from those seeking to modernize Islam to those believing the relative decline of Islamic societies lies with the departure from religious orthodoxy. Al-Qaeda would side with the latter and with those calling for a return to the straight path of Islam to restore pride and identity to the Islamic community.

This division contributed to the emergence of Wahhabism or Wahhabi Islam, which first emerged in the eighteenth century seeking to purify Islam to rid it of the accretions it had gained since the death of the Prophet. The founder of the movement was Muhammad ibn 'Abd al-Wahhab (1703–92) and its origins lie in Arabia. Bin Laden's religious outlook is shaped by Wahhabism, which is a deeply conservative interpretation of Islam (Oliveti, 2002). Yet it has proved to be enormously influential and has come to be associated with Islamic fundamentalism and a range of militant jihadi groups as well as becoming the official state doctrine of Saudi Arabia.[5] It is an important source of the tensions within the Islamic community in the sense that its adherents seek to spread and impose their literalist interpretation of Islam upon other Muslims. In this vein, the Saudi government has been promoting Wahhabi Islam – funding colleges and madrasas and building mosques and other institutions – through its petrodollars across the globe in order to counter the Iranian government's attempts to export its Shii revolution.

However, a greater influence upon bin Laden, Al-Qaeda and many Islamist groups are the writings of Sayyid Qutb (1909–66). Qutb, an influential figure within the Muslim Brotherhood in Egypt, was jailed by Nasser's regime for anti-state activity from 1955 to 1964 and eventually hanged in 1966. During his imprisonment he wrote *Milestones*, which sets out many of the ideas subsequently taken up by radical Islamic movements. He built upon the work of Hasan al-Banna (1906–49), founder of the Egyptian Muslim Brotherhood, who was himself highly critical of both European imperialism and Westernized Muslim elites. In particular, al-Banna called on Muslims to rid their own lands of European invaders. Qutb broadened these ideas to urge Muslims to resist the encroachment of secularism. Many commentators believe Qutb's ideas developed during his stay in the US in the late 1940s. During his time there Qutb had been appalled by what he considered to be the decadence and promiscuity of American society. He also saw how this secular culture was spreading across the globe displacing Islam's God-centred universe (Esposito, 1992: 128). More specifically, he maintained that Muslims throughout the world were living in atheistic and repressive societies, including those headed by Muslim elites and governments. In this respect, Qutb made a comparison between *jahiliyyah* (the 'ignorance' and barbarism of the pre-Islamic period that the Prophet had fought) and our own time. And he urged true believers to resist the modern *jahiliyyah* of the West. Al-Qaeda has chosen to employ violence in pursuing the path outlined by Qutb. Ayman al-Zawahiri, the Egyptian hard-line Islamist and the chief ideologue of Al-Qaeda, is known to have played an important role in steering it in that direction. It is believed he has had an important influence upon Osama bin Laden, especially with regards to turning him against America and convincing him to internationalize their cause (Burke, 2001; Kepel, 2002).

Another important influence upon Qutb was Mawlana Mawdudi (1903–79). Mawdudi, a journalist and member of the Muslim Brotherhood in Pakistan, also made a major contribution to the debate about the future direction of Islam, arguing that secularization and Western domination threatened the very existence of Islam. Mawdudi was particularly critical of Islamic modernists or reformists for taking a secular path and becoming too dependent upon the West. Instead, he argued, it was vital that Muslims should come together to resist these forces and defend their faith (Adams, 1983; Choueiri, 1997; Esposito, 1992). This approach was reflected in his political activity. He founded the influential Jamaat-i Islami (Islamic Society or Group), which resisted attempts to run Pakistan along secular lines and helped to ensure that the 1956 constitution formally defined the country as an Islamic Republic. But arguably Mawdudi's most significant contribution to Islamism was his call for a universal 'jihad' in order to resist the West. Jihad, 'striving in the path of God', is recognized by all Muslims but it is not one of the five pillars of Islam, which are the basic principles or observances to which every Muslim must adhere. In that sense it is not a religious duty imposed upon the individual. Moreover, jihad can assume many forms, such as learning, missionary activity, good works, self-control, as well as an armed struggle to defend the faith. Many Islamists, however, have chosen to pursue a narrow interpretation of jihad, viewing it primarily as decreeing a holy war against the infidels. This is certainly how the Al-Qaeda leadership has chosen to interpret it. More specifically, Mohammed made a distinction between two jihads – the greater, against oneself, and the lesser, against another – and it is the latter that Al-Qaeda has adopted (Burke, 2003).

Not all Muslims, however, shared the attitudes of Qutb, Mawdudi et al. In the early twentieth century there was considerable admiration for the West and its achievements among Muslim and Arab intellectuals and politicians. This was reflected in the attempts to imitate Western approaches and the confining of Islam to the private sphere, of which Atartuk's project in Turkey was the most notable instance. But also the Ba'th of Iraq, the Shah of Iran and Nasser in Egypt embraced Western notions, such as socialism and nationalism, ensuring that Islam played a significantly reduced role in public life. It is for this reason that Qutb and Mawdudi, and their supporters, were so opposed to them. They gained support from the House of Saud, which sought to internationalize Wahhabism in the 1960s. As a conservative monarchy it had obvious political concerns about the rise of Arab socialist governments (Esposito, 2002: 106).

This then was the background to the rise of Islamism in the late 1960s and 1970s. Al-Qaeda has inherited and continued to articulate the Islamist dissatisfaction with Muslim and Arab nationalist regimes. For those who adhere to the path of bin Laden and Al-Qaeda, such regimes are an obstacle to their desire for the return of the caliphate. But while many of the regimes are unpopular, and for this reason have helped Islamist groups gain support, the states have come to be accepted by indigenous populations and are now established political realities in the Middle East. To date therefore Al-Qaeda has had to content itself with simply urging Muslims to join its global jihad, and has proved able to attract Muslims from all over the world, evident in the many nationalities that attended its training camps in Afghanistan.

Beyond colonialism and its multiple legacies, Western powers have, albeit often unwittingly, contributed in a number of ways to the rise of Islamism and Al-Qaeda, in particular. A key episode in this regard was the Cold War and in particular the situation in Afghanistan where it was the policy of the West to arm and finance the *mujahidin* who were attempting to oust the Soviet forces that had invaded in 1979. Leaving aside debates about whether the West abandoned Afghanistan after the withdrawal of Soviet forces, the chaos that followed the withdrawal in time paved the way for the Taliban to take control in 1996. The Taliban leader, Mullah Omar, offered Osama bin Laden and his supporters sanctuary, which afforded them the opportunity to train and plan for the global jihad. Having fought to oust the Soviet Union from Afghanistan – albeit with CIA training and backing – bin Laden now directed his energies to removing the US from the Arabian peninsula, regarded as the Muslim Holy Land. In other words, having helped to defeat one superpower bin Laden now had the confidence to take on another one.

Another legacy of the Cold War and the collapse of the Soviet Union has been instability in Central Asia. The replacement of Soviet rule – which for many decades had sought to suppress religion – by a number of relatively weak and fragmented states has provided militant Islamist groups, such as the Islamic Movement of Uzbekistan (IMU), with an opportunity to spread their influence – although the support they have been gaining is in large part due to the brutal and incompetent nature of their respective governing authorities, rather than their own appeal (Paton Walsh 2003; Rashid, 2003). As Craig Murray, the British ambassador to Uzbekistan, has observed: 'The intense repression here combined with the inequality of wealth and absence of reform will create the Islamic fundamentalism that the regime is trying to quash' (Paton Walsh, 2003: 13). Ahmed Rashid concurs with this point, arguing that '[t]he real crisis in Central Asia lies with the state, not with the insurgents' (2003: 245). Moreover, the oil and gas reserves of countries like Kazakhstan and Uzbekistan ensure continued Western and in particular American involvement in the region. This is a further source of Muslim resentment, with the US accused of propping up some of these authoritarian regimes or at the very least not doing enough to condemn them for their human rights abuses.

There are other similarities with the Middle East. As well as having corrupt and authoritarian governments, Central Asia has a population which is getting younger – '60 per cent of the region's 50 million people are under the age of 25' – and is similarly faced with few employment opportunities (Rashid, 2003: 11). The region also has its global jihadi movement in the form of Hizb ut-Tahrir al-Islami (HT or the Party of Islamic Liberation) that like Al-Qaeda seeks a return of the caliphate, though by non-violent means, while the IMU, and specifically its leader Juma Namangani, forged close links with Osama bin Laden during the period of Taliban rule in Afghanistan and is now considered by the US to be a part of Al-Qaeda's global jihad (Rashid, 2003).

As for the Middle East, the Cold War and, of course, the desire for oil have ensured that, even since decolonization, the West has sought to maintain a presence in the region. This has ranged from covert operations – in 1953 the British intelligence service and the CIA engineered the overthrow of Iran's Prime Minister, Mossadegh, in order to restore the Shah Muhammad Reza Pahlavi to the throne – to military intervention, as in the Suez Crisis of 1956. Above all the West has supported selective and often autocratic regimes across the Middle East. This is an approach Washington in particular has actively pursued, siding with the Shah's Iran against Iraq, the Lebanon and Jordan against Nasser's Egypt, Iraq against Iran during the 1980s, and Kuwait against Iraq. There is considerable disquiet among Muslims and Arabs about the authoritarian rule of the regimes that Western powers have been supporting, with many of them tainted by human rights abuses. More generally, there is a widespread perception that the secular nationalist regimes have been a failure. This became especially apparent with the Six Day War of 1967. The humiliating defeat of the Arab armies and the loss of the holy places in Jerusalem to Israel led many Muslims and Arabs, especially scholars, to look hard at why their states seemed to be failing so miserably.

Thus, since the days of Sayyid Qutb criticism of Arab nationalist regimes has if anything intensified. Indeed, numerous Islamist groups have been seeking their overthrow viewing them as both un-Islamic and corrupt. In this regard, Al-Qaeda has been targeting what it considers to be the decadent oligarchy ruling Saudi Arabia arguing that it has lost the right to be the Guardian of the Two Holy Places. Bin Laden further criticized the Arab nationalist regimes for allowing the US and other coalition forces to set up bases in the region during the Gulf War of 1990–91. Malise Ruthven (1995) considers these states to be vulnerable to Islamism because they lack democracy, and therefore legitimacy. Yet democracy in the Middle East has enabled Islamists to organize and attract popular support to the extent that in Algeria and Egypt the authorities intervened when it appeared that Islamist parties were likely to gain power. For instance, in the case of Algeria, a military takeover prevented the Islamic Salvation Front party from taking power following the 1991 national elections. Such episodes ensure continuing support for Islamist groups, and at the same time make it more difficult for liberal Muslims to make their case for reform and democracy.

A further source of resentment against Western powers is the issue of Palestine. As is well known, the plight of the Palestinians provokes deep anger among Arabs and Muslims, and this has helped to generate support for radical Islam, notably for groups like Hamas. Israel is considered to be one of the legacies of European colonialism and to be propped up in our own time by the financial, military and diplomatic support of the US and the West in general. This support has continued despite Israel's territorial expansion in the region and frequent disregard for UN resolutions condemning its actions. Israel is therefore one of the most important Muslim grievances against the West. But Samuel Berger and Mona Sutphen (2001) believe Al-Qaeda has simply commandeered the Palestinian cause to broaden its support base and justify its extremism. Prior to the September 11 assault, they maintain, there was little mention of Palestine and the Palestinians. It is also the case that Al-Qaeda has little in common with the Palestinian Liberation Organization (PLO), which is a secular nationalist movement geared to achieving Palestinian independence, and is therefore at odds with bin Laden's desire for the return of the caliphate. And despite being part of the same Wahhabi–Salafist tradition, there are even differences between Al-Qaeda and Hamas because of the latter's national agenda, which stems from operating in a particular rather than a global context (see Doran, 2001). However, some commentators, such as John Esposito (2002), believe bin Laden has been consistent in his support for the Palestinians and in his condemnation of Israel and what he considers are its backers, the Crusader governments of the West. In this debate, Paul Rogers (2002) is probably correct in arguing that Israel is certainly not as important to the Al-Qaeda leadership as the US military presence in Saudi Arabia.

Finally, there is a widespread feeling within the Arab and Muslim world that the West, through its financial institutions, controls the world market and the price of commodities. Muslim and Arab oil states have long struggled against Western interests to retain full control over how much oil to sell and how much to sell it for, and oil revenues have declined from a peak of $225 billion per year in 1980 to $55 billion today (Hill, 2001: 97–8). In 1973, Western powers went as far as threatening to impose a food embargo on the region in response to the oil price increase imposed by the Organization of Petroleum Exporting Countries (OPEC). It also led to the US becoming even more closely interested in the affairs of the region, making it effectively part of its sphere of interest. In practical terms this entails not allowing any power to gain control of the Persian Gulf. This in part helps to explain some of the interventions in the region by the US, notably the wars against Iraq (1990–91 and 2003–4), although there were a range of contributory factors in both conflicts (see, for example, Matthews, 1993).

The cumulative effect of these policies leads many Muslims, and not just the fundamentalists, to conclude that the West is hostile to Islam and seeks to discredit it. Furthermore, terrorist incidents are seemingly automatically linked with Muslims. A notable example of this tendency was the 1995 bombing of the federal building in Oklahoma City, which at the time was blamed upon Islamic extremists but was actually the work of an American, Timothy McVeigh. Anti-Muslim sentiment was also evident, it is claimed, in the failure of Western governments do anything substantive to stop the ethnic cleansing of Bosnian Muslims in the early 1990s – although the West did intervene in the Kosovan conflict of 2000, which did benefit the mainly Muslim ethnic Albanians. And now the 'war on terror' is widely perceived to be an attack on Islam, despite the denials emanating from the Bush administration. Some commentators consider this may be leading to a sense of victimhood, whereby the West serves as a convenient scapegoat and Muslims avoid addressing problems within their own societies (Makiya, 2001). And as Fred Halliday (2002) has noted, not all of the conflicts and disputes involving Muslims are directly connected. Some are historically distinct, such as those in Palestine and Kashmir. Nevertheless the view that they are part of a common or general attack upon Islam is becoming increasing popular. As discussed earlier, the development of this view is undoubtedly facilitated by global communications and media organizations, though extremist groups like Al-Qaeda have done much to ensure that connections are made. A regular feature of bin Laden's pronouncements is a list of what he considers to be the crimes against Islam committed by the West.

Thus, there is a general sense within the Islamic world that it is operating from a position of weakness and vulnerability in dealing with the West (Fuller and Lesser, 1995). Any influence that globalization is having upon the Islamic community, and in particular how it is perceived and interpreted, must therefore be understood in relation to this historical and political context. From the perspective of many Muslims, there is a long history of the West trying to dominate and shape their societies. For

Muslims in the Mediterranean Arab world this process dates back to the Crusades (Halliday, 2002). However, the significant episode was Napoleon's entry into Egypt at the end of the eighteenth century, which paved the way for the establishment of European colonialism in the Middle East and arguably the neo-colonialism of our own time. In the light of this history, it becomes more understandable that globalization is considered by many Muslims as yet another stage in the attack by the West upon Islam. Likewise, concerns about the cultural impact of globalization, and Muslim sensitivity over issues such as human rights, the position of women and democracy must be understood in relation to the context described here.

Global Terror after September 11

The focus will now be upon globalization, global terrorism and Islamist extremism in the post-September 11 period. In particular, how have the events of that day informed the debates surrounding these issues? How, if at all, is Al-Qaeda's campaign of global terrorism shaping the nature and course of contemporary globalization? And what are the prospects for radical Islam and Al-Qaeda?

In relation to radical Islam, Gilles Kepel's book *Jihad: The Trail of Political Islam* (2002) has provoked much discussion. In this work, Kepel maps what he considers to be the rise and decline of political Islam. If Kepel is correct in his claim about the decline of political Islam, this has implications for the strategies that radical Islamists will employ in the future, especially in relation to terrorism. Quite simply, if they have diminishing prospects of capturing states there is a greater likelihood of them resorting to terrorism, as the history of groups like ETA and the IRA demonstrates.

An important part of Kepel's case is the failure of the Iranian Islamic revolution to spread. Even at the height of the Ayatollah Khomeini era during the 1980s, Iran's attempt to lead the Islamic revolution was hindered by its Shi'ite and Persian character, which had limited appeal for Sunni Muslims and Arabs. Moreover, there is considerable evidence that it is losing its vigour within Iran. This is reflected in the increasing division between the spiritual and political leadership, with the latter seeking a degree of reconciliation with the West, especially the US. Disillusionment with the Khomeini revolution and living under a theocracy is especially strong among young people (Judah, 2002). They never experienced the Shah and his regime and are becoming frustrated by their lack of freedom and career opportunities. Perhaps tellingly, reformists triumphed in legislative elections of 18 February 2000, and subsequently religious leaders have been determining who can stand in elections.

In other countries Islamism is also having mixed fortunes. As mentioned earlier, Islamist groups have been held back in Egypt and Algeria by strong government action – although in the Algerian election of April 2004 the Islamist candidate, Abdallah Djaballah, secured under 5 per cent of the vote (Saleh, 2004). And while the prospects for Islamists are better in Pakistan and Saudi Arabia there will be strong resistance to them attaining power in these countries, both internally and externally in the form of the US, especially as it is now pursuing its 'war on terrorism'. The House of Saud is unpopular and under pressure but it does not yet look as though it will be losing its grip on power, while the Pakistan government of President Pervez Musharraf shifted its position in the light of the Afghanistan war, most notably restraining the Pakistan Intelligence Service (ISI), which had supported and possibly sponsored the Taliban.

Most importantly, many Muslims have little time for Islamist movements and are especially put off by the violence that is often associated with them. Furthermore, the majority of Muslims do not want to live under the austere regimes established by some Islamist or Islamic fundamentalist groups. The fall of the Taliban, for example, was widely welcomed by Muslims within Afghanistan. Radical Islam lacks broad appeal outside of its Arab and Muslim heartlands and there are limits to what it has to offer to the people living within those areas. More specifically, there is much recent evidence that religious clerics are not the best people to run complex modern economies. As the recent history of Afghanistan and Iran would indicate, regimes headed by religious clerics are unable to improve standards of living, nor generate social and economic progress within their respective countries. For Kepel, this is all evidence of the decline of radical or, as he puts it, political Islam.

However, this does not provide a complete picture of its fortunes. Despite the recent setbacks that Islamist movements have suffered, and maybe even because of them, Islamism is the fastest growing version of Islam in the world. While there is considerable diversity within it, taken as a broad movement pursuing an essentially radical vision of jihad, it is dominating and arguably driving the global Islamic community at this point in time (Esposito, 2002: 116). Put simply, there is a tremendous energy and dynamism behind the Islamic activism that can be seen in contexts ranging from Palestine to Central Asia, while Bassam Tibi argues that Kepel is simply wrong: as the events of September 11 prove, 'the challenge of fundamentalism will continue to be with us, like it or not' (2002: xxiii). Moreover, if radical Islam is in decline, it may well be that – irrespective of debates about its legitimacy and value – the Bush administration's 'war on terrorism' and the wars in Afghanistan and Iraq have aided the ability of Islamist groups to attract support and recruit new members.

As for Osama bin Laden and the rest of the Al-Qaeda leadership, they clearly hoped to ignite a global jihad against America following its predictable military response to the attacks of September 11. This has not happened. Al-Qaeda and its associated groups are now facing considerable pressure in the post-September 11 period. As well as being outlawed by the international community, the world's remaining superpower and its allies are attempting to destroy them. And with the collapse of the Taliban regime in Afghanistan, bin Laden and Al-Qaeda are no longer protected by a state. Even countries like Pakistan and Saudi Arabia are monitoring and arresting

Islamic militants, and capturing and handing over Al-Qaeda suspects to the US authorities. Meanwhile wealthy individuals and groups that donate to Al-Qaeda or related organizations are facing increased monitoring of their financial activities and interests by the international community. Consequently, there are limits to the financial support groups like Al-Qaeda can expect to receive in the future. All of which will make it more difficult for terrorist networks to organize and function.

Furthermore, by resorting to terrorism Al-Qaeda will always face difficulties in sustaining its support base. With the path it has chosen, Al-Qaeda is reliant upon the spectacular event to attract support and is unable to build a constituency through grass-roots activity. As Kepel has noted, images in the media are 'at best capable of provoking only an immediate emotional reaction of solidarity, a fleeting enthusiasm' (2002: 16). This is no substitute for years of campaigning to mobilize Muslim opinion. In contrast, as discussed earlier, it is through such activity that Hamas has been able to develop itself as a credible alternative to the PLO within the world of Palestinian politics. Moreover, Al-Qaeda cannot commit so many terrorist acts that it alienates its existing support base. As is well known, among the innocent civilians killed on September 11 were many Muslims. Moreover, most of the people killed in the recent bombings in Tanzania, Kenya, Saudi Arabia and Morocco were not Westerners but the ordinary citizens of those respective countries. Acts of terrorism and the massive loss of life they entail can weaken the enthusiasm and commitment of even the most ardent supporters, especially when the goals appear unachievable. And it is not just those killed and their families who suffer; following such attacks their societies invariably undergo a downturn in tourism and a reduction in foreign investment and the lives of Muslims living in Western societies often become more difficult. Contrary to how it is often portrayed in the West, there are therefore certain political constraints under which Al-Qaeda operates.

Of course, such constraints are unlikely to lead to a change in Al-Qaeda's approach and strategy. A movement under pressure is likely to be even more dangerous, provoking last gasps of defiance. Moreover, the dispersal of Al-Qaeda and its sympathizers following the fall of the Taliban regime in Afghanistan in many respects makes it harder for Western governments to curtail their activities. No longer based in a particular state, Al-Qaeda, already a fairly loose and fluid network, is in a sense even freer to reek its havoc.

However, the impact of the September 11 attacks might have led commentators and politicians to overestimate the strength, size and significance of Al-Qaeda. In particular, the sheer audacity of the attacks, their horrific nature, as well as their powerful visual image might mean that we have lost a sense of perspective when it comes to Al-Qaeda. In this regard, Al-Qaeda's campaign of global terror may well come to shape the nature and future course of contemporary globalization. For example, one immediate effect of terrorist atrocities is that in their aftermath there is a reduction in the amount of travel to those countries that have been targeted. Attacks upon Westerners in non-Western countries invariably lead to Western governments discouraging their citizens from travelling to those countries. In October 2002, the Australian and British governments went further following the bomb explosion in Bali and urged their citizens to leave Indonesia. Meanwhile Western companies rethink their investment strategies and possibly withdraw from regions perceived as unsafe. Terrorism therefore has a direct impact upon the global economy and is particularly damaging for airlines and travel companies. For example, the British government suspended all flights to Kenya in May 2003 following intelligence reports of the likelihood of an attack by terrorist groups operating in that country. And post-September 11 the authorities in the US have introduced stricter controls over the movement of peoples and capital flowing in to and out of the country. All of which is not to suggest that globalizing processes will be halted or reversed by these acts of global terrorism, merely that their form will be affected by them.

The attacks of September 11 also vividly revealed that isolationism for a nation-state is no longer an option in our global age. The events of that day demonstrated that even the most powerful nation in the world is vulnerable to attack from a combination of modern technology and fanaticism. And the end of its isolation has both internal and external ramifications for the US. In the case of the latter, it means America will pay a price for its actions elsewhere in the globe and cannot expect to remain immune or detached from them. And internally the imposition of security measures to prevent the repeat of such attacks may well infringe upon the rule of law and democracy within America. Likewise, the use of interrogation and torture, the lack of full judicial trials and so forth further undermine these values. Indeed, many citizens within Western societies may witness some erosion of their civil liberties as well as periods of disruption to their daily lives in the fight against terrorism.

Conclusion

The argument of this chapter has been that to understand how globalization may be contributing to the global terrorism pursued by Al-Qaeda, it is necessary to examine this issue within the context of the history of relations between Islam and the West. In this regard, globalization is widely perceived as a form of Westernization and part of an ongoing Western threat to Islam, which has provoked Muslim resistance from Qutb to Al-Qaeda. Indeed, as we have seen Islamism or Islamic fundamentalism emerges from debates within the Islamic community, instigated in part by the encounter with the West and the sense of Islam being under pressure or siege. The rise of Islamist and fundamentalist movements is therefore at least in part a defensive response to these developments, reflecting a desire to hold on to the Islamic way of life. And, arguably, the resort to terrorism by some groups is a reflection of their powerlessness.

Thus, it is when globalization is viewed as a continuation of Western exploitation and injustice that groups like Al-Qaeda benefit. The more direct linkage between globalization and global terrorism lies with the use Al-Qaeda has made of the different forms of global interconnectedness. In particular, global transportation, communications technologies and financial networks have been utilized in order to carry out terrorist attacks throughout the world. Furthermore, Al-Qaeda has justified its actions and sought to recruit new members through global media organizations and networks. The movement is also believed to be using Islamist global networks to acquire radiological and biological weapons materials. In sum, the multiple forms and processes of globalization have played a vital role in Al-Qaeda's ability to organize and sustain itself.

In a single chapter it is only possible to discuss Al-Qaeda and global terrorism in relation to globalization in broad terms. Even talking about 'the Islamic world', 'the Muslim perspective' as well as 'the West' is problematical in that it subsumes diversity. Consequently, a rather generalized account has been presented here. But in trying to understand the wider historical, political and cultural context from which Al-Qaeda has emerged, a broad-brush approach is inevitable. However, future investigations will need to be more specific and localized, taking into greater account, for example, theological differences and divisions within Islam, as well as focusing upon particular Muslim states and societies. The fact that Al-Qaeda, as a global network, has been adapting to local conditions, further emphasizes the need for this type of analysis. It is for this reason that throughout this chapter the necessity of examining local contexts in order to determine why certain Islamist groups have emerged in particular societies and why some groups choose to associate with Al-Qaeda and others do not has been stressed. This type of analysis is also needed if we want to determine more accurately the influence of globalization. As we have seen throughout this work globalization is constituted by an uneven set of processes. For this reason it will be impacting upon Islamic societies and movements in different ways and therefore provoking divergent responses, dependent upon the nature of the interaction as well as local conditions. Nevertheless, by outlining global-Islamic relations or dynamics at a general level this chapter is intended to pave the way for such investigations.

Summarizing Points

- Globalization is perceived by many Muslims as a form of Westernization and as part of an ongoing Western threat to Islam.
- Some states in the Middle East and Central Asia remain largely disconnected from the processes of economic globalization.
- While Al-Qaeda considers globalization to be one of its targets, it has utilized many of its products and processes, such as global communication and information technologies and global financial networks.

–5–

China and Globalization

This chapter will consider the nature of China's engagement with contemporary globalization. Such a study is made more difficult by the vast size of the country and the regional, social, cultural and ethnic differences that exist within it. The experiences and perceptions, and hence any effects, of the multiple processes of globalization will be extremely varied. For example, a province like Guangdong on the eastern coast has become a global region intensively and extensively connected to the international economy and other global processes. In contrast, in some rural areas in the interior and in China's western provinces, the signs of globalization are more difficult to detect. It is also the case that some cities are more globally connected than other cities. A city like Shanghai is more outward-looking and tied into global economic, financial and information flows than, say, Beijing. With this diversity and complexity in mind, in order to assess the primary features of China's relationship with globalization the focus will be upon the party-state, the country's dominant institution, which will be considered in relation to its different dimensions, economic, political, and so forth. While globalization is affecting all sections of Chinese society, this cannot be covered in any detail in a single chapter, though a number of important global–local dynamics will be raised. It will be argued that China is globally interconnected and interdependent in relation to some dimensions of globalization, notably the economic, but more regionally orientated with regards to other dimensions, such as the military-strategic.

Given that China is effectively just starting to engage with contemporary globalization, the emphasis here will be upon thinking through the potential implications, both for the country and the international community, of its increasing engagement with gobalization's processes. This will include considering whether this engagement may contribute to the break-up of China, a possibility raised by a number of writers (see Chang, 2002). In this vein, to what extent does globalization undermine the position of the Chinese Communist Party (CCP), and how is the CCP responding to it? Many commentators maintain that communism is in terminal decline in China and that only the rhetoric remains, notably claiming that the leadership is pursuing 'socialism with Chinese characteristics'. In what ways, if at all, has globalization contributed to this development?

The China we know today did not exist until the twentieth century, emerging as a result of modern nationalism (see Goodman, 2004). Prior to that time it was essentially an empire, with a history of shifting borders and expansion into neighbouring states and provinces. It was also generally ahead of Europe in areas such as the arts, science and literature up until the Renaissance, and is credited for inventing gunpowder, paper and printing. For this reason there was a fairly widespread feeling within China, especially within ruling circles, that the 'Middle Kingdom' had little to gain from engaging commercially, intellectually or diplomatically with 'foreign barbarians'. Consequently, China's emperors consistently shunned contact with Europeans. However, by the nineteenth century the perils of insularity were brought home to many Chinese as they suffered military defeat to the technologically superior Europeans in the Opium Wars. This national humiliation and the imposition of what the Chinese termed 'the unequal treaties' paved the way for Western encroachment into the Chinese economy, as the European powers sought to carve out spheres of economic influence for themselves. These developments also sounded the death knell of the Qing dynasty and saw China start to incorporate foreign political ideas. This was a process that began with Sun Yat-sen's Republican revolution in 1911 and culminated in communism, another European idea, becoming the state ideology when Mao Zedong proclaimed the establishment of the People's Republic of China on 1 October 1949. Arguably, this intellectual trend was further in evidence when Deng Xiaoping declared the opening of China to the global market economy (that is, capitalism) in 1978, a moment that marked the beginning of the country's modernization programme.

Where this path takes China and how it engages with the different processes of globalization are the central concerns of this chapter. Writers such as Liu Kang (1998) consider that the official state response to dealing with globalization is inextricably linked to debates about how China modernizes. This will be another theme of this chapter. Some consideration will also be given to the concern that is being expressed within East Asia and the wider international community about the type of power China will be when it finally realizes its potential.[1]

China and Globalization: The Economic Dimension

It is in the economic sphere that China has most deeply engaged with the processes of globalization and in so doing contributed to greater global interdependence. As mentioned above, China began to take this course when Deng Xiaoping instituted the policy of 'reform and opening to the outside' in 1978, establishing market-orientated reforms and the adoption of an 'open-door policy' in relation to trade and investment.[2] It is with this policy that the link between China's modernization and globalization was explicitly made. Subsequently, China's global economic interdependence has increased, with many of its industries, notably textiles and electronic goods, becoming export-driven. These developments mark a significant departure from China's economic strategy prior to 1979, which was based upon state-driven import substitution and neglectful of export markets. Deng sought to justify this new approach by claiming that it was part of the development of the 'socialist market economy', and the wealth generated would trickle down to the poor. As he later put it, 'to get rich is glorious'. Jing Zemin, Deng's successor, sought to ensure that the CCP remained in control of the social and economic changes this policy stimulated with his strategy of 'The Three Represents'. This established that the party would represent advanced economic forces (the new business elite), the national culture (Confucianism) and the emerging new social constituencies. It has been widely viewed as an attempt by the CCP to become the national party of China, a point returned to later.

Greater integration with the international economy has enabled China to enjoy spectacular economic growth in the recent period, with annual growth rates of 8 to 9 per cent in the final years of the twentieth century.[3] China's international trade rose from $112 billion in 1989 to $474 billion in 2000, and the country has now overtaken the US as the prime site for foreign investment, attracting $53 billion in 2002.[4] In 2005, it is expected to overtake the UK as the world's fourth largest economy. China is also projected to become the world's largest economy by 2050, when its GDP will surpass that of the US and all other countries. Underpinning this development is an unlimited supply of cheap labour, which is a consequence of having a population of 1.3 billion and the reason China is coming to be viewed as the workshop of the world. But China also has one of the world's highest domestic savings rates, some 30 per cent in recent years, which has provided an important source of investment capital for the country's economic expansion. This means that China's economic growth should not be viewed as simply a result of it engaging with economic globalization and pursuing liberal trade polices. Despite the official line of the 'open-door policy', as Robert Hunter Wade (2003) has noted, China retained many of its protective tariff barriers, only starting to liberalize after it had enjoyed significant economic growth for some years.

A further sign of China's global interconnectedness is that it formally became a member of the WTO towards the end of 2001. While this secured China increased access to foreign markets, the WTO does place certain demands upon its members. As well as abiding by WTO rules and regulations, China is accepting the disciplines of a liberal-trading regime. This has entailed reducing tariffs for manufacturing, mining and agricultural products and automobiles. Moreover, as part of China's accession agreement, foreign-affiliated banks must be allowed access to the domestic market without restrictions at the end of 2005. In November 2004, Beijing published for the first time the annual report on its economy by the IMF, which is viewed as the first sign of greater transparency.

Yet China remains a protected economy, one which has been liberalizing but largely on its own terms. Above all the party-state is still seeking to manage aspects of economic globalization. This is because China's development and integration into the global economy will have implications for who controls the economy. Increasingly foreign-owned MNCs and TNCs will become more important to China's economy and they will not want state interference, nor to be associated with a regime that has a poor human rights record. Does the CCP turn its back on these corporations and the employment and FDI that they bring with them? Will the CCP leadership always accept the daily judgements the Chinese economy – and by the same token its economic competence – receives from international financial markets? In a similar vein, will it continue to accept the international consensus on the need for a reduced role for the state within the economy? Meanwhile WTO membership will mean ongoing pressure upon China to reform its financial sector and legal system to ensure greater openness and independence, and hence less political intervention by government. And to ensure fair and free competition, government involvement in economic life will have to become even more transparent. In short, by entering an established liberal international economic order, the CCP has been unable to shape it to make it more amenable to its own views.

Greater global economic integration also means that China is more susceptible to international economic recessions. This was reflected in the Asian financial crisis of 1997, which saw China suffer a dip in its own economic fortunes, though China's experience was nothing like the experiences of other East Asian countries. China's economic growth was 7.1 per cent in 1999, in the aftermath of the crisis, compared with 14.2 per cent in 1992. Furthermore, economic globalization entails Chinese businesses must become globally competitive. In this vein, Thomas Moore (2002) has emphasized that China's participation in and adaptation to the international economy, rather than domestic sources, have driven the country's economic development. He considers that this has been especially evident in reforms that have taken place within the textile and ship-building industries. In contrast, those (generally state-run) businesses unable or unwilling to adapt to the new conditions have been under enormous pressure, with many falling by the wayside. Reflecting these developments, public control of the economy has retreated with many state-owned enterprises being privatized. Moreover, 79 million jobs were lost in the state sector between 1997 and 2002. Today, the private sector accounts for most of China's economic output.

It will steadily become more difficult for Beijing to manage a national economy that is increasingly diverse, dynamic and globally interdependent. For example, since 1990 it has been unsuccessful in fixing minimum prices and limiting production. But this does not mean that the Chinese government will seek to withdraw from aspects of economic globalization in order to preserve its political control. It made considerable efforts to join the WTO (see Panitchpakdi and Clifford, 2002). Moreover, China is now engaged in the creation of the world's largest free trade zone. This follows an agreement by the Association of South-East Asian Nations (ASEAN) in October 2003 to form an integrated tariff-free trading and economic community that would include Japan, India and China by 2012 (Aglionby, 2003). But the main reason that Beijing is unlikely to disengage from forms of economic globalization is that economic growth, new employment opportunities and higher living standards are viewed by the CCP as the best way of convincing the population of the benefits of the existing political system. However, the party leadership is going to have to make difficult decisions about China's further integration into the international economy. For instance, it will have to respond to pressure from the US and Europe to float its currency – the renminbi (yuan) – which is pegged to the dollar (at the time of writing Beijing was showing signs of conceding to this demand and moving towards a more flexible currency regime).

The domestic effects of China's engagement with globalization have been numerous and varied. As mentioned earlier, coastal regions like Guangdong are fully integrated into the global economy and flourishing, whereas regions in the interior are not. Economic globalization is therefore exacerbating regional inequalities. There is also overcrowding in urban areas as a result of massive migration from the rural areas, a development that is highlighting the lack of infrastructure, services and amenities. More than 10 million peasants move into cities and economic zones every year and it is estimated that 345 million will migrate from rural to urban areas in the next 25 years. Higher levels of internal migration are also making it more difficult to tackle poverty because the poor are scattered more widely than in the past, while efforts spread the benefits of economic growth to the rural areas continue to be undermined by corrupt and inefficient regional officials.

The rural–urban divide is creating additional problems for the CCP. In many of China's flourishing cities communism has effectively been displaced by capitalism, while in the rural areas, the extent of peasant poverty is undermining party rule. In 2003, according to Beijing, the number of civic disturbances in rural areas rose by 14 per cent to 58,000 and involved more than 3 million people. Average rural incomes are now four times lower than urban incomes. Indeed, throughout China there has been a significant rise in income inequality, reflected in the emergence of new economic elites (Khan and Riskin, 2001). Such is the income disparity that there are concerns it will lead to social tensions and instability, which in turn have implications for the future survival of the party-state. Moreover, according to government figures, 800,000 of the country's citizens fell into poverty in 2003, with being in poverty defined as having an income of less than $77 per annum (Watts, 2004b). The CCP's response was to place the blame upon natural disasters, of which there were a number during that year, and to stress that more than 220 million had been lifted out of poverty in the past 25 years as a result of its economic reforms (Lim, 2004a). Nevertheless, the extent of the poverty within China will continue to exert a drag upon its economy, ensuring that it both lacks a strong domestic market to sustain its economic growth and remains heavily reliant upon its export trade. At the same time, high unemployment and feelings of widespread insecurity, which are at least in part a consequence of integration into the global market economy and the greater competition this entails, mean that the fate of the party leadership is now closely linked to China's continued economic growth.

One feature of China's economy and society that may well shape its future inter-action with the processes of economic globalization is the level of corruption that exists. Corruption is a particular problem for China because government and party officials control access to business licences and other permits, and also infiltrate the legal system (Gittings, 2002). Indeed, China has been rated as one of the most corrupt economies in the world by Transparency International (Levy, 2002). Moreover, to date the regime's anti-corruption policies have proved unsuccessful in tackling this problem – although many critics consider that it is the regime itself, and the lack of political accountability and openness within the political system, which is actually fuelling the corruption. The extent of the corruption has the potential to deter FDI and foreign companies moving to China. Thus, Beijing's success or otherwise in tackling this problem will impact upon China's future economic relations with the rest of the international community. At the same time the level of corruption has internal political implications, a point acknowledged in a policy paper by the CCP's Central Committee issued in September 2004, which declared that corrupt party members and officials were causing so much popular discontent that it threatened the continuation of communist rule (Hennock, 2004).

China's economic development and deepening engagement with the different forms of economic globalization will obviously have consequences for the environ-ment. In fact, of all the major powers, China is likely to face some of the most challenging environmental problems. This is due to a combination of factors, notably its large population, the environmentally insensitive nature of much of its rapid development and insufficient natural resources. For example, China has to feed a fifth the world's population but possesses only 7 per cent of its arable land. Indeed, it is already feeling the impact of environmental degradation. Sixteen of the world's twenty most polluted cities are in China and large parts of Beijing can be under smog for weeks at a time. Deforestation has worsened the periodic floods the country faces. Stretches of many of its rivers are drying up and dust deserts are not uncommon. As a result of urbanization China's arable land is shrinking at the rate of 1 million hectares a year, which means the country is increasingly reliant upon imported food and has recently become a net importer of food, especially grain, for the first time in its history (Luard, 2004a; Watts, 2004c). Moreover, much of China's development has been based upon reliance upon coal, which provides for 75 per cent of the country's energy needs and is doing considerable harm to the environment. Similarly, the dramatic growth in car ownership – car sales increased by 81 per cent for the year 2002/3 – will have environmental consequences. China is expected to become the second largest car producer by 2010 and as car production is not at this stage export-driven the cars produced are essentially for the domestic market (McRae, 2004). In fact, within a few years China will be the world's second largest car market, after the US. The International Energy Agency predicts the cumulative effect of these developments will be that China will account for more than a quarter of the increase in greenhouse gases in the next 25 years.

China's integration into the global economy has considerable implications for the rest of the international community (see Lardy, 2002). Already China's emergence as a major trading power has been increasing the world's shipping rates. But arguably the key area where China's rise will be felt is in the energy markets. China has become the second largest importer of oil after the US. Indeed, China's development is consuming a range of the world's resources at a staggering rate; in 2003, for example, China used over half of the world's cement and 36 per cent of its steel. As result of its economic transformation China is also now the world's largest consumer of aluminium and copper. All of which means the prices of oil and commodities such as metals and ores have risen significantly, affecting countries and consumers throughout the world – although because China is likely to be extremely productive for the next 25 years, and given that it is a low-cost producer, prices will be forced down, which may serve to counterbalance the rise in the price of mineral resources.

Furthermore the international community will have to decide whether it can keep buying China's goods at current rates. This is especially a problem for the US, which has a growing trade deficit with China. China's exports to the US have risen from $5 billion in 1990 to over $92 billion in 2003, and arguably this has only been tolerated by Washington because many of these manufactured products are produced by US companies operating in the country. This does not mean the US and the rest of the world will turn to protectionism, but other countries will have to factor into their future growth strategies the reality of an emerging new economic superpower.[5]

Finally, it is also the case that China's economic rise should be treated with some caution. To begin with, while China's economic growth has been rapid it started from a very low base. Hence, it is unlikely that levels of 9 per cent growth per year can be sustained, especially as the rest of the world may not always carry on buying China's products at current rates. Furthermore, as well as the problems already cited that will hold back China's economic development, such as inefficient state-owned enterprises and financial corruption, there are also weaknesses in China's banking sector, which is struggling with bad debts to the extent that it could undermine future economic expansion. And as has been shown, China's economic transformation is uneven, with signs that it is provoking resentment in those rural areas being left behind. All of which raises concern about how secure are the foundations of its economic boom are, a point that China's premier, Wen Jiabao, raised repeatedly during 2004 as part of his call for better co-ordinated growth. Lastly, it is highly unlikely that the rest of the international community will continue to tolerate Beijing's selective adherence to WTO rules and regulations, evident in it not respecting intellectual property rights and maintaining forms of protectionism.

China and Globalization: The Political Dimension

Greater integration into the global economy would seem to present the Chinese party-state with considerable political challenges. As mentioned, the liberal economic order that China has entered insists upon openness, transparency and rule-based governance, which will or at least should entail changes to its legal and political systems. Moreover, economic development is aided by the free movement of people, ready access to information for businesses and entrepreneurs and regular contact with other companies and countries in order to exchange best practice, and these economic freedoms it is claimed can lead to demands for equivalent political freedoms. Having the autonomy to be able to display responsibility and initiative in the economic realm makes the denial of this in the political realm stand out all the more. The social forces unleashed by the party leadership's dual globalization–modernization agenda would also seem to demand political changes. In the cities, for example, it has led to a consumer revolution as millions of Chinese forge their own lifestyles through their patterns of consumption, expressing their personal autonomy in the process, behaviour that they may well want to extend into the political realm. In particular, as a result of its economic transformation, China has a rapidly expanding middle class that is likely in the foreseeable future to push for a greater say in a running of its own country and consequently will be demanding political reform.

However, while China's government has been implementing economic reforms and restructuring the state bureaucracy, it has been reluctant to transform the political system. Above all it shows scant signs of introducing democracy and an independent legal system. Indeed, it is in the sphere of politics and culture that the party leadership's attempt to manage globalization has been most apparent. The leadership has adopted more open approach adopted towards economic globalization simply because it is viewed as enhancing state power and hence strengthening the position of the CCP. Critics, however, consider that the lack of political reform actually deters foreign companies who are put off by the lack of rule-based state governance such as clear regulations and enforceable contracts, which necessitates an independent judiciary. They also have to negotiate what are often elaborate party networks in order to conduct their business. All of which it has been claimed will hinder China's ability to become a modern nation-state (see Zheng, 2004). In this vein, the need for reforms to facilitate the emergence of a vibrant civil society within China not only is indicative of an improperly functioning state but also hinders the formation of business networks, which require such a space in order to develop. While new social organizations are emerging, in part facilitated by the IT revolution, the omnipresent party-state means that civil society in China cannot yet be classified as 'vibrant'.

The lack of political reform may well lead to the CCP's authority being challenged in the future. There are already signs of trouble ahead. Uneven economic development is making it more difficult for Beijing to control local provinces. And there are some indications that the party organization and discipline are eroding. For example, urban neighbourhood committees, which monitored citizen behaviour on behalf of the party, have declined. Minxin Pei (2002) believes the CCP has lost its ability to orchestrate mass political campaigns and relies more heavily upon repression to deal with opponents, such as the Falun Gong spiritual movement. This organizational decline is due, Pei believes, to the CCP's diminishing economic role and function in society, which are leading to a loosening of the party-state nexus. For example, the privatization of collective farming has reduced the role of the state in the lives of rural peasants. Thus, political reform is needed in order to incorporate more citizens into the political process, which in turn would help to ensure better scrutiny of government, establish greater accountability and reduce corruption.

Greater global interconnectedness will also mean that Beijing will be more scrutinized by the outside world. In particular, INGOs, such as human rights groups, will be monitoring what is happening in China. Meanwhile China's occupation of Tibet will continue to attract international criticism. There is also the issue of how an authoritarian regime wedded to a particular ideology will react to the continuing development of forms of global governance, such as international rule-making. China has steadily been participating in more multilateral treaties and becoming a member of more international organizations (see Kim, 2004). But to date there remain international treaties and conventions that Beijing has not given its signature to or has simply opposed. These include the landmine treaty and the International Criminal Court. In contrast, China signed the International Covenant on Economic, Social and Cultural Rights on 5 October 1997 and the International Covenant of Civil and Political Rights on 27 October 1998. However, China has fallen short of the international standards these covenants demand. The CCP has also tried to resist international monitoring of its record in these areas. Moreover, Beijing has been devolving political authority to the provinces and this in turn is making it more difficult for China to adhere to international rules and agreements. At the same time the resurgence of nationalism within the country is also likely to influence China's relationship with the institutions of global governance. Tony Saich believes the CCP is adhering to an increasingly outdated conception of sovereignty. As he puts it: 'China is essentially an empire anchored to a Westphalian concept of the nation-state trying to operate in an increasingly multilateral world' (Saich, 2000: 213).

However, there are some signs that the CCP is responding to the extent of the recent changes. Capitalist entrepreneurs are now allowed into the party ranks and the concept of 'private property rights' was incorporated into the constitution at the 2004 National People's Congress. Beijing has been experimenting with low-level elections and improving checks and balances on communist rule in order to reduce corruption and the abuse of power, while the party-state is itself no longer a monolithic entity: there are competing factions and interest groups within the CCP and the government (Yan, 2002). There has even been discussion about changing the CCP's name and dispensing with the word 'communist' in the process (Ryosei, 2004). And with regards to political philosophy some commentators detect a shift from communism to corporatism (Dickson, 2000/1).

The promotion of a nationalist discourse enables the party leadership to fill the ideological vacuum created by the demise of communism and strengthen its grip on power. Furthermore, nationalism can serve to counter calls for greater regional autonomy, which is a potential consequence of China's uneven regional development, especially in flourishing areas like Guangdong where the wealth being generated is providing them with a stronger bargaining position in their dealings with Beijing. In some provinces the promotion of regional identity is seen as the best way of attracting global capital (see Oakes, 2000). Indeed, it is one of the claims of the hyperglobalizers, such as Kenichi Ohmae (2000), that nation-states are under threat from region-states, which are considered the more natural economic zones in an era of globalization – although in the case of China this has to be balanced by the fact that the decision by the CCP to increase devolution of power to the provinces has contributed to the growth in regional distinctiveness in areas like South China.[6]

It may be that a reassertion of nationalism will be necessary to prevent the disintegration of China by separatist forces. In particular, the country is facing internal problems with Muslim separatists in Xinjiang province, who are part of its large Turkic Uighur population and seek their own independent state of East Turkestan. There have been a number of disturbances in recent years, including terrorist attacks, which the Chinese government claim are part of global terrorism (Hewitt, 2000). However, Amnesty International has accused the Chinese authorities of using 'the war on terror' as a pretext for implementing more repressive measures, notably making thousands of arrests and executing dozens of people. The CCP leadership is also concerned about the influence of radical Islam spreading from central Asia and across China's porous border.

Further evidence of the need for a unifying nationalist discourse are the increasing incidents of ethnic violence between some of China's ethnic minorities and the majority Han Chinese population.[7] In November 2004, there was a major outburst of ethnic violence between thousands of Han Chinese villagers and Hui Muslims in Henan province. Relations between the Han and some ethnic minorities in China have been sensitive for many years. In part, this is because the minorities have received some benefits, such as easier access to employment and universities, in an attempt to incorporate them into the nation, which has merely provoked Han resentment. Growing regional inequalities, the decentralization of power and the marginalization of minorities in some areas as a result of increasing Han migration have laid bare ethnic and racial prejudices within Chinese society and led to the loyalty of the minorities being questioned.[8]

These developments will strengthen the resolve of the CCP to pose as the guardian of the nation. As part of this approach, Beijing has been reviving China's cultural heritage, developing strategies to ensure international sporting success and making strenuous efforts to host the Olympics Games, which it will now be doing in 2008. This does not mean, however, that Chinese nationalism should be considered as simply a product of elite manipulation, and hence a superficial phenomenon. On the contrary it pervades Chinese society, evident in the publication of numerous nationalist books and pamphlets in the recent period, and contains a strong anti-western and in particular anti-American sentiment (see Song et al., 1996). This was especially evident with the Belgrade Embassy bombing in 1999, which led to an outburst of popular outrage including physical damage done to the US Embassy in Beijing.[9] Such a widespread reaction was facilitated by Internet chat rooms, which provided a forum for Chinese people to vent their anger (Shen, 2004). China's engagement with globalization therefore not only paves the way for the emergence of new social forces, it threatens the revival of older ones as well. In this regard, Edward Friedman (1996) argues that many ordinary citizens are playing the national card as a form of protest against the CCP. It is difficult for the state to clamp down on citizens engaging in patriotic activities and expressing patriotic sentiments, especially when the CCP is pursuing a similar agenda itself.

Thus, the changes ushered in by globalization and modernization are presenting China's leaders with enormous challenges that potentially threaten the survival of the party-state itself. It is for this reason that the party leadership is seeking to manage globalization. Tony Saich (2000) believes that the CCP has been quite adept at adjusting to the demands of economic globalization, but less so when it comes to responding to the social and political changes generated by this development. The CCP has made the state bureaucratic system and other economic institutions more market-orientated, reformed the taxation and financial systems and encouraged individual enterprise and the development of an entrepreneurial class, in order to enable China to operate in a globalized market economy. At the same time Beijing has largely resisted implementing any measures to facilitate greater pluralism and democracy in order to accommodate new and emerging social forces. But such is the strength of these forces that the party leadership may come to conclude that a different response is required. At this stage, however, the link that is often made between economic development and political liberalization, between capitalism and democracy, has not yet been demonstrated in the case of China. An important reason for this is that too many people have a stake in the existing system, notably the 66 million members of the CCP who enjoy benefits such as exclusive access to certain jobs and better schooling for their children. Moreover, the relationship between capitalism and democracy is not as straightforward as is suggested in the works of some writers (see Huntington, 1984; Lindblom, 1977; Lipset, 1963). The role that culture can play in informing and even disrupting this relationship must be taken into account (see Kinnvall, 2002). Should China ever go down the democratic path, it may simply emulate the model of democracy found elsewhere in East Asia, which is generally more state-centred and often dominated by a single party. This is all the more likely given that China's President Hu Jintao publicly declared in September 2004 that 'copying Western political systems is a blind alley for China'. It is also perhaps why the CCP is repositioning itself as the national party.

China and Globalization: The Military Dimension

What impact may a rising power like China have upon the stability of the international system? Will China want to gain international status to match its growing economic power, much as Germany did in the late nineteenth century? China's military capability is enhanced by the country's rapidly developing economy, its vast territory, which contains fossil fuels, such as coal, and a huge population. The People's Liberation Army (PLA) is the largest army in the world at 2.3 million, though it has not fought a war since 1979. China already possesses nuclear weapons and has been acquiring advanced weapons such as ballistic missiles and strategic nuclear warheads from other countries, notably Russia. It is also a significant exporter of arms and weapons technology, especially to Middle Eastern regimes. Yet despite these factors there are reasons to suggest that China should not currently be viewed as an active contributor to military globalization. In essence they are the same reasons why Beijing will seek to avoid engaging in a global ideological or geopolitical struggle with the US, as the Soviet Union did during the Cold War.

First, there are certain factors that limit China's military potential, which mean that it will be unable to match America's military power for the foreseeable future. To begin with size of territory is no longer viewed as a key determinant of power in the contemporary period. Multi-ethnic empires spanning large areas or regions are invariably confronted with regional and separatist forces, both of which China is indeed confronted with, though the size of the Han Chinese population means that to date this has not been a major problem. More significantly, as will be discussed in Chapter 6, China cannot match the US in terms of the 'revolution in military affairs' (RMA). It lacks the requisite scientific infrastructure to deploy technologically advanced forces for several decades (Goldstein, 2000). China also currently lacks an effective modern air force, and its navy is also inferior to that of the US, though Beijing is endeavouring to modernize aspects of both forces. Moreover, to date, China's growing economic power has not significantly enhanced its military power. In fact, its total military budget declined from 2.5 to 2 per cent of GDP during the 1990s (Nye, 2002: 21). This means that China's defence budgets come nowhere near to the levels spent by the US upon its military forces (see Chapter 6). In sum, Beijing is almost certainly aware that at present it cannot match US military power and is unlikely to be a global competitor for most of this century. Indeed, should China wish to harm the US it could best do so by economic means, curtailing the loans that it has been giving to America. As will be discussed in the next chapter, China, along with Japan, has been lending America hundreds of billions of dollars, facilitating its huge spending sprees. However, given that China has greatly benefited from American consumers purchasing vast amounts of Chinese goods, such an action is also unlikely.

Second, as has been mentioned, the CCP has already effectively lost the ideological battle at home, where communism is a diminishing force. It is for this reason that the

CCP leadership is insecure about its own survival, and it would be unlikely to go out of its way to test its popularity by fighting a major conflict. The alternative view is that Beijing may come to regard military engagement as a way of strengthening its own position, enabling it to ride on a tide of resurgent nationalism that any conflict is likely to provoke. Yet concern with its own survival entails that the CCP leadership regards global economic interdependence as more important than devising a global military strategy, at least for the time being. This necessitates continued access to foreign markets and technology and hence avoiding tensions with powers like the US and the EU, which could harm China's economic development. Thus, the CCP's concern with China's economy is likely to deter it from being overly aggressive in its conduct within the international arena, both now and in the future.

Third, at present China's military and strategic policy is simply not globally orientated. Rather it is regionally focused upon East Asia, where China believes it has more pressing interests, notably its territorial claims to Taiwan, the Spratly Islands and the Diaoyu (Senkaku) Islands. It is for this reason that Beijing blocks any attempts to establish an Asian collective security system as it would give states in the region a forum in which to challenge such claims (Saich, 2000). Above all the Chinese authorities would like to reintegrate Taiwan into the motherland. Beijing has never accepted Taiwan's breakaway from China in 1949 and is unlikely ever to accept its formal independence. China would also like to establish itself as the regional hegemonic power and arguably it is on the way to doing so. The country's growing economic power, coupled with Japan's continuing economic difficulties, is enabling Beijing to position itself as the major player in the region. But China's ability to get its own way will be dependent upon a range of factors, and not only how the US views such a development. It will depend on how the states of the region respond, on whether they pursue a policy of engagement or containment. In this regard, the late Gerald Segal (2000) wrote of the need for a policy of 'constrainment', containing elements of both approaches, though he doubted that there was the collective will to achieve this. A further complicating factor is that a number of East Asian countries have sizeable ethnic Chinese populations, inevitably affecting relations with China.

It is also important to bear in mind how China views itself and its role within the international community. Obviously, there will be a myriad of perspectives on this issue within China, ranging from the views of policy-makers to those of ordinary citizens. There is also the possibility that there will be unrealistic perceptions of China's power and status. Conversely, future setbacks, such as economic downturns, domestic unrest or environmental problems, may dent some of the confidence currently emanating from China. Ultimately, however, in the current circumstances it is the CCP leadership that will decide on China's future global or regional role and it will do this largely on the basis of domestic political considerations, and in particular the party's future survival. While some political authority has been devolved to the local and regional authorities, foreign policy remains the preserve of the Politiburo and the Central Military Commission. In other words, it is controlled by figures whose outlook is profoundly informed by the events at Tiananmen Square in 1989 and the collapse of communist governments at that time (Shambaugh, 2000).

Thus, if we view military globalization as entailing 'long-distance networks of interdependence in which force, and the threat or promise of force, are employed' (Keohane and Nye, 2002: 196), then for the reasons outlined China cannot be viewed as significantly contributing to this phenomenon at this moment in time. While it is involved in the global arms trade, China has neither the capacity nor the will to maintain long-distance military-strategic networks. Given its current military capabilities, China will have difficulty in projecting its hard power beyond East Asia. Therefore, for the foreseeable future it will be a regional rather than a global power (see Gill, 2004). In fact, at this stage China would find it difficult to overcome other regional powers, despite the overwhelming size of the PLA. Taiwan, Japan and the ASEAN states have independent military capabilities, including advanced weapons that cannot easily be dismissed or defeated. Arguably, if this were not the case, China might already have made a concerted and sustained attempt to recapture Taiwan (Goldstein, 2000).[10]

China and Globalization: The Cultural Dimension

This section will consider the cultural dynamics of globalization in relation to China. Martin Jacques has argued that the rise of China as an economic powerhouse and a key global player 'will be the prelude to the growing global influence of Chinese values' (2004: 23). This is an interesting contention, but the danger is that it essentializes Chinese culture. Given the size of China, the diversity that exists within it and that it is a relatively recent construct, 'Chinese culture' is a problematic concept (Shih, 2002). It is therefore appropriate to ask: what are these distinctive 'Chinese values'? And how do they differ from human values?

Confucianism is often regarded as being a key constitutive element of Chinese values. However, its emphasis upon education and hard work can be found in other cultures (Lingle, 1997). There are other aspects of Confucianism that are more distinctive, such as filial piety, harmonious co-operation (i.e., commitment to the social group over the self) and respect for authority. Indeed, these conformist values are the reason why Beijing, following the Tiananmen Square massacre, has been promoting neo-Confucianism as integral to the new national culture. In addition, neo-Confucianism is presented as an alternative to an American-led globalization (Zheng, 1999). However, given its communist past, there is the issue of whether the CCP can credibly commandeer Confucianism as part of a unifying discourse of nationalism, while the extent of the corruption within the party-state system, and the damage that it is doing to do Chinese society, would also seem to undermine the CCP's promotion of neo-Confucian values. Moreover, there is a further sense in which neo-Confucianism does not neatly fit with the new Chinese nationalism.

This concerns the origins of its recent revival, which began outside of China, in countries such as Hong Kong, Taiwan, Singapore, South Korea and even the US, where it was promoted by North American academics, such as Tu Wei-ming. Indeed, Confucianism or new Confucianism is now increasingly discussed as a model of capitalist development (see Pye, 2000; Rieger and Leibfried, 2003). For a variety of reasons therefore neo-Confucianism would not seem to be a particularly productive means of building a national culture.

Most importantly, Chinese values and culture cannot be reduced to Confucianism. Within China there are traditional folk cultures as well as other ethical–religious traditions, such as Buddhism and Taoism. However, returning to the theme of this work, Chinese culture in all its diverse forms is facing certain challenges from aspects of globalization. China has been undergoing a consumer revolution, and Western brands and products, from films to furniture, as well as chain stores, are proving extremely popular (see Link et al., 2002).[11] Western advertising is everywhere, especially in China's major cities. In addition, China in its rush to develop has been destroying much of its cultural heritage, especially in clearing ground to build new skyscrapers, enormous malls and shopping plazas. In this way it has continued the destructive practices of the twentieth century that culminated in the Cultural Revolution (Luard, 2004b). More recently, however, as part of its attempt to revive national culture, the CCP has been taking a greater interest in China's cultural heritage and attempting to preserve and restore artefacts and rebuild monuments and ancient pagodas.

Similarly, cultural and economic globalization has implications for Chinese (Confucian) values. Given Beijing considers engagement with globalization to be an integral part of China's modernization programme, then the changes these combined processes will usher in may well have detrimental consequences for these values and ways of life. For example, filial piety, harmonious co-operation and respect for authority would seem to be challenged by rapid urbanization, greater travel and social mobility, the rural–urban division of wealth, and access to new cultures and ideas. In particular, rising individualism runs counter to the Confucian emphasis upon the wider social group and social stability over the self. Of course, the extent to which China has become a more individualistic society as a result of its economic transformation is a source of debate. There may be signs of individualism among China's growing middle class, with many adhering to Western lifestyles and consumption patterns. However, this social class covers many different groups and sectional interests, and it is unwise to generalize about how it is behaving. Furthermore the need even for entrepreneurs to work with the party-state system in order to conduct their business means they cannot simply ignore the wider social framework.

As regards the export of Chinese culture abroad, and how China is informing cultural globalization more generally, it is a mixed picture. There are aspects of Chinese culture that have gained a wide audience, such as its cuisine, martial arts and exercise regimes, partly because of the Chinese diaspora. More recently, there are also signs that Chinese action films are becoming increasingly popular abroad. There is also growing interest in the West in traditional Chinese medicine, art and Taoism, and new Buddhist monasteries and temples in the Chinese tradition are being built in the US and Europe. But other aspects of Chinese culture, ranging from Confucianism to music, have not caught on beyond East Asia. Gerald Segal (1999) believed Chinese culture had a limited global reach, noting that the Chinese party-state has spent much of the last two decades fighting a rearguard action against external cultural influences. Yet this needs to be balanced by the fact that China is poised to make inroads into the world of the Internet. By the end of 2004 China had 111 million Internet users, making it the largest online community in the world after the US, and it is estimated that within a few years Chinese Internet users will outnumber American users. Some commentators argue this development is unlikely to lead to Mandarin displacing English as the lingua franca of the Internet. Others predict that by 2010 the Chinese-language Internet will be larger than its English-language counterpart.

A significant factor inhibiting China's ability to inform and influence other societies via global cultural and information flows is the nature of its political system. China's government, and in particular its state-centred communist ideology and human rights record, has little appeal for other countries, which in turn reduces its soft power. Indeed, one area where the CCP attracts considerable criticism is over its tight control of the media. China has over 25,000 newspapers and magazines but the authorities determine whether they report on sensitive political issues and provide guidance on how to do so. Likewise, the state censors television news coverage, determining the stories that must not be reported. And while there are many terrestrial television channels in China, they are all run by the state or provincial government. Beijing also routinely blocks access to Internet web sites, notably those of Falun Gong, human rights groups and some foreign news organizations. It also jams the short-wave radio broadcasts of foreign news providers, while in 2004 television presenters were instructed by the State Administration of Radio, Film and TV to stop aping Western ways in their appearance and manner and to refrain from using English words (Watts, 2004a).

However, controlling global cultural and information flows is difficult even for an authoritarian regime, and the more China integrates with the rest of the world the more difficult it will become for the CCP. In particular, Beijing appears unable to deal with the scale of pirating and distribution of foreign films and television programmes within China. Likewise it cannot monitor and block all satellite television and Internet usage. New global information and communication technologies therefore present ordinary Chinese citizens with greater access to the outside world and to different perspectives on news and global affairs. This means that the state no longer has a monopoly over information. The long-term political consequences of this development are difficult to determine. While it would seem to work against an authoritarian regime, whether the CCP falls or not will be determined by many other factors, such as the domestic political situation and the extent of corruption within China.

For Mayfair Mei-hui Yang (2002), what really concerns Beijing about global cultural flows is not so much Westernization, but the influence that Chinese communities overseas might exert. Based upon a case study of Shanghai, Yang identifies the makings of a transnational Chinese cultural identity that increasingly eludes state influence. In particular, Hong Kong and Taiwanese popular culture, from pop songs to karaoke singing, are permeating Chinese society as a result of the emergence of a genuinely transnational media, one that is starting to challenge the national media. All of which will make it harder, Yang argues, for the Chinese party-state to shape the national subject. However, there are four factors that suggest the CCP leadership will not be unduly concerned about this development. First, most of the financial flows going into China are from the Chinese communities of Hong Kong, Taiwan and Southeast Asia, which suggests that many within them are not overly hostile to Beijing. Between 1979 and 1997, the overseas Chinese were responsible for 80 per cent of the foreign investment and loans that China received (Cohen, 1997: 161). Second, as mentioned earlier, Shanghai has since the arrival of the Royal Navy in the nineteenth century been one of China's most outward looking cities. This raises questions about how representative it is of the rest of China. Third, Yang's identification of a transnational cultural subjectivity resulting from exposure to an ethnic overseas Chinese capitalism must be weighed against the growth of popular (as opposed to government orchestrated) nationalism in China. Fourth, as David Goodman (2004) has argued, we should not homogenize 'the Chinese'. Many of the Chinese living elsewhere in East Asia are assimilated into those societies, speak no Chinese language, and will therefore have only limited cultural appeal for Chinese living on the mainland.

There is a further aspect of the cultural dynamics of globalization that needs to be considered in relation to China, and this concerns the possibility of global cultural conflict. In this vein, Samuel Huntington (1997), who considers that globalization brings different cultures into closer contact with the each other and thereby increases the likelihood of conflict, detects an emerging global Islamic–Confucian connection seeking to challenge Western hegemony. But there are numerous problems with this claim. In China there is little evidence of this development. As we have seen Beijing is currently fighting, as it sees it, its own 'war on terror' against Islamic extremists. Moreover, with regard to Muslims in China, there is a further factor that both undermines the connection Huntington makes and reveals how the country, in order to retain its distinctiveness, still remains detached from some global processes. This concerns the way in which Islam in China is at odds with global trends within the Islamic world. There are 20 million Muslims in China, and what is emerging in some parts of China, notably in Ningxia province, is what has been termed 'Islam with Chinese characteristics' (Lim, 2004b). Quite simply, the CCP's control of religion has ensured that a distinctly Chinese conception of Islam has developed, something that is especially evident in the emergence of female imams as well as female Muslims setting up their own independent mosques in China. In short, globalizing Islam, which as we saw in Chapter 4 is dominated by the Wahhabi and Salafi traditions, has found it difficult to have any impact upon China's Muslims. All of which would suggest that there are significant obstacles in the way of a global Confucian–Islamic connection.

In sum, any claims about the spread of Chinese cultural values should be treated with caution, especially if this is asserted to be a consequence of globalization. This is because as has been shown there are many aspects to the cultural dynamics of globalization. But also because cultures are not neat and discrete entities. Nor are they stable. Rather they absorb a range of influences and traditions, a process that globalization facilitates.

Conclusion

Having examined how China has been dealing with globalization, two main conclusions can be drawn. First, globalization is conceived of by the party-state as central to its modernization programme. Second, China has been pursuing multifarious strategies in relation to the processes of globalization with the party-state engaged to a varying extent and in distinct ways with its different dimensions. More specifically, China is economically interconnected and interdependent with the rest of the world, whereas militarily and strategically it is less so. As for the political and cultural dimensions of globalization, the party-state is seeking to manage any domestic effects that global forces and flows can have through such measures as promoting a nationalist discourse and monitoring the Internet usage of its citizens (Yan, 2002). The consistent theme underlying the CCP's multidimensional approach to the different aspects of globalization is simply its own survival.

Having been a leading civilization for many thousands of years, China arguably lost its way because it remained closed to the outside world and new ideas. Today, China's engagement with globalization is enabling it to tackle its relative decline. Via foreign companies based in China, it is absorbing new ideas and technologies and adapting them to suit its own purposes. Meanwhile other aspects of economic globalization – notably more intensive and extensive trading and financial relations with the rest of the international community – are facilitating the country's economic transformation. All of which holds out the possibility of China eventually returning to its pre-eminent position in the world. At the same time it raises the issue of how the international community should respond to the rapid rise of this power. Some Western commentators predict conflict with China is the likely and even inevitable outcome of this development (see Bernstein and Munro, 1997). The US since the mid 1990s has been pursuing a policy of both containment and engagement, limiting

China's access to military technologies and building alliances with Japan but also backing China's entry into the WTO in the hope that it will liberalize. But whatever response is adopted one thing that a more interconnected and interdependent world ensures is that China cannot be ignored.

Summarizing Points

- China is engaged with economic globalization, but more regionally orientated with regards to globalization's other dimensions, such as the military-strategic.
- Economic globalization is viewed by the CCP as essential to China's modernization programme and as a way of strengthening the party-state.
- It is in the areas of politics and culture that the CCP leadership's attempt to manage globalization is most evident.
- It is too early to tell whether the economic success of globally integrated regions like Guangdong will come to challenge China itself.

−6−

The United States and Globalization

As was the case with China, determining the influence of globalization upon the United States is made more difficult by the size of the country and the sheer diversity that exists within it, notably in the form of ethnic cultural, class and regional differences. Americans living in parts of the rural Midwest are likely to have different experiences and perceptions of globalization from their fellow Americans living in New York, for example. Indeed, the extent of the divisions within American society is attracting considerable comment (Himmelfarb, 1999; Huntington, 2004; Wolfe, 1998). It was evident in the voting at the 2000 presidential election, with the Republican Party receiving the bulk of its support from rural areas and the inner heartland of America, and the Democratic Party gaining most of its support from the larger cities, the industrial Midwest and America's coastal regions. As for the presidential election of 2004, arguably its most notable feature was that it showed up the profound differences that existed between the religious right and the secular left within the US. In this vein, there are also considerable political divisions over America's role in the world, including isolationists, multilateralists and unilateralists or neo-conservatives. Hence it is perhaps appropriate to conceive of the US as many Americas, rather than just the one (see Slater and Taylor, 1999).

America is also a dynamic and ever-changing society, a society on the move, as it is sometimes described. This merely exacerbates the difficulty of determining how the processes of globalization are operating at any one moment. And as has been stressed throughout this work, there are many dimensions to globalization. Moreover, the varying intensity and extent of contemporary global flows, networks and interconnections will not be having a uniform impact upon American society. As a consequence, while the intention is to consider the multiple forms of globalization in relation to particular contexts, there will inevitably be something of a broad-brush approach employed here, as with previous chapters. And as with China, a number of different aspects of globalization will be considered in relation to American society, notably the cultural, economic, military and human migration dimensions, in order to determine how they are being engaged with and any possible effects that they might be having.

Finally, an examination of America raises the issue of whether it is reasonable to consider the multiple forms of global interconnectedness that constitute globalization as non-political developments. That is, as being largely beyond the political control of any single power like the US. Consequently, as well as examining how the different processes of globalization are impacting upon American society, this chapter will consider the extent to which the US is shaping their nature and form elsewhere in the globe. This in turn will help us to decide whether it is appropriate to view globalization as essentially Americanization. Addressing this issue will further highlight the contested nature of globalization, or at least the debates surrounding it. The position taken here is that there are aspects of globalization that the US is indeed dominating and informing, notably in the economic and military spheres, but that it is not in control of all of globalization's processes. In fact it is possible that aspects of globalization will in time serve to erode some of America's power.

Global Migration and America

America has a long history of accepting the world's migrants. The issue concerning many commentators and politicians is whether, during the contemporary phase of globalization, this trend has increased in intensity and extent. In other words, are more people entering America? And are they coming from more parts of the world? Obviously, this is dependent upon the periods our own era is being contrasted with. Using official figures, David Held and his co-writers estimate that between 1945 and 1995 around 25 million people emigrated to the US, which as they note is less than the 30 million to the US during the period 1880 to 1920 (1999: 311–12). However, these figures focus upon legal migration and it is estimated that there were between 4 and 5 million irregular ('illegal') migrants in the US during the 1990s with many coming from Mexico (Jordan and Düvell, 2003). Moreover, Held et al. note that immigration between 1990 and 1995 did substantially rise to around 1 million legal migrants per year, and taking this figure together with the level of illegal migration, they conclude that '[i]mmigration in the first half of the 1990s was running at a historically unparalleled rate' (1999: 315). This is reflected in the number of foreign-born residents in the US, which in 2000 stood at 10.4 per cent of the population. In 1890 the figure was 14.8 per cent but of course the population was then much smaller than it is now (US Census Bureau, 2001). On balance therefore the levels of immigration in the US today are high though comparable with those of earlier periods, notably the period between 1880 and 1930, known as the Great Migration.[1]

However, arguably perceptions of immigration are more important than the actual numbers arriving, a point returned to at the end of this chapter. As for the origins of migrants, in broad terms, while in the nineteenth century most came from Europe, now increasingly they come from Asia and Latin America. This is reflected in figures presented by the US Census Bureau (2000) which revealed that a quarter of all the foreign-born residents in America were from Asia and half were from Latin America.

The most notable demographic change within the US in the recent period has been the growth of the Hispanic community. In January 2003, Hispanics overtook

African Americans as the nation's largest minority group, comprising 13 per cent of the population (37 million); African Americans now constitute 12.7 per cent of the population (36.2 million). This development is the result of differing birth rates, but it is also due to ongoing Hispanic immigration (Younge, 2004). It is forecast that non-Hispanic whites will only be a bare majority by 2050, with Hispanics constituting 25 per cent, blacks 14 per cent, and Asians 8 per cent of the population (Holmes, 1996). Again differences in birth rates between the groups will partly account for these changes, but patterns of global migration and immigration will also be contributory factors.

The potential cultural impact of demographic shifts is discussed in the next section; but do they have any political implications for America? In this regard, one development worthy of note concerns America's growing Arab and Muslim communities, which again is due to a combination of immigration and relatively high birth rates. Their numbers have grown to the extent that the Democrats and Republicans actively seek their votes. The issue of whether this might lead in time to a change in America's traditionally supportive approach towards Israel is raised. However, this needs to be balanced against the continuing influence and effectiveness of Israeli lobbying groups in Washington. Moreover, September 11 will continue to exert an influence upon how US administrations view the Middle East for the foreseeable future.

At a party political level, many ethnic minority groups and recently settled immigrants have in the past voted for the Democratic Party. This has led to discussion about whether we are likely to witness the emergence of a permanent democratic majority. This point has been made by in the book *The Emerging Democratic Majority* John B. Judis and Ruy Teixeira (see Kettle, 2002), who believe that demographic and cultural changes in the US, notably a growing Latino population, are in the long term working against the Republican Party. However, it is unlikely the political situation in America will be this straightforward. In the case of America's Hispanic community, many within it are now native-born and English-speaking and, having grown up in the US, they have different life experiences and hence attitudes from earlier generations, making it more difficult to predict their voting habits (Younge, 2003). For example, George W. Bush secured 35 per cent of the Hispanic vote in the 2000 presidential election. Moreover, an opinion poll conducted in 2003 found that 52 per cent of Hispanic Americans considered themselves to be politically independent (Borger, 2004). This would suggest that such communities are integrating into American society and that the melting pot is still working, a conclusion supported by a poll carried out by the *Washington Post* in 2001. The poll identified different degrees of assimilation among America's Hispanic community, but crucially revealed that those born in the US or living there for many years had assimilated many of its attitudes and beliefs without forgetting their cultural heritage (Goldstein and Suro, 2001).

Such surveys may help to reassure figures like Samuel Huntington. He is concerned that aspects of globalization might weaken the commitment of recent immigrants to America and to becoming 'American', and further encourage the phenomenon of hyphenated Americans. His argument is that, while in the past people came to the US to become Americans and to integrate into the American way of life, aspects of contemporary globalization mean that it is now easier for them to go back and forth to their countries of origin. In particular, jet air-travel and modern communication technologies make it possible for them to stay in regular contact with family and friends in their homelands.[2] However, while these developments enable them to retain their ethnic and cultural identities, as we have seen this need not prevent them from developing a sense of 'Americanness'.

What are the economic implications for the US should immigration continue at current levels? In brief, if it is managed effectively, ongoing immigration should provide the country with a number of benefits. First, it will help to ensure that America avoids the difficulties many European countries are having sustaining ageing populations. New immigrants mean new workers paying taxes that can contribute to provision for the elderly, and some will be employed in jobs that care directly for them. Second, it can help to fill any skill shortages that arise in sectors of the US economy. Many immigrants are university graduates and go to America for the opportunities it can afford them. For example, one-third of Silicon Valley's scientists and engineers were foreign-born in 1990. Third, new economic migrants and immigrants inevitably retain ties with their former countries, and these can serve as potential business and trading contacts and links in the future. Many of them will also bring new ideas to America, and will in time set up new businesses providing fresh sources of employment. Finally, immigration will help America to maintain its position of power. Unlike other developed nations, the US according to the Population Reference Bureau will continue to experience significant population growth. The population is estimated to rise from 294 million people in 2004 to 420 million people by 2050 (BBC, 2004). Indeed, if its population did not continue to rise the US would be at a disadvantage in relation to India and China, as both countries have huge populations able to sustain future economic growth.

Globalization and American Culture

How are the multiple processes of globalization impacting upon American culture? To begin with, migration and immigration are provoking considerable discussion within the US about the fate and condition of the national culture. As was mentioned in the previous section, writers like Samuel Huntington (1997, 2004) are worried about the long-term social and cultural implications of this trend for America and American identity. In particular, immigration is contributing to debates about multiculturalism (see Brimelow, 1995; Kivisto, 2002), which in turn are provoking concerns about assimilation and whether multiculturalism is leading to the 'disuniting of America' (Schlesinger, 1998). Some writers detect a change in attitude among minority groups in the US with the emphasis upon self-assertion rather than assimilation and simple equality (Dickstein, 1993). Peter Brimelow (1995), for example, believes the pressure to become 'American' and to Americanize is lessened by the promotion of multiculturalism in public life, especially in schools and colleges. This is being played out in disputes over the content of educational curricula, bilingualism and affirmative action policies. All of which has led some commentators to declare that America is inflicted by 'culture wars', a development that has raised profound questions about what it means to be an 'American' (Lapham, 1992).

As Joseph Nye (2002) has noted, if tensions between different cultures became a part of everyday life there would be implications for America's hard and soft power in the world. In the case of its hard power, a culturally divided society would make it more difficult for the US to pursue a coherent foreign policy and to play a leading role in international affairs. In relation to its soft power – defined as a country's ability to get what it wants because others are attracted to it – a culturally divided society would be unattractive to other nations, and America would lose some of its cultural influence.

However, Alan Wolfe (1998) has questioned the significance of these so-called culture wars, arguing that many Americans simply do not view their country in these terms. While researching of the attitudes of middle-class Americans, he discovered a strong degree of toleration and acceptance of other cultures. Although Wolfe's research tells us nothing about other sections of American society, it nevertheless provides a useful counterbalance to some of the gloomier predictions about cultural relations within the US. In a similar vein, Nye places faith both in the need for people to work and in modern communications and media, which taken together require a mastery of the English language and create attendant cultural homogenizing pressures. This entails newly settled immigrants being given not only inducements, but also the means to integrate into American society.

Looking more broadly at the issue of American culture and society, the charge often raised against the US is that it is culturally conservative and inward-looking. It is noted that many Americans do not travel abroad, do not even have passports and have scant knowledge of foreign affairs. Insularity is reinforced, in the view of some commentators, by its media organizations and their news coverage, which can be parochial, conservative and uncritically patriotic. Moreover, isolationist sentiments have a long history within America. It has been suggested that the end of the Cold War, and the removal of 'the evil empire' from the international scene, enabled a return to isolationism or at the very least to a greater preoccupation with internal concerns (Lindsay, 2000; Reilly, 1999). In this regard, President Bill Clinton successfully promoted an 'America First' agenda, prioritizing domestic rather than foreign policy objectives, during his first election campaign against George Bush. During the 1990s this attitude was further evident in the growing hostility towards the UN, especially among many conservatives who considered that America's own foreign policy interests were being subordinated to it. There were calls for withholding or cutting back America's financial commitment to the UN, an approach that the administration of George W. Bush has in fact pursued, an issue returned to later.

However, it is important not to caricature Americans and American culture. The danger of this type of analysis is that it not only stereotypes but homogenizes 'America', when in reality there are many Americas and its citizens have a plethora of different views and outlooks. There is no single American culture. At best it may be possible to identify a number of dominant themes – such as individualism, consumerism and materialism – but even this risks playing down the extent of cultural diversity that exists. Moreover, are these themes exclusively 'American'?

As for isolationism, this was dispensed with as a serious policy strategy many decades ago. The Second World War and the Cold War led the US not just to engage with international affairs, but to play a leading role. Even the administration of George W. Bush seeks, as it sees it, to spread democracy abroad, and is in this sense far from being inward-looking. At a more profound level, America has historically been a remarkably open society. So much so that numerous commentators consider America to be a product of globalization, forged from waves of different peoples, cultures and ethnic groups dating back to its 'discovery' by Christopher Columbus in 1492. It is too early to tell if the attacks of September 11 fundamentally changed this approach or philosophy, but it would be to run counter to the history the US were they to do so.

It is often claimed that globalization is ushering in a homogenized global culture, one that is dominated and defined by America.[3] And it can seem as if American culture is everywhere: US films, television programmes, music, news organizations, software programmes and other products can be found all over the globe. For example, the US exports significantly more television programmes than any other country in the world (Held et al., 1999: 359). US media-entertainment conglomerates, such as Time-Warner, CBS and Walt Disney, are significant players within the global culture industry. However, some of the most powerful studios in Hollywood, such as Columbia Tristar and Fox, are owned by Japan's Sony organization and Australia-based News Corporation (*The Economist*, 1998). Indeed, given the nature of corporate ownership in the contemporary period, we should perhaps not be preoccupied about the national origins of corporations and conglomerates. Furthermore, American cultural dominance is not even complete within the US. There are countless television channels and radio stations within the country that broadcast in a foreign language, such as Spanish or Japanese, and are geared to particular ethnic or cultural groups.

As for whether the US controls or dominates the global media, while US news and media organizations, like CNN, are extremely influential, they do not determine national news agendas. Moreover, the emergence of a media organization like al-Jazeera and the launch in 2005 of CII (International Information Channel) –

dubbed the 'French CNN' – suggest that in the future there will be a greater range of perspectives upon global affairs. America's inability to control the international news agenda was evident in the extensive international news coverage of human rights abuses of Iraqi prisoners. It is also the case that the international media, in all its myriad of forms, has an impact upon American society. This was apparent in the few days leading up to the 2004 presidential election, when there was much speculation in the US about the extent to which a message released at the time by Osama bin Laden via the al-Jazeera news network would influence the final outcome.

The US is widely viewed as leading the field in the area of information technology and enjoys certain advantages over its competitors. In particular, by being there at the start of the information revolution, the US and its corporations have been able to shape information systems and processes. However, these advantages will erode over time. The new technologies will become cheaper, allowing other countries, particularly developing countries, to incorporate them and develop their own productive capacity. Indeed, the information revolution allows some countries to skip or speed through stages along the path to development.

America benefits from the fact that many of the global flows and interconnections that make up globalization are conducted in the English language. This has been particularly evident with the spread of the Internet. But again it is questionable whether the US will always enjoy this advantage. Spanish and Chinese are growing in popularity and are set to become during this century, along with English, the dominant global languages. While Spanish poses less of a problem for the US given its large Hispanic population, Mandarin – the most widely spoken form of Chinese and the official language of China – is clearly a challenge for it. And as we saw in the previous chapter, Internet usage in China is growing dramatically.

A combination of the English language being at the forefront of the information revolution and successful global distribution companies and networks has enabled America's music industry and youth culture, in particular, to enjoy considerable influence across the world. But there are other aspects of American culture that have not gained such international acceptance. In this regard, a number of American political ideas, such as a minimal state, have not gained universal currency and are rejected by most European countries, in particular. There also appears to be something of a backlash against American cultural influence in many parts of the world, which may well restrict its future spread. This phenomenon has been noted by numerous commentators, who cite reasons ranging from envy of American power to the unpopularity of the George W. Bush administration (see Hertsgaard, 2002; Sardar and Wyn Davies, 2002).[4] It is reflected in the campaigns against McDonalds that have sprouted up in many countries. Even Western governments, such as the Canadian and French governments, have pursued polices designed to resist what they consider to be forms of American cultural hegemony, especially in the area of popular entertainment. Such anti-Americanism may in part be a response to the sheer amount and volume of American cultural products that are exported abroad, but there is frequently an element of cultural reductionism at work. Anti-Americanism assumes that American culture can be pinned down and defined, and as we have seen this is problematic. It is invariably based upon a particular conception of what American culture *is*, and a notion that this culture is both uniform and stable, neither of which is the case.

Moreover, to view American culture as defining the cultural dynamics of globalization is to misunderstand the nature of globalization. Global cultural flows do not just or even mainly emanate from the US. At any one moment they will be coming from multiple sources and going in multiple directions across the globe, and many will have little or nothing to do with America. For example, there are forms of cultural interaction taking place between Europe and Asia all the time, and this has been the case for many centuries. Thus, it is highly debatable whether the complex processes and interconnections that constitute globalization serve as a homogenizing force. In this vein, is it possible for any country or power to dominate global cultural flows and processes?[5] Indeed, the very notion of a global culture does not do justice to the complex and plural nature of globalization and neglects the particular ways dominant cultures are interpreted and indigenized rather than passively accepted or embraced. Writers such as Roland Robertson (1992) employ the term 'glocalization' to express this global–local dynamic. As is well known, American companies such as McDonalds have recognized the need to adapt their products to local and regional markets and sensitivities. MTV, for instance, broadcasts Chinese music in China and Hindi pop in India (Eckes and Zeiler, 2003).

Furthermore, to insist upon a homogenizing global culture emanating from the US is to neglect the possibility of cultural flows and influences, in the form of food, fashion, religion, music and so forth, travelling from elsewhere in the world to America, something which happens daily through immigration and other means. The US can absorb, for example, Asian, Latin American or European business practices, political ideas and popular tastes. Indeed, as a result of its demographic make-up America has been absorbing new cultural influences throughout its history. This is evident in the US constitution, which borrowed much from European revolutionary ideas and ideals. Joseph Nye describes America as a 'cultural sponge, a syncretic society that can assimilate influences from all over the world' (Eckes and Zeiler, 2003: 242). Thus, American culture is an eclectic mixture subject to ongoing change.

In sum, there is a two-way relationship between globalization and American culture. America has been informing global cultural flows as well as being informed by them. The recent forms of resistance to American culture are a further example of how perceptions of globalization can be at odds with the realities of globalization.

Globalization and America: The Economic Dimension

As with the previous discussion on culture, the extent to which the US is shaping or being shaped by the economic dynamics of globalization is difficult to determine and can only be discussed in broad terms. There are some areas of economic global interconnectedness in which the US is either leading the way or has an edge over other countries. For example, many of the major MNCs and TNCs in the world are American and run from headquarters in the US. The American retailer Wal-Mart became the world's largest corporation in 2002, and is continuing to open up new markets, notably in Europe and Asia. Critics consider these corporations to be instrumental in establishing American global hegemony, enabling in particular the spread of American corporate culture and managerial practices. Whether we consider this to be a valid charge will depend in part upon our individual political views, but also on our conception of globalization. Many globalists, for example, consider MNCs and TNCs to be largely autonomous economic actors operating primarily in their own interests rather than serving the agenda of a particular nation-state, and that in fact they are actually undermining the nation-state (Ohmae, 1990). In contrast, as we saw in the Introduction, sceptics such as Hirst and Thompson (1996) emphasize the national attachments and connections of MNCs and challenge the existence of TNCs. The issue of the extent to which the US government is in control of US-based MNCS and TNCs is therefore raised. Many ordinary Americans are likely to consider that their government needs to take more control. This is because large American companies are increasingly outsourcing parts of their business, sending work abroad, notably to India and elsewhere in Asia where labour costs are cheaper.

Irrespective of this debate about who controls MNCs and TNCs, these corporations have contributed to the globalization or internationalization of production and helped to ensure that in the mid 1990s 26 per cent of total world FDI originated from the US (Dicken, 1999: 36).[6] US-owned or -based MNCs and TNCs are therefore significant economic players on the global stage. However, this point needs to be counterbalanced by the fact that the number of non-US MNCs and TNCs is steadily growing and expanding into more and more sectors, and as a result US corporations are facing increasing global competition. This is reflected in the fact that US MNCs have lost significant market shares to their competitors, notably European and Japanese firms, since the 1970s (Held et al., 1999: 278).

With regards to information flows, the US is similarly open and its citizens and companies are intensively connecting with countries throughout the world every day. By 2000, there were nearly 100 million users of the Internet in the US. Moreover, as mentioned in the previous section, the US is also the dominant player in the production and use of information technology, with companies like Microsoft pioneers in this field (Nye, 2002). And the very nature of information technology has served to integrate America more closely into new areas of the international economy. It is also widely held that the economic growth the US enjoyed during the 1990s stemmed from the emergence of its 'new economy', which was founded upon developments facilitating globalization, such as technology, media and telecommunications as well as an increased openness to the global economy.

Furthermore, the US has via international trade treaties played a pivotal role in facilitating the free flow of information across the globe (Comor, 1999). Of course, America itself benefits from this development, with US-based corporations being dominant global players in information-based services and commodity activities. However, while markets are shaped by flows of information, it does not follow that America is controlling global markets. This is because the speed of information flows makes it difficult even for a superpower like the US to control.

In relation to the issue of who or what is controlling economic globalization, the US is regularly accused of imposing its own neo-liberal version of globalization upon the rest of the world. In particular, it is charged with using such institutions as the WTO, the IMF and the World Bank to push through polices such as trade liberalization that facilitate access for American companies to new markets, especially in the developing world (see Sardar and Wyn Davies, 2002). Moreover, critics believe that when the US cannot get its own way within the multilateral framework of the WTO, it seeks bilateral and regional agreements, such as the US–Jordan Free Trade Agreement and the Free Trade Area of the Americas. Invariably, the US response to criticism of its neo-liberal agenda is to argue that free trade facilitates the development of less developed countries (LDCs) allowing them to gain access to the goods and services that they lack, thereby contributing to their economic growth. However, more damagingly it has been claimed that the US is actually pursuing a selective free trade agenda calling for it only in those sectors, such as intellectual property rights, in which its interests lie (Woods, 2002: 40). Arguably, such selectivity is also apparent in the recent implementation of protectionist measures by US governments, notably in the form of increasing farm subsidies and the imposition of steel tariffs.

The extent to which the US is controlling and informing the economic dynamics of globalization, and specifically whether it is dictating the rules of global trade and commerce, has become a highly contested and politicized debate (see Amin, 1996; Callinicos et al., 1994; Gill, 1992). In relation to this debate, it is important to remember that a defining feature of a globalizing economy is greater economic interdependence, something that even a country as powerful as America is affected by. For example, the deindustrialization that America is undergoing is in part a reflection of a more integrated global economy, whereby manufacturing is increasingly located within newly industrializing countries (NICs), such as Mexico, Singapore and Malaysia, where labour costs are cheaper. At the same time there has been a concomitant rise in the number of service sector jobs within the US economy.

It is also the case that the sheer volume of world trade, the increasing internationalization of production as well as the complexity of global financial flows and transactions prevent any single country, including the US, from controlling all of these processes. There is a myriad of financial flows and trading networks that lie outside the American sphere of influence. China, for example, is seeking to develop its relationship with African states. Similarly, countries in Asia and Europe have their own respective networks and interconnections, including of course with each other. The spread of the East Asian financial crisis of 1997 to several continents is also an indication of both the interdependence and instability of the global economy, and a further indication that no single power is really in control.[7]

There are also aspects of increasing global economic interconnectedness that are not serving US interests. In particular, global flows of trade and finance are exacerbating America's huge debt problems, while the promotion of global free trade and open markets has also led to low-priced goods entering America at an ever-growing rate, especially from India and the Far East. In 2004, the US twelve-month trade deficit approached $600 billion, contributing to its massive current account deficit. A consequence of the US being the world's largest importer is that it is the world's largest debtor nation, with its cumulative international debts reaching approximately $3 trillion at the end of 2004 (Hutton, 2004). For the US, servicing these debts ensures that government deficit spending remains high, and the country is heavily dependent on foreign investment and borrowing.[8] The other countries of the world accept America's enormous current account deficit and the endless supply of dollars because it provides a ready market for their goods. Or rather the international community accepted this state of affairs until the dollar hit record lows against the euro in November 2004, suggesting a change in attitude. Increasingly there is talk of declining confidence in the dollar as the currency of international trade and finance and of the euro emerging as a global reserve currency. There is also speculation that investors in Japan and China are rethinking the wisdom of heavily investing in American debt and may turn to euros. From the globalist perspective, economic globalization entails that national economies and the policies of their respective governments receive daily judgements upon their performance by international financial markets. It would seem that even the most powerful country in the world is not immune to such judgements.[9]

A globalizing economy will also enable some countries and regions to begin catching up with the US, economically speaking.[10] They will have access to new markets and hence greater trading opportunities and increased prospects of FDI, and any TNCs and MNCs that set up in those countries will provide sources of employment. And the US further facilitates their development by offering them a ready market in which to export their goods. The economies of Asia, notably China and India, have been enjoying good trading relations with the world's superpower in the recent period. As numerous commentators have noted, such developments will entail America suffering relative economic decline (see Kennedy, 2001; Wallerstein, 2003).

However, it is important not to overemphasize the detrimental effects of economic globalization upon the US, nor to underestimate its economic power. There are worrying developments within the America economy, such as the decline in research and development and the low level of domestic saving, that are a product of domestic circumstances and decision-making and have little or nothing to do with globalization. Moreover, economic globalization might serve to reinvigorate the American economy because it ensures greater competition, and this may also stimulate a response forcing American businesses to be more dynamic, to absorb new business methods, and so forth. Such developments are necessary because the US is falling behind in certain manufacturing sectors, such as automobiles and consumer electronics while America's 'large internal market makes it less dependent on and less sensitive to other countries, so there is little economic incentive to take on foreign horizons' (Nederveen Pieterse, 2004: 128).

Globalization and America: The Military Dimension

If military globalization entails 'long-distance networks of interdependence in which force, and the threat or promise of force, are employed' (Keohane and Nye, 2002: 196) then the US is clearly at an advantage in relation to other powers. As well as having military capability, notably possessing more intercontinental missiles than any other country, it plays a key role in the key strategic-security alliances of our time in Europe (NATO) and the Pacific (US–Japan Security Alliance). The US is also the only country that has the economic power to play a global policeman role, possessing 152 military installations overseas in 2003 (Traynor, 2003). By the end of the last century, that is, even before the 'war on terror' began, the US was spending $270 billion a year on defence, while China and Russia, America's nearest competitors, were spending approximately $35 billion each per year (Rosendorf, 2000: 127). The US defence budget for 2004 stood at $401.3 billion, excluding $150 billion special appropriations that were mainly for the occupation of Iraq. Furthermore, global information technology ensures there is a new and important aspect of military globalization in which America leads the way. This is the so-called 'revolution in military affairs' (RMA), which is largely information- and technology-driven and enables the US to project missiles over vast distances and with great precision. It means the US itself sustains fewer casualties, certainly in comparison with wars earlier in the twentieth century, which in turn makes it easier for US administrations to convince the American public of the need to enter or initiate military conflicts.

However, this technology, especially satellite digital technoloy, and global information flows make it harder for all governments to keep their military secrets and undertake military planning. Military information is now much more readily available, even to ordinary citizens (and hence to terrorists), with the Internet allowing its rapid dispersal. Moreover, the information systems that give the US an edge in so many spheres are an obvious target for terrorists, and one which is relatively risk-free in that the attacks can come in the form of computer viruses. Nevertheless the RMA is enabling America to fight wars with relatively few casualties among its own troops. This was evident in the wars in Afghanistan, Kosovo and the Gulf. Joseph

Nye and William Ovens (1996), among others, consider that America's information systems give it a significant edge over potential rivals.

As we saw in Chapter 4, global terror is a by-product of globalization. Deepening forms of global interconnectedness mean that the US is now more vulnerable to external attack than at any time in the past, as September 11 so vividly demonstrated. The events of that day reminded Americans that they are not separated from the rest of the international community, and raised concerns that any future attacks might involve biological or chemical agents, whose impact might be more widespread and lasting. Moreover, there is another aspect of globalization that can act as a constraint upon US foreign policy and military action, in particular. A globalized media ensures that any US military engagement abroad receives international scrutiny. In this regard, good investigative journalism aligned with the potential of reaching a global audience can serve to undermine the case made for intervention by particular US governments. Conversely, of course, the international media skilfully managed can help to make the case for aspects of US foreign policy.

The question of how the US should respond to global terrorism is likely to shape US military and foreign policy for at least a generation. There are unilateralist, multilateralist and isolationist tendencies within America competing to inform policy. This is reflected in differing attitudes towards global institutions, international treaties and the need for consultation with other countries (see Ruggie, 1996). But even though it is the dominant military power, the US is unable to pick and choose the aspects of globalization that it deals with. And in many respects its military preponderance will not be of great use in tackling some of the problems globalization. For example, looming environmental problems, transnational criminal organizations, financial instability in some countries and regions and drug trafficking are all aspects of globalization. At the same time the complaint against the Bush administration is that it is not recognizing the realities of global interdependence preferring instead to employ America's military power to pursue its own agenda. Furthermore, the Bush approach requires considerable military expenditure, which is said to be distorting the US economy as well as damaging America's soft power (Nye, 2002).

Globalization as Americanization?

Many critics on the left view globalization as a form of Americanization and/or imperialism (González Cazanova, 1999; Harvey, 2003; Petras and Veltmeyer, 2001). In contrast, globalists and transformationalists would contest the notion that globalization can be reduced to Americanization. For these groups, globalization constitutes a more profound process entailing changes to contemporary social life and patterns of social, political and economic organization. As Anthony Giddens notes, globalization 'affects the United States as it does other countries' (2000: 22). One way of determining who is right in this debate is to examine the influence that the US has had upon the institutions of global governance whose development is both a reflection and an expression of the intensification of forms of global interconnectedness.

From a realist perspective, global governance is the means by which dominant states like the US are able to shape global affairs. And there is an established tradition on the left of viewing forms of global governance and order as simply a cover for US hegemony (see, for example, Chomsky, 1994; Gowan, 2001). It is certainly the case that successive US governments have been contributing to globalization by seeking to reduce trade and investment barriers, notably through the different rounds of General Agreement on Tariffs and Trade (GATT) negotiations, and to global governance by helping to set up the WTO in 1995. As we have seen, the US has also been exerting its influence within and upon the IMF and the World Bank. In the case of the IMF, for example, the US has been aided by its unilateral veto power. However, America has found some multilateral institutions to be less pliable and less to its liking. This is reflected in the US withdrawal from UNESCO in December 1984 for pushing what it considered to be a 'third world' agenda. There have been ongoing budgetary disputes with the UN and its agencies, with the US owing the UN $1,774 million at the end of May 2000 (UN Association of the USA, 2000: 275). Moreover, the tensions between the US and the UN are unlikely to ease if as has been proposed membership of the UN Security Council is increased to include representatives from Africa, Latin America, Asia and the Muslim world (*Guardian*, 2004: 27). US administrations are likely to view inclusion of these representatives as further curtailing their influence within the UN.

Other examples of America being at odds with recent developments in relation to global governance and legislation include the US campaigning against the International Criminal Court, refusing to ratify the Kyoto Protocol and withdrawing from or refusing to sign up to a number of arms control treaties and agreements. In its treatment of prisoners at Guatanamo Bay, the US government has flouted numerous articles of international law, while in its foreign policy the Bush administration has often preferred to construct 'coalitions of the willing' rather than working through multilateral institutions. Indeed, the UN and its agencies are considered in some quarters as an unnecessary fetter upon US policy (see Krauthammer, 2001b). However, this unilateral stance takes us beyond the concern of this discussion, which is with the institutions of global governance that are continuing to evolve despite recent US attempts to by-pass them. Indeed, America's ability to shape their development is reduced if it acts alone.

In reality, the US has to engage with the rest of the international community, rather than go it alone, if it wants to enjoy good trade relations, gain access to resources such as oil, ensure decent standards of living for the majority of its citizens and maintain its international status. A crude assertion of its military and material power will not be enough to secure these ends. Instead, the US needs allies and influence, and to court international opinion, which requires working with and through multilateral institutions. As the recent war in Iraq has shown, it is difficult as well as costly even for a superpower to enforce its will by military means alone. It is far better to be considered a member of the international community, observing it rules and working through its institutions, than its ruler. Such an approach is more likely to ensure that the US gains a favourable hearing from other countries whenever issues involving its key interests arise. In this vein, the reputation of the US will be harmed if much of the rest of the world proceeds with developing international law and institutions without it, as has been the case with regards to the International Criminal Court Treaty and the Ottawa Convention on landmines.

Despite the current influence of neo-conservative thinking within Washington, the US government – presumably recognizing the realities described above – continues to participate in multilateral institutions which hinder its unilateral exercise of power (Michael Reisman, 1999). And while the US has certainly shaped these institutions during the post-war period, they are being developed and extended to ensure wider participation and, it has been claimed, a more genuinely international as opposed to US-centred structure (see Germain, 2002). In this regard, there must be some doubt about whether the US will be able to impose its agenda upon the WTO to the extent that it has in the past. There are now 147 members, with others set to join in the near future, and Japan and the EU have become key players within the organization often being at odds with the US. Europe, for example, has successfully contested trade disputes with the US through the WTO, notably the Bush administration's imposition of steel tariffs to protect America's steel industry. Moreover, WTO decisions are absolute and every member, including the US, must abide by them.

Furthermore, aspects of globalization, such as the spread of global communications technologies, the increased flows of information and the formation of global networks, contribute to America's difficulties in acting autonomously. This is because they make it easier for INGOs to organize enabling them to put pressure upon the US and other major states to behave in accordance with international rule-based decision-making.[11] Being at the forefront of the information revolution does not enable the US to control the technologies involved. Moreover, if cumulatively these developments are, as is often claimed, leading to the formation of a global civil society, then this will concern those US administrations that pursue unilateral agendas. Indeed, there may already be evidence of the difficulties that INGOs can present US governments. As was mentioned in the Introduction, arguably INGOs were central in blocking the American-backed Multilateral Agreement on Investment, which would have reduced barriers to investment by multinationals. They have also challenged the neo-liberal Washington Consensus pursued by the IMF and the World Bank. In response the American Enterprise Institute has set up a web site to monitor the activities of INGOs, which it considers have – along with UN organizations – been placing undue pressure upon national governments and corporations (Reus-Smit, 2004: 86).

Finally, as was discussed earlier, aspects of globalization are entailing greater economic competition for America, the prospect of other countries catching up with it and hence the prospect of the US suffering relative economic decline. Indeed, Immanuel Wallerstein (2003) considers contemporary globalization to be another phase of the modern world system, marked by the US fading as a global power (also see Taylor, 1999, 2001). For the US to undergo a reduction in its relative economic strength would in the long term have implications for it military power and dominant status in the world. 'The unipolar moment' in which the US can get its own way in global affairs is therefore just that: a 'moment' (Waltz, 1999).

In sum, the notion of globalization as Americanization is an oversimplification of what is taking place. The multiple processes and complex dynamics of what we call globalization lie beyond the control of even the world's only superpower. There is simply too much going on. As James Rosenau more eloquently puts it, the 'world is simply too interdependent, and authority is too dispersed, for any one country to command the global scene as fully as was the case in the past' (2002: 76).

American Perceptions of Globalization

In assessing America's relationship to the different dimensions and processes of globalization, it is important to take into account American people's perceptions of it. Their responses will be dependent upon the particular dimension of globalization that they are being asked about and their particular or individual experiences of it. There is also the wider issue of their knowledge of what globalization actually *is*, a point that is applicable to citizens of other countries. In addition we need to acknowledge the range or plurality of attitudes and opinions that will exist among Americans, reflecting the diversity of American society itself. Nevertheless, putting aside all of these caveats, a poll conducted by the Chicago Council on Foreign Relations after September 2001 revealed that 87 per cent of American leaders and 54 per cent of the American public consider that globalization is mostly beneficial for the United States (Nye, 2002: 133). In short, there are interesting divisions between the American electorate and their politicians over aspects of globalization. Broadly speaking, and allowing for differences between the major political parties, national politicians in the US are more in favour of economic liberalization and an aggressive or pro-active policy to deal with terrorism than the citizens that they represent (Nye, 2002).

It is also the case that there are particular aspects of global interconnectedness that concern many Americans, notably the amount of foreign direct investment in the American economy and a sense that the US is being flooded by foreign imports (Scheve and Slaughter, 2001). Further, there is a general unease about global migration and immigration. Opinion poll surveys reveal that more, often twice as many, Americans are sceptical about immigration than are sympathetic to it (Nye, 2002; Wolfe, 1998). As might be expected, less skilled employees particularly feel under threat from new immigrants and would favour tighter entry restrictions, but above all seek greater governmental assistance to protect their jobs (Nye, 2002: 136). As a result of global migration a steady stream of immigrant labour is coming to the US from all over the developing world, including Latin American, and this labour is significantly cheaper than indigenous labour. In a similar vein, there is disquiet about the loss of jobs as American corporations either outsource or relocate to developing countries where labour is cheaper. Thus, there is considerable concern about globalization and its consequences among many ordinary Americans (Eckes and Zeiler, 2003). This is borne out by a 2004 report published by the International Labour Office, which measured how national workforces were experiencing and perceiving globalization and ranked the US twenty-fifth in the world in its economic security index (Seager, 2004).

However, as has often been the case during the course of this work, perceptions of globalization are at odds with reality. Empirical studies consistently reveal that it is primarily technological developments, which require skilled workers, rather than the globalization of trade and migration, that constitute the major reason for the diminishing employment prospects and wage levels of unskilled workers in industrialized countries of the northern hemisphere. Thus, technological developments account for 80 to 90 per cent of this phenomenon and globalization for between 10 and 20 per cent (Thompson, 2000: 120) – although, as was mentioned earlier, it is important not to forget that technology, in the form of new communication and information technologies, is making it easier for companies to relocate abroad.

Conclusion

As we have seen, there are a number of aspects of globalization that the US is unable to control or at best can only partially influence. First, the products of globalization, such as aeroplanes, the Internet and global communications technologies, which were used in the attacks of September 11 and facilitate global terror generally lie beyond the scope of Washington. The same applies to the global media and media organizations, which publicized the attacks throughout the world. In this regard, while US media corporations and networks exert a powerful influence, they do not control the global media agenda. National governments and national media organizations continue to determine their own news agendas, though many of them are extremely interested in developments within the US, evident in the extensive international news coverage of the 2004 elections. Second, global migration, another important feature of globalization, also lies beyond the control of America. As we have seen, there are potentially profound social and political consequences for American society of the demographic changes brought about by global population shifts.

As for economic forms of globalization, the extent to which the US is able to exert its influence or control is a source of debate. Is the US dictating the nature and organization of the global economy and trade patterns? The imposition by the first Bush administration of steel tariffs and quotas suggests that the global economy is not always operating in America's interests, while in the medium and long term multiple global flows and forms of interconnectedness are facilitating the rise of powers such as China and India, which will eventually challenge America's economic dominance.

There is, however, a feature of globalization that has not yet been considered in this chapter. Aspects of globalization, such as increased flows of trade and people, are having a harmful impact upon the environment. To deal effectively with this problem will require US administrations recognizing the importance of collective action. But at present America appears unwilling to go down this path. Indeed, it is widely criticized for doing considerable damage to the global environment, and in particular for contributing to greenhouse gas emissions – it was responsible for 36 per cent of total emissions in 1990. But this is a complaint about how it runs its domestic economy, the lack of regulation of its industries, as well as the lifestyles of many of its citizens. The more intensive and extensive movements of trade and people that are integral features of globalization, the US along with the rest of the international community is unable or unwilling to control. To restrict such movement would have a significant impact upon everyday human existence and how national economies are organized, and at present there does not appear to be the political will to implement such measures. Continuing global climate change that will result from this policy inertia will have numerous consequences for America and the other countries of the world.

In summary, this chapter has sought to consider the internal and external dynamics of globalization. It has examined how the different processes of globalization are impacting upon American society, as well as the extent to which the US is shaping their nature and form elsewhere in the international arena. Of course, in reality such a neat distinction does not exist: the internal and external dimensions of globalization intersect. For example, immigration levels can affect economic performance and levels of economic productivity, which can in turn have an influence upon America's wider role in the world. Following on from this it has been shown that there are aspects and processes of globalization that America as the dominant power of our time is contributing to and informing, but is also being shaped by. In this regard, the multiple ways in which the different forms and aspects of globalization are impacting upon American society serve to counter the claim that globalization is a form of American imperialism or McDonaldization (Ritzer, 1998), as it is sometimes termed. While in a number of respects it is indeed an American-led project, globalization is not Americanization. To paraphrase, Jan Nederveen Pieterse's excellent book *Globalization or Empire?* (2004): 'while empires come and go, globalization – as a profound historical process – persists'.

Finally, as with all of the case studies undertaken here it is often difficult to determine which developments are due to the processes of globalization and which are the result of 'local' factors and conditions, such as political decisions, cultural and historical influences, national self-interest and so on. In reality, there will often be a combination of both. And again much depends upon ideas about what globalization *is* and these in turn will influence responses to it. In the case of the US, there is the additional complicating factor of September 11, which has arguably shaped attitudes about America's role in the world for a generation.

Summarizing Points

- Globalization is not Americanization: there are aspects of globalization that the US is shaping, notably the economic and military spheres, but it is not in control of all of its processes.
- America faces a challenge from some elements of contemporary globalization, such as the development of global governance.
- Levels of immigration in the US today are high though comparable with those of earlier periods.
- America has been informing global cultural flows as well as being informed by them.

Conclusion: Living with Globalization

So, then, what does it mean to be living with globalization? How do we experience the intensive global flows and forms of interconnectedness that constitute contemporary globalization? In what ways are its processes shaping and informing contemporary life? And how should we think about and investigate globalization? These have been the concerns of this work. It has been argued that in order to enhance our understanding of globalization we must take a *differentiating* approach and examine how its multiple processes and dimensions are encountered and informed by different social groups and other agencies within particular *contexts*. Thus we must take into account such factors as local conditions, including historical, cultural and political influences, which shape perceptions and experiences of the different forms of global interconnectedness.[1] Any effects of globalization emerge from a range of interacting contexts, those points or moments where the global and the local intersect. Hence, our analyses must centre upon the myriad of global–local connections and interactions. As a result of such investigations, it has been argued, we are likely to discover that complexity and heterogeneity are the dominant themes that emerge from living with globalization. For this reason it is appropriate to think of globalization in plural terms as *globalizations*.

As well as examining how the multiple processes of globalization are operating within particular contexts, the case studies that we undertake should recognize its *multidimensional* nature, consisting as it does of economic, cultural and political dimensions, to cite but a few. And that these dimensions are constituted by different *global flows* and types of *interconnectedness*, in the form of more internationally intensive and extensive movements of information, ideas, images, people, finance, and products. Global interconnectedness is also reflected in the expansion of international law and the institutions of global governance, which shape how countries, regions and peoples interact. Moreover, such developments will be informed by ideas and ideologies about how a more interconnected world is operating or should operate. In short, there is an *ideational* dimension to globalization. This is evident in the championing of neo-liberal globalization by institutions such as the World Bank, the WTO and the IMF as well as some national governments. Of course, conceptions of globalization are not confined to governments. Ordinary citizens, religious and cultural groups, business people, nationals of particular countries and so forth will all have their own views of what it is and what it entails for them. The ideational element to globalization raises the issue of who or what is shaping globalization's different processes and dimensions as well who or what is deciding how to respond to them (*agency*). Globalization therefore generates questions about the nature of *power* and power relations in the contemporary period. Consequently, determining whether there are dominant influences or forces informing its multiple processes and global–local dynamics must also be a part of our investigations. An obvious focus of interest, one that dominates much of the current globalization literature, is the extent to which some powers are attaching a neo-liberal agenda to economic globalizing processes.

Globalization is also a *contested* phenomenon. This is reflected in the debates and interpretations that it generates and the ways in which it is used for political ends, and not only by its supporters and opponents. For example, the CCP leadership considers economic globalization to be a means of strengthening the position of the party-state in China (Chapter 5), while many New Labourites believe globalization lends support to their project to the extent that it has become a self-fulfilling prophecy (Chapter 1). But as has been shown, frequently ideas about globalization do not stand up to scrutiny, and rarely are they politically and culturally neutral. Indeed, there is much rhetoric surrounding globalization, though this is not to suggest that there is no substance to it. Even writers who are sceptical about globalization acknowledge that changes are afoot, merely questioning the extent and nature of the changes. Forms of global interconnectedness exist and are evident in the growing volume of international trade, the movement of peoples, MNCs and TNCs setting up in different countries and new communication technologies facilitating the formation of global networks. There is then a *material* quality to globalization. Further, it can have *structural* consequences. For example, it is claimed, and not just by globalists, that the continuing relocation of MNCs and TNCs to cheap labour areas is transforming the international division of labour, with manufacturing increasingly concentrated in non-Western societies (see Brewer, 1990; Hoogvelt, 1997; Johnston et al, 1995). In time this development may even come to influence the policies of the world's superpower, with Washington forced to take action to prevent the flood of goods into America from these countries. This means that we also need to consider the extent to which structural constraints in the global economy can compel states and societies to act in particular ways. In this regard, a case has been made that such external constraints have shaped the New Labour project (see Coates, 2002), though as was suggested in Chapter 1 perceptions of what globalization is and entails have also influenced policy (see Hay, 2002).

Thus, when we investigate these global–local encounters, as well as taking into account the historical, cultural and political influences that shape 'local' experiences of the global, we need to employ a sociological approach to the nature of this interaction focusing upon structure and agency. Of course, in reality a combination of these elements will be at work. As we saw in Chapter 1, the New Labour government and some of its leading figures (agency) have a conception of how globalization is operating (ideational), which may well have some grounds in reality (material and structural) – though not for its critics (contested) – and they are formulating policy accordingly (power). Policy in turn has implications for how UK citizens experience globalizing processes (context). In contrast, many of their European counterparts will have a different experience of these processes because to date their governments, sceptics maintain, do not perceive globalization in neo-liberal terms and have persisted with a social democratic mixed economy. Again a differentiating approach is better able to recognize our particular experiences of the multiple processes and dimensions that constitute globalization.

In sum, the watchwords informing our analyses of globalization should be: *differentiating, global flows and interconnectedness, multidimensional, agency, ideational, structural, material, power, contested* and *context*. It has been maintained here that by employing these guiding principles our understanding of globalization will be enhanced and we will gain a clearer insight into its dynamics. These principles have been variously employed or followed in each of the above chapters. This has entailed making a critical judgement about the appropriate ways in which to consider the particular areas being examined. For example, in relation to China (context), in order to ascertain the primary ways in which global flows and forms of interconnectedness are being engaged with and to consider the wider issue of China's rise to power, the investigation centred upon the party-state (power, agency). Chapter 5 looked at how the party-state conceives of globalization (ideational, contested), identifying its discriminating strategy with regards to globalizing processes (multidimensional), which is impacting upon the lives of its citizens (material) as well as having implications for the rest of the international community (structural). The type of analysis undertaken in relation to China may be considered by some to be inappropriate and the insights gained from it insignificant, but the broad aim has been to stress the value of employing such a differentiating approach to the study of globalization. In a similar vein, while the specific claims and arguments of individual chapters may well be disputed, something that is almost inevitable given the range as well as the nature of the topics covered, the overall purpose has been to defend a particular way of approaching globalization. Having argued for the merits of this approach and striven to pursue it during the course of this work, what conclusions can we draw about the influence of contemporary globalizing processes?

To begin with, the case studies undertaken here suggest that general claims about globalization, ranging from the argument that it spreads democracy to the argument that it exacerbates cultural conflict, or that it is assuming particular forms, such as Americanization or Westernization, must be viewed with scepticism. What is occurring is much more complex than can be encapsulated by these linkages and interpretations. Often there will be multiple responses and adaptations to globalizing processes within the same country, region or locality. As we saw with China, as a result of the CCP leadership's conception of globalization, the country has largely embraced economic globalization but sought to resist its political and cultural dimensions. Meanwhile, in the case of the US, it is both informing and being informed by global flows and the different types of global interconnectedness

(Chapter 6). For this reason globalization is not Americanization. Its multiple processes do not emanate from a single source, national or otherwise. Globalization is
therefore not just multidimensional; it is also multidirectional. Thus it follows that
overarching accounts of global processes and developments will always struggle to
represent the complexity, unevenness and sheer unpredictability of what is actually
taking place. And we need to bear in mind these points whenever claims about the
consequences of globalization are made. Indeed, as has been maintained throughout
this work, globalization is not a uniform process, but a complex set of processes that
have numerous and often contradictory effects. In Europe, for example, it is possible
to detect both nationalist (Chapter 2) and cosmopolitan (Chapter 3) reactions to
different aspects of globalization. Above all, to repeat, what globalization *is* or means
for many of us only really emerges when these processes intersect with particular
settings, where they are interpreted and experienced by different social and cultural
groups and other agencies.[2] This can range from an individual sitting down in front
of their computer and sending out emails across the globe to a national government
deciding how to respond to the challenges presented by a more interconnected and
interdependent world.

It is important to consider the possible shortcomings of this differentiating and
contextualist approach to globalization. One of the difficulties with analyzing
globalization in relation to different contexts is determining the level at which
the investigation should be conducted. Considering the influence of globalizing
processes upon different countries, regions, political movements and cultural groups
can overlook the degree of diversity that exists within each of these geographic and
social formations. It is for this reason that the examination of European responses
to globalization (Chapters 2 and 3) stressed the importance of taking into account
the variations that exist between different countries and regions. Yet even focusing
upon a single country can present problems. As was shown in Chapter 6, the US is
a diverse society containing within it a range of opinions and cultural and ethnic
groups, as well as regional differences. Consequently, the notion of an 'American
response' to globalization is difficult to sustain. There will inevitably be a plethora of
perceptions, interpretations and experiences of globalizing processes within the US.
Therefore, a valid criticism of the case studies undertaken here is that they have not
been sufficiently localized and specific. This has meant, for example, in the case of
the EU and the US, that given their size only the dominant or defining features of their
relationship to globalization have been delineated. However, an important additional
aim here has been to examine key recent developments in order to ascertain the
ways in which, if at all, contemporary globalizing processes are influencing them. In
this regard, a problem with focusing upon how particular individuals and relatively
small groups are responding and contributing to globalization is that it tells us little
about what is happening in our time. We also need to take into account that these
globalizing processes are encountered and engaged with at many different levels.
For example, how a national government responds to globalization will often filter

down and have an influence upon how local groups and ordinary citizens experience its processes.

When it comes to analyzing the local and the specific in relation to globalization, it should be acknowledged that contemporary anthropology is in many respects leading the way. Anthropologists are mapping how global flows, whether in the form of commodities, people, images or ideas, are operating within particular contexts (see Xavier Inda and Rosaldo, 2002). They are seeking to explore the ways in which our local everyday experiences are shaped by the broader processes of globalization. And they are discovering a plurality of perceptions and adaptations, as has been emphasized here. In reality, of course, even within particular streets in any town or city in the world there will be some households that are more integrated into different forms of global interconnectedness than other households. Some will be making extensive use of global communications technologies and have members who regularly travel abroad, others will not (McGrew, 1996).

There is a tendency within other disciplines to focus upon globalization at the macro level, considering it in relation to capitalism, modernity and Westernization, for example. In the case of both economics and politics, neo-liberalism and Marxism form a prominent part of the ways of examining globalization and often little attention is given to global–local dynamics. In these disciplines there is little emphasis upon analyzing how globalizing processes intersect with particular contexts and how these contexts are shaped by factors such as history and culture. Furthermore, there are frequently problems of analysis and approach at the macro level. In this regard, a common problem with neo-liberal and Marxist accounts is their lack of appreciation of the long history of globalization. Studies which focus upon the global free market and global capitalism tend to, respectively, neglect pre-modern forms of globalization and underplay non-economic globalizing processes. This is not to deny that global capitalism is providing much of the momentum behind contemporary globalization. Yet our own accounts will be inadequate if we do not acknowledge those forms of global interconnectedness, such as the increased opportunities to travel and experience new cultures and the emergence of INGOs, which are not driven by global capitalism, and may even be opposed to it. As we have seen, the notion of global flows and processes being driven by any single force or power is problematic. Likewise, there are non-economic factors that have facilitated contemporary globalization, notably technological developments and the end of the Cold War. However, this does not mean we should lose sight of the importance of considering the wider picture in relation to globalization, such as issues to do with global governance, geopolitics and the global environment. Thus, we must seek to balance the micro and macro in our investigations into globalization.

A concern with macro globalizing processes is similarly evident within current approaches to globalization, often classified as globalist, sceptical and transformationalist accounts. However, these broad schools of thought provide useful analytical frameworks for mapping the different forms of globalization and generate important questions and debates about the subject. In particular, these approaches provide informative, though competing, historical accounts of the different forms of global interconnectedness. Where appropriate therefore the respective insights provided by globalists, sceptics and transformationalists should be considered as part of our examination of the global–local nexus. For example, if writers that are sceptical about the extent and even existence of contemporary globalization are correct in their assessments, then the influence it is exerting upon government policy (Chapter 1) and regional developments (Chapters 2 and 3) is very much due to ideas about what it entails. We would need therefore to consider ideational as much as actual globalization in these contexts.

As stated in the Introduction, this work is closest to the transformationalist perspective, as articulated by David Held and his co-writers (1999), with its stress upon the indeterminate path of globalization. However, there are differences in emphasis and approach. Rather than a focus upon the unpredictable ways in which more intensive and extensive forms of global interconnectedness are operating, here there has been stress upon global–local dynamics within particular contexts and the complexity and heterogeneity that these dynamics generate. Held et al. (1999) do examine a number of countries in relation to globalization, but a concern with this phenomenon at the macro level permeates their albeit excellent work. This includes viewing globalization as driven by the combined forces of modernity and considering how globalizing processes are reconstituting the nation-state and transforming political community and world politics. Consequently, these writers put little emphasis upon the ways in which individuals and groups are experiencing, interpreting and responding to globalizing processes and developments. They also give little consideration to the ideational and power dimensions of globalization, notably to how claims about it can serve political ends, such as justifying policy approaches and political positions. To be fair to David Held and his co-writers, their stated primary objective was to consider what was happening to the nation-state in the context of intensifying global processes.

Thus, we need to examine the myriad points at which the global and the local meet in order to understand the nature and effects of globalizing processes. It is at these meeting points that social groups experience and contribute to the multiple processes and dimensions of globalization, and where the ideas, ideologies and power relations surrounding globalization come into play. Moreover, as we have seen, globalizing processes are not working in the same way in different settings or contexts. In this vein, there are groups, societies and localities that are globally integrated and interdependent, and others that are less so. All of which highlights the uneven and complex nature of globalization and suggests we need an additional way of looking at and thinking about globalization to complement existing approaches. More specifically, alongside globalist, sceptical and transformationalist accounts we need to add what might be termed a contextualist approach, examining the particular ways in which more intensive forms of global interconnectedness are being played out in different locations.

We have also seen from this study that globalization is having a variable impact upon some of the major developments of the recent period. This is because any potential effects that globalizing processes might have are contingent upon local conditions and perceptions. Any influence that global flows and forms of interconnectedness is exerting must therefore be considered in relation to other contributory factors. For example, as much as governments may like to blame globalization for downturns in the performance of their respective national economies, their own mismanagement must also be taken into account. In many instances, globalization has merely exacerbated trends and developments already afoot. As we saw in Chapter 4, many Muslim societies have harboured concerns about spreading Western influence for generations; contemporary globalization has merely intensified these feelings. In contrast, China's engagement with globalizing processes is arguably changing its economy and society in quite profound and lasting ways (Chapter 5).

Yet we should be careful not to overestimate the impact that the different aspects of globalization are having in the contemporary period. In this vein, as we saw in Chapter 2, the revival of ethnic nationalism in the Balkans is due primarily to local conditions, in the form of the region's particular histories, cultures and political developments, rather than being a reaction against an all-pervasive global culture, assuming that such a culture actually exists. Often therefore the influence of globalization will be negligible. This is not only because there may be other domestic or local influences at work, but also because, as Paul Hirst and Grahame Thompson have argued, globalizing processes may be of a more limited nature that we imagine. In this vein, Robert Gilpin (2001) notes that even in the most globalized economy, America, imports in 1995 constituted just 13 per cent of total US production. There is of course the danger that because this work on the dynamics of contemporary globalization its significance has been overplayed in some or all of the case studies undertaken here. This is for the reader and experts in the various areas or fields to judge. But at least in principle considering globalization in relation to particular contexts reduces the likelihood of overgeneralizations.

We should also acknowledge that determining the effects of globalization is a difficult task. For example, within a number of European states there are complaints about the erosion of national sovereignty. This is due to regional developments and specifically the growing importance of the EU; however, as was suggested in Chapter 3, the development of the EU is in part a response to globalization: the countries of Europe are pooling their sovereignty to ensure that they continue to be a force in a globalizing world. Globalization in this case is having an indirect influence. But in many instances, there simply will not be coherent and identifiable responses to globalizing processes. Meanwhile, in other cases, detecting the influence of globalization will be more straightforward. As we saw in Chapter 1, globalization is a theme running through New Labour publications and speeches, and informs government policy.

In general, however, detecting the influence of globalization is difficult, and it is therefore unwise to make general claims about it. For example, how does one prove

that globalizing processes are undermining indigenous cultures and threatening traditional ways of life? Such developments are very difficult to measure objectively
and may be the result of other influences. Similarly, how does one demonstrate that
more intensive and extensive forms of global interconnectedness are generating nationalist and fundamentalist reactions? Inevitably, there will be a range of factors at
work, including the role played by charismatic leaders, the history of a region, local
political developments and so on. There is also a danger that we may seek to find the
influence of globalization everywhere and that globalization becomes an all-purpose
phenomenon, robbed of any meaning. Or, that we may view globalization as an
omnipresent and omnipotent force or agent operating autonomously in the world. As
we have seen, in many instances any effects that 'globalization' is having are due as
much to ideas about what it is as to the actual processes and forms of connectedness
that constitute it. Globalization does not have a separate existence that stands outside
of societies and cultures; rather its flows and processes circulate and permeate
societies and cultures, which are in turn informed by them. It is an expression of
forms of global interconnectedness. In short, we need to avoid the reification of
globalization that can sometimes be found in general accounts.

In order therefore to enhance our understanding of globalization we need to
employ a differentiating and contextualist approach to the subject, examining the
particular ways in which its macro processes are engaged with by different social
groups and societies, each with their own cultures and histories. The speeding-up of
social and economic processes (Harvey, 1989) and the stretching of social life across
time and space – that Anthony Giddens (1990) terms 'time–space distanciation'
– entail a degree of adjustment for all societies. But by focusing upon particular contexts we can allow for the fact that people are experiencing these changes and forms
of global interconnectedness in a myriad of ways and that some are doing so only
in a very limited sense. Some people, for example, are taking advantage of greater
opportunities to travel or migrate, to encounter new cultures and to communicate
and conduct business with other parts of the world (and are being changed by these
experiences) and others are not. Of course, many people due to certain constraints,
financial, cultural or otherwise, are simply unable to act in such manner.

It is clear that the multiple aspects and processes of globalization are provoking
numerous and diverse responses. This undermines any notion that more intensive
forms of global interconnectedness compel us to act or respond in particular ways.
Further, it has implications for any attempts to employ globalization in support
of grand narratives about the nature of global affairs, in the manner of Huntington, Fukuyama, Barber and others. As a powerful, dynamic and multidimensional
phenomenon, globalization encapsulates processes which are simply too complex,
uneven and indeterminate for us to be able to make such bold claims. Hence, rather
than focusing upon globalization in general and macro terms, we need to consider
the global–local nexus, examining how particular groups, states and societies are
informing and contributing to its processes, as well as being informed and influenced

by them. It is only upon the basis of this type of work that any broader claims about the nature of globalization should be made, and then only in a tentative manner. In other words, we need to pay greater attention to what it means to be living with globalization.

Summarizing Points

- We should conceive of globalization in plural terms as *globalizations*.
- Often it is ideas about globalization as much as its actual processes that are shaping responses to it.
- The watchwords informing our analyses of globalization should be: *differentiating, global flows and interconnectedness, multidimensional, agency, ideational, structural, material, power, contested* and *context*.

Notes

Introduction Globalization and Complexity

1. There is already a vast globalization literature. Two works that have especially influenced my own approach to globalization are Colin Hay and David Marsh's *Demystifying Globalization* (2001) and David Held, Anthony McGrew, David Goldblatt and Jonathon Perraton's *Global Transformations: Politics, Economics and Culture* (1999). In particular, Colin Hay's work has informed my thinking in relation to globalization (see Hay, 1999, 2000 and 2002).
2. However, D. Henderson (1999) has questioned the extent of the influence exerted by INGOs during this episode.
3. These developments also present something of a challenge to Leslie Sklair's (1991) thesis that there is one dominant global system structured around TNCs, a transnational capitalist class and the culture-ideology of consumerism. In his more recent book *Globalization: Capitalism and its Alternatives* (2002) Professor Sklair acknowledges the emergence of 'competing alternative global systems' during the 1990s. For example, he notes how transnational social movements and networks have contributed to the development of competing forms of globalization.
4. In this regard, Heliose Weber (2002) considers one such measure – the microcredit and microfinancing programmes trumpeted by the IMF and the World Bank as self-help initiatives geared to facilitating development – actually serves to extend a disciplinary neo-liberalism.

Chapter 1 Globalization and the Third Way

1. To be fair to Anthony Giddens, he is trying to tackle a number of important topics, such as democracy and the family, in a book designed only to present a brief overview of these areas, and he has articulated how he considers globalization is working elsewhere (see Giddens, 1990). Nevertheless, as far as I am aware, he has not responded in detail to the sceptical thesis in any of his works. And given globalization is so integral to the third way project, it would seem to

require a more in-depth analysis of its nature and form, as well as the critical interpretations of it.

2. The Labour Party's intellectual and political heritage is a source of considerable debate (see Coates, 1975; Jones, 1996; Leys, 1996; Shaw, 1996). In particular, whether the Labour Party was ever a socialist party is a much contested issue.

3. As might be expected, these processes or epochs have been challenged. For example, some writers dispute the notion that we have entered a post-Fordist or post-industrial epoch (Kumar, 1978; Tomaney, 1994). It is pointed out that basic capitalist relations maintained by the system of wage-labour and private property persist in Western societies as do traditional industrial organizations and practices.

4. In promoting this Anglo-Italian agreement, Tony Blair argued that economic liberalization was the best way for Europe to compete with Japan and the US in the 'new global economy'.

5. For example, David Dolowitz (2004) has argued that the consistent theme behind New Labour's governing approach has been the pursuit of an endogenous growth strategy, which is viewed as facilitating its social-welfare agenda. However, Dolowitz's thesis has been challenged (see Matthew Watson, 2004).

6. Colin Hay (2002) has suggested that New Labour's conception of globalization was shaped by the 'new times' thesis (see Hall and Jacques, 1989).

Chapter 2 Globalization and Conflict in Contemporary Europe

1. A great deal has been written about the recent upsurge in 'tribalist' patterns of behaviour in Europe. For example, on the rise of the far right in Western Europe see Betz (1994) and Harris (1994). For useful edited works that cover this development across Europe, see Hainsworth (2000) and Merkl and Weinberg (1997). Hockenos (1993) provides a detailed account of the rise of the right in post-communist Eastern Europe. For the rise of racism and racist violence see Björgo and Witte (1993), Ford (1992) and Fekete and Webber (1994). And for the resurgence of ethnic nationalism and national conflicts see Bugajski (1995), Caplan and Feffer (1996) and Denitch (1994).

2. Walker Connor (1978) is critical of the overlapping or 'interutilization' of these concepts. However, the aim here is merely to delineate key trends in the contemporary period, rather than establish precise definitions.

3. The appropriateness and definitional accuracy of terms such as 'extreme right', 'far right', 'radical right' and 'neo-populist' have been the subject of much discussion (see Betz and Immerfall, 1998; Hainsworth, 2000). However, there will be no attempt to engage in these debates here as to do so would distract from the

primary purpose of this chapter, which is to plot and account for a range of 'tribalist' forms of behaviour. Consequently, these terms will be employed interchangeably.

4. The general position of the extreme right in Europe, as Hans-Georg Betz has noted, is that if each country is allowed to preserve its own culture and identity this will help to ensure a 'Europe of diversity' (Betz, 1994: 184). In defending this notion, a contrast is made with the American 'melting pot' society, which it is claimed has simply led to the blurring of cultures and hence the destruction of individual cultures.

5. This of course raises the question of what we mean by American culture. Joseph Nye (2002), for example, argues that the US is an open society and therefore has always had a syncretic culture. This is evident, he notes, with Pizza Hut: an American company selling food of Italian origin.

6. It is not just in the realm of culture that the US is considered a threat. With the collapse of the Soviet bloc, the intellectual and political elites of the New Right in Europe view the spread of American influence to be the main challenge to the continent's independence (see Minkenberg, 1997).

7. French concerns were expressed as part of a wider dispute between Europe and the US during the Uruguay Round of GATT talks in 1993, in which the Europeans sought to limit the number of American films and television programmes coming into Europe. See Tomlinson (1997) and Van Hemel (1996) for a fuller discussion of this dispute.

8. There are other aspects to the cultural imperialism thesis, such as the debate about the 'Westernization of the rest of the world', but in Europe the focus is firmly upon America.

9. In a number of works, George Ritzer has discussed other aspects of Americaniza-tion or, as he puts it, 'McDonaldization'. In particular, he identifies the ways in which American business practices and principles have permeated European societies and much of the rest of the world. See Ritzer (1998), especially Chapter 6, for his views on the impact of 'McDonaldization' upon Europe.

10. However, the relationship between Europe's radical-right parties and free trade is more complicated than this portrayal as many of them embrace neo-liberalism. Indeed, it is only relatively recently that the FN and the Freedom Party have come to pursue protectionist programmes.

11. One writer who is even more forthright on this issue is Anthony Smith (1995). He argues that to understand nations and nationalisms in the modern world we must recognize they are products of deep-rooted historical cultures and ethnic ties, rather than the 'consequences of global interdependence' (Smith, 1995: vii). However, Smith's ethno-symbolist approach has been criticized – particularly by modernists – for not recognizing how ethnic identities and national cultures change and evolve. For an overview of some of the major criticisms of ethnosymbolism see Özkirimli (2000).

12. However, there are certain shortcomings with this line of reasoning. In particular, it implies that when economic conditions improve racism and far-right activity will diminish. In reality, the economic recession in Western Europe has been over since the mid 1990s, yet still the extreme right continues to thrive. This would suggest that there are profounder processes at work behind such patterns of behaviour.
13. A similar case has been made to account for recent developments in the former Yugoslavia (see Vujacic and Zaslavsky, 1991).
14. And, arguably, when examining different contexts in relation to globalization we should go beyond the national level and concentrate upon the local level and particular localities, a theme that is returned to in the Conclusion to this work.

Chapter 3 Globalization, Cosmopolitanism and the European Union

1. There is an expanding literature on the cultural and sociological dimensions of cosmopolitanism (see for example Beck, 2000a; Breckenridge et al., 2002; Urry, 2000).
2. The focus of this chapter is upon how the EU as a regional body is responding to globalization. But of course we should bear in mind the point made in the previous chapter about the variety of perspectives that will exist among, and within, European countries towards globalization (see Hay and Rosamond, 2002).
3. Often there are direct or explicit connections made between these developments and globalization. For example, Adam Tickell believes that the much of the financial 'restructuring that took place in the EU during the early 1990s was a response to existing processes of globalization in financial markets' (1999: 64).
4. George Ross believes that the project of European integration was at its creation 'strongly conditioned by processes of globalization', which were 'at work long before the concept was used in popular discourse' (1998: 179). Moreover, the decisions taken within Europe to deepen integration after 1985 have actually served to promote globalization.
5. While the Schengen Agreement involves many EU states it is not part of the European Treaties and is therefore outside of European law. This means there is no single official EU policy on asylum and immigration – although there is currently much discussion about harmonizing the national policies of member states.
6. For a full explanation and discussion of how globalization fosters individualism, see my book *Rebuilding Communities in an Age of Individualism* (2003), especially Chapter 3.

7. In this vein, Gerard Delanty (1998, 2000) believes the 'knowledge society' may serve as the basis for the social dimension of European integration. Given the difficulties Europe faces becoming a properly functioning community, he believes it would be wiser to develop it as a virtual community, a 'civic communication community', as he terms it.

8. This can provoke a range of cultural reactions. In particular, the dominant group will often seek to hold on to its own conception of the nation. The French policy of assimilationism and the German *gastarbeider* approach should perhaps be viewed in this way. But such approaches can not conceal the fact that minority cultures are now a permanent presence within these societies.

9. Writers like Homi Bhabha (1990) would undoubtedly challenge the notion that the nation has ever been unitary and stable. Rather, from a post-colonial/post-structuralist viewpoint, nations have always been hybrid constructions.

10. Ulrich Beck (2002) draws similar conclusions in relation to his discussion of the 'Second Age of Modernity', which globalization has helped to ensure that we are entering. In particular, Beck regards cosmopolitanism as an ally of globalization in that it challenges the nation-state: 'globalization means that an increasing number of social processes are indifferent to national boundaries' (2002: 62). Although Beck warns this does not mean that we are all going to become cosmopolitans as countermovements will remain.

11. There have been recent attempts to address some of the EU's shortcomings, such as the EU Charter of Fundamental Rights. However, this has been criticized for not tackling the democratic accountability of EU institutions (see Venables, 2001).

Chapter 4 Globalization, Al-Qaeda and Global Terror

1. Osama bin Laden's own life and career as well as the emergence of Al-Qaeda have already received considerable critical attention. See Bergen (2001), Bodansky (2001), Burke (2003), and Gunaratna (2002).

2. For an informed insight into the different forms of Islam and Islamism, see Burgat (2003), Hiro (2002), Roy (1999) and Saikal (2003). For example, Amin Saikal (2003) identifies a number of different approaches and strands of opinion within the Muslim world. As well as radical Islamists, he identifies neo-fundamentalist Islamists and grass-roots networks made up of ordinary Muslims. Saikal recognizes, however, that there is considerable overlap between the different groups, including the forging of close links and alliances, such as those which existed between Al-Qaeda (radical Islamist) and the Taliban (neo-fundamentalist).

3. These developments are often articulated as an example of Muslim societies being at odds with modernity, generally conceived of as a Western project (Fukuyama, 2002; Huntington, 1997; Lewis, 2002, 2003). However, there is currently much debate about Islam and modernity (see Thompson, 2003), with many commentators identifying Islamic conceptions of modernity (Cooper et al., 2000) as part of a general insistence upon multiple modernities (Eisenstadt et al., 2000).
4. From a Muslim perspective, human rights and democracy are significant issues within the Islamic world. Human rights are the subject of a lively and ongoing debate centred mainly around Islamic human rights schemes (see Meyer, 1995). Meanwhile liberal Muslims contend Islam and democracy are not incompatible, and note that representative government is a feature of the Islamic political system. Critics, however, point to the fact that there are few examples of stable democracies in Muslim majority states (Çaha, 2003).
5. As a result of Wahhabi becoming something of a blanket term, some prefer the term *Salafi* to refer to groups beyond the borders of Saudi Arabia (Oliveti, 2002). This term reflects the desire to return to the Islam of Mohammed and the early believers as well as indicating that it is an approach or worldview common to many groups. But as John Esposito has noted: 'both Wahhabi and Salafi can be misleading, as they are used as umbrella terms that incorporate diverse ideologies and movements' (2002: 106).

Chapter 5 China and Globalization

1. Concern about China's untapped resources and potential dates back many decades. For example, during his tour of the country in 1898, Rudyard Kipling declared, 'What will happen when China really wakes up?'
2. Although China was engaged in pre-modern globalization with the Silk Route, a network of trade routes connecting Asia with Europe.
3. The reliability of some of China's economic statistics, especially in relation to its growth rates and the recording and measurement of poverty, has hampered both researchers and commentators alike. As a result there continues to be debate about the actual economic size of China, with some writers presenting a more cautious appraisal of China's economic growth (see for example, Rawski, 2002; Segal, 1999).
4. However, Yasheng Huang (2003) questions whether the level of foreign direct investment (FDI) is evidence of a dynamic and competitive economy. Huang maintains that there is the huge demand for FDI in China because resources are unfairly allocated to inefficient state-owned enterprises.

5. While it is widely predicted that China will overtake the US as the world's largest economy at some point this century, though estimates vary as to when this will be, it will still be well behind America in per capita terms.

6. For an extensive analysis of China's dynamic coastal region between Shanghai and Hong Kong and its interaction with globalizing processes, see Carolyn Cartier, 2001.

7. The Han Chinese community make up 93 per cent of China's population and there are around fifty-five so-called 'national minorities' in China.

8. For an informative analysis of the discourse of race in Chinese society, see Frank Dikötter, 1992.

9. However, based upon his study of this episode, Simon Shen believes that contemporary Chinese nationalism 'is unlikely to become the new Chinese foreign policy framer in the future' (2004: 122). The nationalist feelings of the Chinese people and the rhetoric frequently employed by Chinese leaders are not leading to nationalist foreign policy formulation. Indeed, Shen detects a pragmatic strain within the third-generation CCP leadership.

10. Continuing US support for Taiwan has also undoubtedly shaped Beijing's approach towards the country. However, some Taiwanese commentators are now expressing concern that China's growing economic muscle will enable it to exert pressure upon the US to rethink its close support for Taiwan.

11. Interestingly, Perry Link and his co-editors note that none of the Chinese people portrayed in their book *Popular China: Unofficial Culture in a Globalizing Society* (2002) considered their local culture to be in opposition to global culture. Rather, as they put it, 'they employ aspects of their local traditions to interpret that culture and to negotiate their way through it' (Link et al., 2002: 5).

Chapter 6 The United States and Globalization

1. It should also be borne in mind that current levels of immigration have only been possible because of an amendment to the Immigration and Naturalization Act in 1965, which ended racial and ethnic restrictions on immigration.

2. Roger Rouse (2002) has studied this phenomenon in the case of labour migrants from the rural Mexican town of Aguililla who have relocated to Redwood City in the US. His study highlights the intensity of the connections and communication between Aguililla and Redwood City.

3. There are variants of this charge that consider globalization in relation to cultural imperialism (Tomlinson, 1991), McDonaldization (Ritzer, 1998) and Westernization (Latouche, 1996). More broadly, the claim that cultural

homogenization is an inevitable consequence of global processes dates back to Marshall McLuhan's conception of 'the global village' (McLuhan, 1964).

4. Such has been the spread of anti-Americanism that the US State Department organized a conference in September 2002 specifically to address this phenomenon (Kettle, 2002).

5. And even if we allow for the existence of a global culture, some writers note the possibility of cultural flows moving from the local to the global (for example, Cvetkovich and Kellner, 1997; Friedman, 1990; Giddens, 1994; Tomlinson, 1999).

6. Indeed, in relation to direct foreign investment, the US economy is the most open of all economies, investing and receiving nearly twice as much as the UK, its nearest competitor (Nye, 2002: 36).

7. However, the US government arguably took decisive action to prevent the crisis from spreading further, with the US Federal Reserve cutting domestic interest rates to boost the world economy. The Clinton administration also played a key role in shaping the huge financial rescue package for the region.

8. As further evidence of a more integrated global economy, should the US take the measures needed to tackle this deficit it would have a damaging impact upon countries throughout the world. This is because in the last few years America has been a welcoming market in which other countries can sell their goods, and this would no longer be the case.

9. However, it is important not to forget that writers sceptical about globalization, such as Hirst and Thompson (1996), question the extent of global economic integration and stress the continuing autonomy of the nation-state.

10. This is not to ignore the claim of dependency theorists that it is actually the international economy and the way it is organized that restrict the development of some countries, merely to acknowledge that China, India and the 'Asian Tiger' economies have been developing apace under contemporary conditions.

11. As was discussed in Chapter 4, these developments also make it easier for terrorists groups to organize. It follows that the US by itself will not defeat terrorist groups and must be more strongly orientated toward working with other nations. It must recognize that power in the contemporary period is multifaceted, depending upon factors such as image and gaining influence though coalition-building, and not just based upon military capabilities.

Conclusion Living with Globalization

1. It is for this reason that, for example, in seeking to understand New Labour's conception of globalization in Chapter 1, the UK political context from which

it had emerged was examined, notably the legacy of Thatcherism. Similarly, in attempting to account for the Al-Qaeda view of globalizing processes, much of Chapter 4 was devoted to a consideration of the historical, political and cultural context from which the phenomenon has emerged.

2. For a range of interesting case studies on the local effects of, and reactions to, globalization, see John Eade (ed.), *Living the Global City: Globalization as a Local Process* (1997). For example, Martin Albrow in an essay in the book entitled 'Travelling Beyond Local Cultures' charts the ways in which globalization is impacting upon everyday life within the inner London borough of Wandsworth.

Bibliography

Abu-Lughod, J. (1989), *Before European Hegemony*, Oxford, Oxford University Press.

Adams, C.T. (1983), 'Mawdudi and the Islamic State', J. Esposito (ed.), *Voices of Resurgent Islam*, Oxford, Oxford University Press.

Aglionby, J. (2003), 'Economic Superpower Rises in the East', *Guardian*, 8 October, p. 20.

Ahmed, A. (1995), 'Ethnic Cleansing: A Metaphor for Our Time', *Ethnic and Racial Studies*, 18, 1, pp. 2–25.

Ahmed, A.S. (2003), *Islam under Siege*, Cambridge, Polity.

Alam, F. (2004), 'Give Our Boys a Future', *Observer*, 4 April, p. 27.

Albrow, M. (1997), 'Travelling Beyond Local Cultures', J. Eade (ed.), *Living the Global City: Globalization as a Local Process*, London, Routledge.

Alibhai-Brown, Y. (2001), 'Ramadan's True Spirit is Threatened', *Independent*, 19 November.

—— (2002), 'Reformist Muslims are Bringing New Hope to Islam', *Independent*, 9 September.

Amin, A. (2001), 'Immigrants, Cosmopolitans and the Idea of Europe', H. Wallace (ed.), *Interlocking Dimensions of European Integration*, Basingstoke, Palgrave, pp. 280–301.

Amin, S. (1996), 'The Challenge of Globalization', *Review of International Political Economy*, 3, 2.

Andersen, J.G. and Bjørklund, T. (2000) 'Radical Right-Wing Populism in Scandinavia: From Tax Revolt to Neo-liberalism and xenophobia', P. Hainsworth (ed.), *The Politics of the Extreme Right: from the Margins and the Mainstream*, London, Pinter, pp. 193–23.

Anderson, S. and Sloan, S. (1995), *Historical Dictionary of Terrorism*, London, The Scarecrow Press.

Anderson-Gold, S. (2001), *Cosmopolitanism and Human Rights*, University of Wales Press, Cardiff.

Anker, C. van den (2001), 'Dutch Social Democracy and the Poldermodel', L. Martell et al., *Social Democracy: Global and National Perspectives*, Basingstoke, Palgrave, pp. 129–59.

Annesley, C. (2003), 'Americanised and Europeanised: UK Social Policy since 1997', *British Journal of Politics and International Relations*, 5, 2, pp. 143–65.

Appadurai, A. (1996), *Modernity at Large*, Minneapolis, University of Minnesota Press.

—— (2000), 'Disjuncture and Difference in the Global Cultural Economy', D. Held and A. McGrew (eds), *The Global Transformations Reader*, Cambridge, Polity, pp. 230–8.

Archibugi, D. (1995), 'Immanuel Kant, Cosmopolitan Law and Peace', *European Journal of International Relations*, 1, 4, pp. 429–56.

Archibugi, D. and Held, D. (eds) (1995), *Cosmopolitan Democracy*, Cambridge, Polity.

Armstrong, K. (2001), 'The War We Should Fight', *Guardian*, 13 October.

—— (2002), 'The Curse of the Infidel', *Guardian*, 20 June.

—— (2003), *Islam: A Short History*, London, Phoenix.

Axford, B. and Huggins, R. (1999), 'Towards a Post-National Polity: The Emergence of the Network Society in Europe', D. Smith and S. Wright (eds), *Whose Europe?*, Oxford, Blackwell, pp. 173–206.

Ball, D. (2002), 'Desperately Seeking Bin Laden: The Intelligence Dimension of the War Against Terrorism', K. Booth and T. Dunne (eds), *Worlds in Collision: Terror and the Future of Global Order*, Basingstoke, Palgrave, pp. 60–73.

Barber, B. (1996), *Jihad vs. McWorld: How Globalism and Tribalism are Reshaping the World*, New York, Ballantine.

Barry Jones, R.J. (2000), *The World Turned University Pressside Down? Globalization and the Future of the State*, Manchester, Manchester University Press.

Batha, E. (2000), 'Austria's Problem with Foreigners', *BBC News Online*, 4 February.

Bauman, Z. (1993), *Postmodern Ethics*, Oxford, Blackwell.

—— (1996), 'Morality in the Age of Contingency', P. Heelas, S. Lash and p. Morris (eds), *Detraditionalization: Critical Reflections on Authority and Identity*, Oxford, Blackwell, pp. 49–58.

—— (1998), *Globalization: The Human Consequences*, Cambridge, Polity.

—— (2001), *The Individualized Society*, Cambridge, Polity.

BBC (2003a), 'Arab Economies "Must Reform"', *BBC News Online*, 11 September.

—— (2003b), 'Jobs "Key" to Middle East Growth', *BBC News Online*, 19 September.

—— (2004), 'India's Population "to be Biggest"', *BBC News Online*, 18 August.

Beaumont, P. (2001), 'The Roots of Islamic Anger', *Observer*, 14 October.

Beck, U. (1992), *Risk Society: Towards a New Modernity*, London, Sage.

—— (1999), *World Risk Society*, Cambridge, Polity.

—— (2000a), *What is Globalization?*, Cambridge, Polity.

—— (2000b), *The Brave New World of Work*, Cambridge, Polity.

—— (2002), 'The Cosmopolitan Perspective: Sociology in the Second Age of Modernity', S. Vertovec and R. Cohen (eds), *Conceiving Cosmopolitanism*, Oxford, Oxford University Press, pp. 61–85.

Beck, U. and Beck-Gernsheim, E. (1996), 'Individualization and "Precarious Freedoms": Perspectives and Controversies of a Subject-Orientated Society', P. Heelas, S. Lash and P. Morris (eds) *Detraditionalization: Critical Reflections on Authority and Identity*, Oxford, Blackwell, pp. 23–48.

—— (2002), *Individualization*, London, Sage.

Beck, U., Giddens, A. and Lash, S. (1994), *Reflexive Modernization*, Cambridge, Polity.

Becker, J. (2000), *The Chinese*, London, John Murray.

Bellamy, R. (2000), 'Citizenship Beyond the Nation State: The Case of Europe', N. O'Sullivan (ed.), *Political Theory in Transition*, London, Routledge, pp. 91–112.

Bellamy, R. and Castiglione, D. (1998), 'Between Cosmopolis and Community: Three Models of Rights and Democracy within the European Union', D. Archibugi, D. Held and M. Kohler (eds), *Re-imaging Political Community*, Stanford, Stanford University Press, pp. 152–78.

Bergen, P. (2001), *Holy War, Inc.: Inside the World of Osama bin Laden*, New York, The Free Press.

Berger, P.L. and Huntington, S.P. (eds) (2002), *Many Globalizations*, Oxford, Oxford University Press.

Berger, S.R. and Sutphen, M. (2001), 'Commandeering the Palestinian Cause: Bin Laden's Belated Concern', J.F. Hoge and G. Rose (eds), *How Did This Happen? Terrorism and the New War*, Oxford, Public Affairs, pp. 123–8.

Bernstein, R. and Munro, R.H. (1997), *The Coming Conflict with China*, New York, Knopf.

Betz, H.-G. (1994), *Radical Right-Wing Populism in Western Europe*, Basingstoke, Macmillan.

—— (1998), 'Introduction', H.-G. Betz and S. Immerfall (eds) (1998), *The New Politics of the Right: Neo-Populist Parties and Movements in Established Democracies*, Basingstoke, Macmillan, pp. 1–10.

Betz, H.-G. and Immerfall, S. (eds) (1998), *The New Politics of the Right: Neo-Populist Parties and Movements in Established Democracies*, Basingstoke, Macmillan.

Bevir, M. (2000), 'New Labour: A Study in Ideology', *British Journal of Politics and International Relations*, 2, pp. 227–301.

Bhabha, H. (1990), *Nation and Narration*, London, Routledge.

Biersteker, T.J. (2002), 'Targeting Terrorist Finances: The Challenge of Financial Market Globalization', K. Booth and T. Dunne (eds), *Worlds in Collision: Terror and the Future of Global Order*, Basingstoke, Palgrave, pp. 74–84.

Billig, M. (1995), *Banal Nationalism*, London, Sage.

Bin Laden, O. (2001), 'Bin Laden's Warning: Full Text', *BBC News*, 7 October, <www.news.bbc.co.uk/newsid_1585000/1585636.stm>

Björgo, T. (1993), 'Role of the Media in Racist Violence', T. Björgo and R. Witte (eds), *Racist Violence in Europe*, Basingstoke, Macmillan, pp. 96–112.

Björgo, T. and Witte, R. (eds) (1993), *Racist Violence in Europe*, Basingstoke, Macmillan.

Black, I. (2003), 'Europe Nears Agreement on Constitution', *Guardian*, 7 June, p. 17.

Blair, T. (1996), *New Britain: My Vision of a Young Country*, London, Fourth Estate.

—— (1997), *Speech to the Party of European Socialists Congress*, Malmö, 6 June, London, Labour Party.

Blair, T. (1998a), 'The Third Way', speech to the French National Assembly, 24/3/98, <www.fco.gov.uk/speeches>

—— (1998b), *The Third Way: New Politics for the New Century*, London, Fabian Society.

—— (1999), *Facing the Modern Challenge: The Third Way in Britain and South Africa*, speech in Cape Town, South Africa.

Blair, T. and Schroeder, G. (1999), 'Europe: The Third Way/Die Neue Mitte', K. Coates (ed.), *The Third Way to the Servile State*, Nottingham, Spokesman, pp. 38–59.

Bodansky, Y. (2001), *Bin Laden: The Man Who Declared War on America*, New York, Prima.

Booth, K. and Dunne, T. (eds) (2002), *Worlds in Collision: Terror and the Future of Global Order*, Basingstoke, Palgrave.

Borger, J. (2004), 'Bush Woos Hispanic Immigrants', *Guardian*, 7 January, p. 13.

Breckenridge, C.A., Bhabha, H.K., Pollock, S. and Chakrabarty, D. (eds) (2002), *Cosmopolitanism*, Durham, Duke University Press.

Brenner, R. (2002), *The Boom and the Bubble: The US in the World Economy*, London, Verso.

Brewer, A. (1990), *Marxist Theories of Imperialism*, 2nd edition, London, Routledge.

Brimelow, P. (1995), *Alien Nation: Common Sense About America's Immigration Disaster*, New York, Random House.

Brown, M.E., Coté, O.R., Lynn-Jones, S.M. and Miller, S.E. (eds) (2000), *The Rise of China*, Cambridge MA, MIT Press.

Browne, M. and Akbar, Y. (2001), 'Globalization and the Renewal of Social Democracy: A Critical Reconsideration', L. Martell et al., *Social Democracy: Global and National Perspectives*, Basingstoke, Palgrave, pp. 49–73.

Brubaker, R. (1996), *Nationalism Reframed*, Cambridge, Cambridge University Press.

—— (1998), 'Myths and Misconceptions in the Study of Nationalism', J.A. Hall (ed.), *The State of the Nation*, Cambridge, Cambridge University Press, pp. 272–306.

—— (2000), *Fundamentalism*, Cambridge, Polity.

Bruce, S. (2003), *Politics and Religion*, Cambridge, Polity.

Bruff, I. (2003), 'The Netherlands, the Challenge of Lijst Pim Fortuyn, and the Third Way', *Politics*, 23, 3, pp. 156–62.

Bugajski, J. (1995), *Nations in Turmoil: Conflict and Cooperation in Eastern Europe*, Boulder, Westview Press.

Burbach, R., Nunez, O. and Kagarlitsky, B. (1997), *Globalization and its Discontents*, London, Pluto.

Burgat, F. (2003), *Face to Face with Political Islam*, London, I.B. Tauris.

Burke, J. (2001), 'The Making of the World's Most Wanted Man', *Observer*, 28 October.

—— (2003), *Al-Qaeda: Casting a Shadow of Terror*, London, I.B. Tauris.

Busch, A. and Manow, P. (2001), 'The SPD and the Neue Mitte in Germany', S. White (ed.), *New Labour: The Progressive Future*, Basingstoke, Palgrave, pp.175–89.

Çaha, Ö. (2003), 'The Deficiency of Democracy in the Islamic World', M.J. Thompson (ed.), *Islam and the West: Critical Perspectives on Modernity*, Oxford, Rowman and Littlefield, pp. 39–48.

Callinicos, A. (2001), *Against the Third Way*, Cambridge, Polity.

—— (2003), *An Anti-Capitalist Manifesto*, Cambridge, Polity.

Callinicos, A., Rees, J., Harman, C. and Haynes, M. (1994), *Marxism and the New Imperialism*, London, Bookmarks.

Caplan, R. and Feffer, J. (eds) (1996), *Europe's New Nationalism: States and Minorities in Conflict*, Oxford, Oxford University Press.

Carey, H.F. (1997), 'Post-Communist Right Radicalism in Romania', P.H. Merkl and L. Weinberg (eds), *The Revival of Right-Wing Extremism in the Nineties*, London, Frank Cass, pp. 149–76.

Carroll, R. (2002), 'Blair and Berlusconi Frame Deal to Free Up EU Markets', *Guardian*, 16 February.

Cartier, C. (2001), *Globalizing South China*, Oxford, Blackwell.

Castells, M. (1996), *The Rise of the Network Society*, vol. 1, Oxford, Blackwell.

—— (1997), *The Power of Identity*, vol. 2, Oxford, Blackwell.

Castles, S. (2000), *Ethnicity and Globalization*, London, Sage.

Castles, S. and Miller, M.J. (1998), *The Age of Migration*, 2nd edition, Basingstoke, Macmillan.

Chang, G.C. (2002), *The Coming Collapse of China*, London, Arrow.

Chang, M.H. (2001), *Return of the Dragon – China's Wounded Nationalism*, Boulder, Westview Press.

Cheah, P. and Robbins, B. (eds) (1998), *Cosmopolitics: Thinking and Feeling beyond the Nation*, Minneapolis, University of Minnesota Press.

Chomsky, N. (1994), *World Orders, Old and New*, London, Pluto.

Choueiri, Y.M. (1997), *Islamic Fundamentalism*, London, Pinter.

Christensen, T.J. (2001), 'Posing Problems Without Catching Up: China's Rise and Challenges for US Security Policy', *International Security*, 36.

Clammer, J. (2001), 'In But Not Of the World? Japan, Globalization and the "End of History"', C. Hay and D. Marsh (eds), *Demystifying Globalization*, Basingstoke, Palgrave, pp. 147–67.

Clift, B. (2002), 'Social Democracy and Globalization: The Cases of France and the UK', *Government and Opposition*, 37, 4.

—— (2004a), 'New Labour's Second Term and European Social Democracy', S. Ludlam and M.J. Smith (eds), *Governing as New Labour*, Basingstoke, Palgrave, pp. 34–51.

—— (2004b), 'New Labour's Third Way and European Social Democracy', S. Ludlam and M.J. Smith (eds), *New Labour in Government*, Basingstoke, Macmillan, pp. 55–72.

Coates, D. (1975), *The Labour Party and the Struggle for Socialism*, Cambridge, Cambridge University Press.

—— (2002), 'Strategic Choices in the Study of New Labour: A Response to Replies from Hay and Wickham-Jones', *British Journal of Politics and International Relations*, 4, 3, pp. 479–86.

Coates, K. (ed.) (1999), *The Third Way to the Servile State*, Nottingham, Spokesman.

Cohen, R. (1997), *Global Diasporas*, London, Routledge.

Cohen, S.J. (1999), *Politics Without a Past: The Absence of History in Postcommunist Nationalism*, Durham, Duke University Press.

Colás, A. (2002), *International Civil Society*, Cambridge, Polity.

Comor, E.A. (1999), 'Governance and the Nation-State in a Knowledge-Based Political Economy', M. Hewson and T.J. Sinclair (eds), *Approaches to Global Governance Theory*, Albany, State University of New York Press, pp. 117–34.

Connor, W. (1978), 'A Nation is a Nation, is a State, is an Ethnic Group, is a …', *Ethnic and Racial Studies*, 1, 4, pp. 379–88.

Cooper, J, Nettler, R. and Mahmoud, M. (eds) (2000), *Islam and Modernity: Muslim Intellectuals Respond*, London, I.B. Tauris.

Cox, M. and Shearman, P. (2000), 'After the Fall: Nationalist Extremism in Post-Communist Russia', P. Hainsworth (ed.), *The Politics of the Extreme Right*, London, Pinter, pp. 224–46.

Cox, R. (1997), 'Economic Globalization and the Limits to Liberal Democracy', A.G. McGrew (ed.), *The Transformation of Democracy? Globalization and Territorial Democracy*, Cambridge, Polity.

Crouch, C. (1999), 'The Parabola of Working-Class Politics', A. Gamble and T. Wright (eds), *The New Social Democracy*, Oxford, Blackwell, pp. 69–83.

—— (2001), 'A Third Way in Industrial Relations', S. White (ed.), *New Labour: The Progressive Future*, Basingstoke, Palgrave.

Cvetkovich, A. and Kellner, D. (eds) (1997), *Articulating the Global and the Local*, Boulder, Westview Press.

Davies, N. (1997), *Europe: A History*, London, Pimlico.

Davis, H. and Rootes, C. (eds) (1994), *A New Europe?*, London, UCL.

Davison Hunter, J. and Yates, J. (2002), 'In the Vanguard of Globalization: The World of American Globalizers', P.L. Berger and S.P. Huntington (eds), *Many Globalizations*, Oxford, Oxford University Press, pp. 323–57.

Dawood, N.J. (trans.) (1997), *The Koran*, London, Penguin.

Dawoud, K. (2002), 'Egypt terror leaders renounce violence', *Guardian*, 2 August.

Delanty, G. (1995), *Inventing Europe: Idea, Identity, Reality*, Basingstoke, Macmillan.

—— (1998), 'Social Theory and European Transformation: Is there a European Society?', *Sociological Research Online*, 3, <www.socresonline.org.uk>

—— (2000), *Citizenship in a Global Age*, Buckingham, Open University Press.

Delanty, G. and O'Mahony, P. (2002), *Nationalism and Social Theory: Modernity and the Recalcitrance of the Nation*, London, Sage.

Denitch, B. (1994), *Ethnic Nationalism: The Tragic Death of Yugoslavia*, Minneapolis, University of Minnesota Press.

—— (1996), 'National Identity, Politics and Democracy', *Social Science Information*, 35, 3, pp. 459–83.

Dicken, P. (1998), *Global Shift: The Transformation of the World Economy*, 3rd edition, London, Paul Chapman.

—— (1999), 'Global Shift – the Role of United States Transnational Corporations', D. Slater and P.J. Taylor (eds), *The American Century: Consensus and Coercion in the Projection of American Power*, Oxford, Blackwell, pp. 35–50.

Dickson, B.J. (2000/1), 'Co-optation and Corporatism in China: The Logic of Party Adaptation', *Political Science Quarterly*, 115, 4, pp. 517–40.

Dickstein, M. (1993), 'After the Cold War: Culture as Politics, Politics as Culture', *Social Research*, 60, 3, pp. 531–44.

Dikötter, F. (1992), *The Discourse of Race in Modern China*, London, Hurst.

Dolowitz, D.P. (2004), 'Prosperity and Fairness? Can New Labour Bring Fairness to the 21st Century by Following the Dictates of Endogenous Growth?', *British Journal of Politics and International Relations*, 6, 2, pp. 213–30.

Doran, M.S. (2001), 'Gods and Monsters', *Guardian*, 8 December.

Downs, E.S. and Saunders, P.C. (2000), 'Legitimacy and the Limits of Nationalism: China and the Diaoyu Islands', M.E. Brown, O.R. Coté, S.M. Lynn-Jones and S.E. Miller (eds), *The Rise of China*, Cambridge MA, MIT Press, pp. 41–73.

Doyle, L. (1996), 'EU Slams the Door on Fleeing Victims', *Guardian*, 23 March, p. 14.

Driver, S. and Martell, L. (1998), *New Labour: Politics after Thatcherism*, Cambridge, Polity.

—— (2001), 'Left, Right and the Third Way', A. Giddens (ed.), *The Global Third Way Debate*, Cambridge, Polity, pp. 36–49.

—— (2002), *Blair's Britain*, Cambridge, Polity.

Dunkerley, D., Hodgson, L., Konopacki, S., Spybey, T. and Thompson, A. (2002), *Changing Europe*, London, Routledge.

Dunn, J. (ed.) (1995), *Contemporary Crisis of the Nation-State?*, Oxford, Blackwell.

Dunn, S. and Fraser, T.G. (1996), *Europe and Ethnicity: World War I and Contemporary Ethnic Conflict*, London, Routledge.

Duroselle, J.-B. (1990), *Europe: A History of its Peoples*, London, Viking.

Eade, J. (ed.) (1997), *Living the Global City: Globalization as a Local Process*, London, Routledge.

Eatwell, R. (1998), 'The Dynamics of Right-Wing Electoral Breakthrough', *Patterns of Prejudice*, 32, 3, pp. 3–31.

Eckes, A.E., Jr. and Zeiler, T.W. (2003), *Globalization and the American Century*, Cambridge, Cambridge University Press.

Economy, E. and Oksenberg, M. (eds) (1999), *China Joins the World: Progress and Prospects*, New York, Council on Foreign Relations.

Eisenstadt, S.N. (2003), *Comparative Civilizations and Multiple Modernities*, 2 volumes, Leiden, Brill.

Eisenstadt, S.N. et al. (2000), 'Multiple Modernities', *Daedalus*, 129, 1.

Elliott, L. (2002), 'Fortress Europe Pulls Up the Drawbridge', *Guardian*, 3 June, p. 21.

Esposito, J.L. (1992), *The Islamic Threat: Myth or Reality?*, Oxford, Oxford University Press.

—— (2002), *Unholy War: Terror in the Name of Islam*, Oxford, Oxford University Press.

Esposito, J.L. and Burgat, F. (eds) (2003), *Modernizing Islam*, New Brunswick, Rutgers University Press.

Fairclough, N. (2000), *New Labour, New Language?* London, Routledge.

Falk, R. (1995), 'The World Order between Inter-State Law and the Law of Humanity: The Role of Civil Society Institutions', D. Archibugi and D. Held (eds), *Cosmopolitan Democracy*, Cambridge, Polity, pp. 163–79.

—— (1996), 'Revisioning Cosmopolitanism', M.C. Nussbaum, *For Love of Country*, Boston, Beacon, pp. 53–60.

—— (1998), 'The United Nations and Cosmopolitan Democracy: Bad Dream, Utopian Fantasy, Political Project', D. Archibugi, D. Held and M. Kohler (eds), *Re-imaging Political Community*, Stanford, Stanford University Press, pp. 309–31.

—— (1999), *Predatory Globalization*, Cambridge, Polity.

Featherstone, M. (ed.) (1990), *Global Culture: Nationalism, Globalization and Modernity*, London, Sage.

—— (1995), *Undoing Culture: Globalization, Postmodernism and Identity*, London, Sage.

Featherstone, M., Lash, S. and Robertson, R. (eds) (1995), *Global Modernities*, London, Sage.

Fekete, L. and Webber, F. (1994), *Inside Racist Europe*, London, Institute of Race Relations.

Finlayson, A. (1999), 'Third Way Theory', *Political Quarterly*, 70, 3.

—— (2002), 'What about the Politics, Tony?', *Observer*, 16 June.

—— (2003), *Making Sense of New Labour*, London, Lawrence and Wishart.

Florini, A.M. (ed.) (2000), *The Third Force: The Rise of Transnational Civil Society*, Washington DC, Carnegie Endowment for International Peace.

Føllesdal, A. (1999), 'Third Country Nationals as European Citizens: The Case Defended', D. Smith and S. Wright (eds), *Whose Europe?*, Oxford, Blackwell, pp. 104–22.

Ford, G. (1992), *Fascist Europe: The Rise of Racism and Xenophobia*, London, Pluto Press.

Freedland, J. (2002), 'What Really Changed', *Guardian*, 4 September.

Freedman, L. (2002), 'A New Type of War', K. Booth and T. Dunne (eds), *Worlds in Collision: Terror and the Future of Global Order*, Basingstoke, Palgrave, pp. 37–47.

Friedman, E. (1996), 'A Democratic Chinese Nationalism?', J. Unger (ed.), *Chinese Nationalism*, New York, M.E. Sharpe.

Friedman, J. (1990), 'Being in the World: Globalization and Localization', M. Featherstone (ed.), *Global Culture: Nationalism, Globalization and Modernity*, London, Sage, pp. 311–28.

Front National (1993), *300 Mesures pour la renaissance de la France*, Paris, Editions Nationales.

Fukuyama, F. (1992), *The End of History and the Last Man*, New York, The Free Press.

—— (2002), 'History and September 11', K. Booth and T. Dunne (eds), *Worlds in Collision: Terror and the Future of Global Order*, Basingstoke, Palgrave, pp. 27–36.

Fuller, G. and Lesser, I. (1995), *A Sense of Siege: The Geopolitics of Islam and the West*, Boulder, Westview Press.

Gamble, A. and Kelly, G. (2004), 'Labour's New Economics', S. Ludlam and M.J. Smith (eds), *New Labour in Government*, Basingstoke, Macmillan, pp. 167–83.

Gamble, A. and Wright, T. (1999), *The New Social Democracy*, Oxford, Blackwell.

Garrett, G. (1998), *Partisan Politics in the Global Economy*, Cambridge, Cambridge University Press.

Germain, R.D. (2002), 'Reforming the International Financial Architecture: The New Political Agenda', R. Wilkinson and S. Hughes (eds), *Global Governance: Critical Perspectives*, London, Routledge, pp. 17–35.

Gessner, V. and Schade, A. (1990), 'Conflicts of Culture in Cross-Border Legal Relations', *Theory, Culture and Society*, 7, 2–3.

Geyer, R. (2003), 'Beyond the Third Way: The Science of Complexity and the Politics of Choice', *British Journal of Politics and International Relations*, 5, 2, pp. 237–57.

Giddens, A. (1990), *The Consequences of Modernity*, Cambridge, Polity.

—— (1994), *Beyond Left and Right: The Future for Radical Politics*, Cambridge, Polity.

—— (1998), *The Third Way: The Renewal of Social Democracy*, Cambridge, Polity.

—— (1999), *Runaway World: How Globalisation is Reshaping our Lives*, London, Profile.

—— (2000), *The Third Way and its Critics*, Cambridge, Polity.

—— (2001), 'The Question of Inequality', A. Giddens (ed.), *The Global Third Way Debate*, Cambridge, Polity, pp. 178–88.

—— (2002a), *Where Now for New Labour?*, Cambridge, Polity.

—— (2002b), 'There is no Alternative – The Third Way is the Only Way Forward', *Independent*, 8 January.

Gilboy, G. and Heginbotham, E. (2002), 'China's Coming Transformation', *The Rise of China*, New York, Foreign Affairs, pp. 102–14.

Gill, B. (2004), 'China as a Regional Military Power', B. Buzan and R. Foot (eds), *Does China Matter? A Reassessment*, London, Routledge, pp. 124–42.

Gill, S. (1992), 'Economic Globalization and the Internationalization of Authority: Limits and Contradictions', *GeoForum*, 23, 3.

—— (1995), 'Globalization, Market Civilization, and Disciplinary Neoliberalism', *Millennium*, 24.

Gilpin, R. (1987), *The Political Economy of International Relations*, Princeton, Princeton University Press.

—— (2001), *Global Political Economy*, Princeton, Princeton University Press.

Gittings, J. (2002), 'Don't Mention Communism', *Guardian*, 13 August.

Glenny, M. (1993), *The Rebirth of History: Eastern Europe in the Age of Democracy*, 2nd edition, London, Penguin.

Goldstein, A. (2000), 'Great Expectations: Interpreting China's Arrival', M.E. Brown, O.R. Coté, S.M. Lynn-Jones and S.E. Miller (eds), *The Rise of China*, Cambridge MA, MIT Press, pp. 3–40.

Goldstein, A. and Suro, R. (2001), 'A Journey in Stages: The Many Faces of Assimilation', *Responsive Community*, 11, 4, pp. 55–64.

González Cazanova, P. (1999), 'Americanization of the World', D. Slater and P.J. Taylor (eds), *The American Century: Consensus and Coercion in the Projection of American Power*, Oxford, Blackwell, pp. 317–37.

Goodman, A. (2001), 'Income Inequality', *New Economy*, 8, 2, pp. 92–7.

Goodman, D.S.G. (2004), 'China in East Asian and World Culture', B. Buzan and R. Foot (eds), *Does China Matter? A Reassessment*, London, Routledge, pp. 71–86.

Goodman, J. (2000), 'Stopping a Juggernaut: The Anti-MAI Campaign', J. Goodman and P. Ranald (eds), *Stopping the Juggernaut*, London, Pluto.

Gould, P. (1999), *The Unfinished Revolution: How Modernizers Saved the Labour Party*, London, Abacus.

Gowan, P. (2001), 'Neoliberal Cosmopolitanism', *New Left Review*, 11, pp. 7–93.

Gray, J. (2003), *Al Qaeda and What it Means to be Modern*, London, Faber.

Green, D.M. (2000), 'The End of Identity? The Implications of Postmodernity for Political Identification', *Nationalism and Ethnic Politics*, 6, 3, pp. 68–90.

Greider, W. (1997), *One World, Ready or Not: The Manic Logic of Global Capitalism*, London, Penguin.

Grundmann, R. (1999), 'The European Public Sphere and the Deficit of Democracy', D. Smith and S. Wright (eds), *Whose Europe?*, Oxford, Blackwell, pp. 125–46.

Guardian (2004), 'United Nations: The Only One We've Got', Editorial, 2 December, p. 27.

Guéhenno, J.M. (1995), *The End of the Nation-State*, Minneapolis, University of Minnesota Press.

Guerrina, R. (2002), *Europe: History, Ideas and Ideologies*, London, Arnold.

Guibernau, M. (1996), *Nationalism: The Nation-State and Nationalism in the Twentieth Century*, Cambridge, Polity.

Gunaratna, R. (2002), *Inside Al Qaeda*, London, Hurst.

Gupta, A. and Ferguson, J. (2002), 'Beyond "Culture": Space, Identity, and the Politics of Difference', J. Xavier Inda and R. Rosaldo (eds), *The Anthropology of Globalization: A Reader*, Oxford, Blackwell, pp. 65–80.

Habermas, J. (1992), 'Citizenship and National Identity: Some Reflections on the Future of Europe', *Praxis International*, 12, 1, pp. 1–19.

—— (1998), 'The European Nation-State: On the Past and Future of Sovereignty and Citizenship', *Public Culture*, 10, 2, pp. 397–416.

—— (1999), 'The European Nation-State and the Pressures of Globalization', *New Left Review*, 235, pp. 46–59.

—— (2001), 'Why Europe Needs a Constitution', *New Left Review*, 11, pp. 5–26.

Haider, J. (1993), *Die Freiheit, die ich meine*, Frankfurt and Berlin, Ullstein.

Hainsworth, P. (ed.) (2000), *The Politics of the Extreme Right: From the Margins to the Mainstream*, London, Pinter.

Hall, S. (1994), 'Son of Margaret', *New Statesman*, 6 October.

—— (1996), 'Ethnicity: Identity and Difference', G. Eley and R. Suny (eds), *Becoming National: A Reader*, Oxford, Oxford University Press, pp. 339–57.

—— (2003), 'The Great Moving Nowhere Show', A. Chadwick and R. Hefferman (eds), *The New Labour Reader*, Cambridge, Polity, pp. 82–7.

Hall, S. and Jacques, M. (eds) (1989), *New Times: The Changing Face of Politics in the 1990s*, London, Lawrence and Wishart.

—— (1997), 'Blair: Is He the Greatest Tory since Thatcher?', *Observer*, 13 April.

Halliday, F. (1996), *Islam and the Myth of Confrontation*, London, I.B. Tauris.

—— (2001), 'Beyond bin Laden', *Observer*, 23 September.

—— (2002), *Two Hours that Shook the World*, London, Saqi.

Harding, L. (2003), 'Swiss Lurch to the Right Follows Trend in Europe', *Guardian*, 21 October, p. 19.

Hardt, M. and Negri, A. (2000), *Empire*, Cambridge MA, Harvard University Press.

Harman, C. (1996), 'Globalisation: A Critique of a New Orthodoxy', *International Socialism*, 73, pp. 3–33.

Harper, T.N. (2002), 'Empire, Diaspora and the Languages of Globalism, 1850–1914', A.G. Hopkins (ed.), *Globalization in World History*, London, Pimlico, pp. 141–66.

Harris, G. (1994), *The Dark Side of Europe: The Extreme Right Today*, Edinburgh, Edinburgh University Press.

Harris, N. (1990), *The End of the Third World*, London, Penguin.

—— (2002), *Thinking the Unthinkable: The Immigration Myth Exposed*, London, I.B. Tauris.

—— (1989), *The Condition of Postmodernity*, Oxford, Blackwell.

—— (2003), *The New Imperialism*, Oxford, Oxford University Press.

Hattersley, R. (2000), 'In the Lingerie Shop: Review of The Third Way and its Critics', *Guardian*, 15 April.

Hay, C. (1994), 'Labour's Thatcherite Revisionism: Playing the Politics of Catch-up', *Political Studies*, 42, pp. 700–7.

—— (1997), 'Blaijorism: towards a one-vision polity', *Political Quarterly*, 68, pp. 372–8.

—— (1999), *The Political Economy of New Labour*, Manchester, Manchester University Press.

—— (2000), 'Globalization, Social Democracy and the Persistence of Partisan Politics: A Commentary on Garrett', *Review of International Political Economy*, 7, pp. 138–52.

—— (2002), 'Globalisation, "EU-isation" and the Space for Social Democratic Alternatives: Pessimism of the Intellect – a reply to Coates', *British Journal of Politics and International Relations*, 4, 3, pp. 452–64.

Hay, C. and Marsh, D. (eds) (2001), *Demystifying Globalization*, Basingstoke, Palgrave.

Hay, C. and Rosamond, B. (2002), 'Globalization, European Integration and the Discursive Construction of Economic Imperatives', *Journal of European Public Policy*, 9, 2, pp. 147–67.

Hay, C. and Watson, M. (2003), 'Diminishing Expectations: The Strategic Discourse of Globalization in the Political Economy of New Labour', A.W. Carfuny and M. Ryner (eds), *A Ruined Fortress? Neo-liberal Hegemony and Transformation in Europe*, Oxford, Rowman and Littlefield, pp. 147–72.

He, B. and Guo, Y. (2000), *Nationalism, National Identity and Democratization in China*, Aldershot, Ashgate.

Heater, D. (2002), *World Citizenship: Cosmopolitan Thinking and its Opponents*, London, Continuum.

Heelas, P., Lash, S. and Morris, P. (eds) (1996), *Detraditionalization: Critical Reflections on Authority and Identity*, Oxford, Blackwell.

Heer, J. and Penfold, S. (2003), 'The Resilience of Regional Identity: Misunderstanding McDonaldization', *Responsive Community*, 13, 3, pp. 6–11.

Heffernan, R. (1998), 'Labour's Transformation: A Staged Process with no Single Point of Origin', *Politics*, 18, pp. 101–6.

—— (2001), *New Labour and Thatcherism: Political Change in Britain*, Basingstoke, Palgrave.

Heitmeyer, W. (1993), 'Hostility and Violence towards Foreigners in Germany', T. Björgo and R. Witte (eds), *Racist Violence in Europe*, Basingstoke, Macmillan, pp. 17–28.

Held, D. (ed.) (2000), *A Globalizing World? Culture, Economics, Politics*, London, Routledge.

—— (2002), 'Cosmopolitanism: Ideas, Realities and Deficits', D. Held and A. McGrew (eds), *Governing Globalization*, Cambridge, Polity, pp. 305–24.

—— (2003), 'From Executive to Cosmopolitan Multilateralism', D.Held and M. Koenig-Archibugi (eds), *Taming Globalization: Frontiers of Governance*, Cambridge, Polity, pp. 160–86.

—— (2004), *Global Covenant*, Cambridge, Polity.

Held, D. and Koenig-Archibugi, M. (eds) (2003), *Taming Globalization: Frontiers of Governance*, Cambridge, Polity.

Held, D. and McGrew, A. (eds) (2000), *The Global Transformations Reader*, Cambridge, Polity.

—— (2002a), *Governing Globalization*, Cambridge, Polity.

—— (2002b), *Globalization/Anti-Globalization*, Cambridge, Polity.

Held, D., McGrew, A., Goldblatt, D. and Perraton, J. (1999), *Global Transformations: Politics, Economics and Culture*, Cambridge, Polity.

Henderson, D. (1999), *The MAI Affair: A Story and its Lessons*, London, Royal Institute of International Affairs.

Hennock, M. (2004), 'China's Graft: Tough Talk, Old Message', *BBC News Online*, 27 September.

Hertsgaard, M. (2002), *The Eagle's Shadow: Why America Fascinates and Infuriates the World*, New York, Bloomsbury.

Hewitt, D. (2000), 'China Clampdown on Muslim Region', *BBC News Online*, 29 May.

Higgott, R., Underhill, G. and Bieler, A. (eds) (1999), *Non-State Actors and Authority in the Global System*, London, Routledge.

Hill, C. (2001), 'A Herculean Task: the Myth and Reality of Arab Terrorism', S. Talbott and N. Chanda (eds), *The Age of Terror: America and the World after September 11*, Oxford, Perseus Press, pp. 81–111.

Himmelfarb, G. (1999), *One Nation, Two Cultures*, New York, Knopf.

Hiro, D. (2002), *War Without End*, London, Routledge.

Hirst, P. and Thompson, G. (1996), *Globalization in Question*, Cambridge, Polity.

—— (2000), 'Global Myths and National Policies', B. Holden (ed.), *Global Democracy: Key Debates*, London, Routledge, pp. 47–59.

Hobsbawm, E.J. (1983), 'Mass-Producing Traditions: Europe, 1870–1914', E. Hobsbawm and T. Ranger (eds), *The Invention of Tradition*, Cambridge, Cambridge University Press, pp. 263–307.

—— (1992), *Nations and Nationalism since 1780*, Cambridge, Cambridge University Press.

Hockenos, P. (1993), *Free to Hate: The Rise of the Right in Post-Communist Europe*, London, Routledge.

Hoge, J.F. and Rose, G. (eds) (2001), *How Did This Happen? Terrorism and the New War*, Oxford, Public Affairs.

Holden, B. (ed.) (2000), *Global Democracy: Key Debates*, London, Routledge.

Holmes, S. (1996), 'Census Sees a Profound Ethnic Shift in U.S.', *New York Times*, 14 March, p. 16.

Holton, R.J. (1998), *Globalization and the Nation-State*, Basingstoke, Macmillan.

Hombach, B, (2000), *The Politics of the New Centre*, Cambridge, Polity.

Hoogvelt, A. (1997), *Globalization and the Postcolonial World*, Basingstoke, Macmillan.

Hopper, P. (2003), *Rebuilding Communities in an Age of Individualism*, Aldershot, Ashgate.

—— (2004), 'Who Wants to be a European? Community and Identity in the European Union', *Human Affairs*, 14, 1, pp. 141–51.

—— (forthcoming), *Understanding Cultural Globalization*, Cambridge, Polity.

Horsman, M. and Marshall, A. (1995), *After the Nation-State: Citizens, Tribalism and the New World Disorder*, London, HarperCollins.

Huang, Y. (2003), *Selling China: Foreign Direct Investment During the Reform Era*, Cambridge, Cambridge University Press.

Huber, E. and Stephens, J. (2001), 'The Social Democratic Welfare State', A. Glyn (ed.), *Social Democracy in Neo-liberal Times*, Oxford, Oxford University Press.

Hunter, J.D. and Yates, J. (2002), 'The Vanguard of Globalization: The Word of American Globalizers', P.L. Berger and S.P. Huntington, *Many Globalizations*, Oxford, Oxford University Press, pp. 323–57.

Hunter Wade, R. (2002), 'The American Empire', *The Guardian*, 5 January.

—— (2003), 'The Disturbing Rise in Poverty and Inequality: Is It all a "Big Lie"', D. Held and M. Koenig-Archibugi (eds), *Taming Globalization: Frontiers of Governance*, Cambridge, Polity, pp. 18–46.

Huntington, S.P. (1984), 'Will More Countries Become Democratic?', *Political Science Quarterly*, 99, pp. 193–218.

—— (1997), *The Clash of Civilizations and the Remaking of World Order*, London, Touchstone.

—— (2004), *Who Are We? America's Great Debate*, New York, The Free Press.

Hutchinson, J. (2005), *Nations as Zones of Conflict*, London, Sage.

Hutton, W. (1996), *The State We're In*, London, Vintage.

—— (2004), 'When America Sneezes …', *Observer*, 14 Novembeer, p. 30.

Inglehart, R. (1990), *Culture Shift in Advanced Industrial Society*, Princeton, Princeton University Press.

Jacques, M. (2004), 'Our Moral Waterloo', *Guardian*, 15 May, p. 23.

Jenkins, B.M. (2001), 'The Organization Men: Anatomy of a Terrorist Attack', J.F. Hoge and G. Rose (eds), *How Did This Happen? Terrorism and the New War*, Oxford, Public Affairs, pp. 1–14.

Johnston, R.J., Taylor, P.J. and Watts, M.J. (eds) (1995), *Geographies of Global Change*, Oxford, Blackwell.

Jones, T. (1996), *The Remaking of the Labour Party: From Gaitskell to Blair*, London, Routledge.

Jordan, B. and Düvell, F. (2003), *Migration*, Cambridge, Polity.

Jospin, L. (2002), *My Vision of Europe and Globalization*, London, Policy Network/ Polity.

Judah, T. (2002), 'Via TV and the Net, Iran's Youth Plot Social Revolution', *Observer*, 25 August.

Juergensmeyer, M. (2001), *Terror in the Mind of God: The Global Rise of Religious Violence*, Berkeley, University of California Press.

Julius, D. (1990) *Global Companies and Public Policy*, London, Pinter.

Kahn, J. (2001), *Modernity and Exclusion*, London, Sage.

Kaldor, M. (1993), 'Yugoslavia and the New Nationalism', *New Left Review*, 197, pp. 96–112

—— (1996), 'Cosmopolitanism Versus Nationalism: The New Divide?', R. Caplan and J. Feffer (eds), *Europe's New Nationalism: States and Minorities in Conflict*, Oxford, Oxford University Press, pp. 42–58.

—— (2003), *Global Civil Society*, Cambridge, Polity.

Kang, L. (1998), 'Is there an Alternative to (Capitalist) Globalization? The Debate about Modernity in China', F. Jameson and M. Miyoshi (eds), *The Cultures of Globalization*, Durham, Duke University Press, pp. 164–88.

—— (2004), *Globalization and Cultural Trends in China*, Honolulu, University of Hawaii Press.

Keane, J. (2003), *Global Civil Society?*, Cambridge, Cambridge University Press.

Keck, M.E. and Sikkink, K. (1998), *Activists beyond Borders*, Ithaca NY, Cornell University Press.

Kelly, G. (ed.) (1999), *The New European Left*, London, Fabian Society.

Kennedy, P. (2001), 'Maintaining American Power: From Injury to Recovery', S. Talbott and N. Chanda (eds), *The Age of Terror: America and the World after September 11*, Oxford, Perseus Press, pp. 53–79.

Keohane, R. and Hoffman, S. (1991), *The New European Community*, Boulder, Westview Press.

Keohane, R.O. and Milner, H.V. (1996), *Internationalization and Domestic Politics*, Cambridge, Cambridge University Press.

Keohane, R.O. and Nye, J.S. Jr. (2002), 'Governance in a Globalizing World', R.O. Keohane (ed.), *Power and Governance in a Partially Globalized World*, London, Routledge, pp. 193–218.

Kepel, G. (2002), *Jihad: The Trail of Political Islam*, London I.B. Tauris.

Kettle, M. (2002), 'Relax the Republicans' Days are numbered', *Guardian*, 2 September.

Khagram, S., Riker, J.V. and Sikkink, K. (eds) (2002), *Restructuring World Politics: Transnational Social Movements*, Minneapolis, University of Minnesota Press.

Khan, A.R. and Riskin, C. (2001), *Inequality and Poverty in China in the Age of Globalization*, Oxford, Oxford University Press.

Kim, S.S. (2004), 'China in World Politics', B. Buzan and R. Foot (eds), *Does China Matter? A Reassessment*, London, Routledge, pp. 37–53.

King, D. and Wickham-Jones, M. (1999), 'Bridging the Atlantic: The Democratic (Party) Origins of Welfare to Work', M. Powell (ed.), *New Labour, New Welfare State? The Third Way in British Social Policy*, Bristol, Policy Press.

Kinnvall, C. (2002) 'Analyzing the Global–Local Nexus', C. Kinnvall and K. Jönsson (eds), *Globalization and Democratization in Asia: The Construction of Identity*, London, Routledge, pp. 3–18.

Kinnvall, C. and Jönsson, K. (eds) (2002), *Globalization and Democratizaion in Asia: The Construction of Identity*, London, Routledge.

Kivisto, P. (2002), *Multiculturalism in a Global Society*, Oxford, Blackwell.

Kobrin, S.J. (1998), 'The MAI and the Clash of Globalizations', *Foreign Policy*, 112, Fall.

Kohn, H. (1945), *The Idea of Nationalism*, Basingstoke, Macmillan.

Krauthammer, C. (2001a), 'The Bush Doctrine: ABM, Kyoto and the New American Unilateralism', *Weekly Standard*, Washington DC, 4 June.

—— (2001b), 'The New Unilateralism', *Washington Post*, 8 June, A29.

Kumar, K. (1978), *Prophecy and Progress: The Sociology of Industrial and Post-Industrial Society*, London, Penguin.

Lacroix, J. (2002), 'For a European Constitutional Patriotism', *Political Studies*, 50, 5, pp. 994–58.

Lane, J-E. and Ersson, S.O. (1994), *Politics and Society in Western Europe*, London, Sage.

Langman, L. and Morris, D. (2002), 'Islamic Terrorism: From Retrenchment to Ressentiment and Beyond', H.W. Kushner (ed.), *Essential Readings on Political Terrorism*, Lincoln, Gordian Knot, pp. 130–84.

—— (2003), 'The Roots of Terror', M.J. Thompson (ed.), *Islam and the West: Critical Perspectives on Modernity*, Oxford, Rowman and Littlefield, pp. 49–74.

Lapham, L.H. (1992), 'Who and What is American?', *Harper's*, 43, January.

Laqueur, W. (1996), 'Postmodern Terrorism', *Foreign Affairs*, 75, 5.

Lardy, N.R. (2002), *Integrating China into the Global Economy*, Washington DC, Brookings Institution Press.

Latouche, S. (1996), *The Westernization of the World*, Cambridge, Polity.

Lees, C. (2001), 'Social Democracy and Structures of Governance in Britain and Germany: How Institutions and Norms Shape Political Innovation', L. Martell et al., *Social Democracy: Global and National Perspectives*, Basingstoke, Palgrave, pp. 160–78.

Lent, A. (1997), 'Labour's Transformations: Searching for the Point of Origin', *Politics*, 17, 1.

Leonard, M. (1998), *Making Europe Popular*, London, Demos.

Levitas, R. (1998), *The Inclusive Society? Social Exclusion and New Labour*, Basingstoke, Macmillan.

Lewis, B. (1998), 'Licence to Kill: Usama Bin Laden's Declaration of Jihad', *Foreign Affairs*, 77, 6, pp. 14–19.

—— (2002), *What Went Wrong? Western Impact and Middle Eastern Responses*, London, Phoenix.

—— (2003), *The Crisis of Islam: Holy War and Unholy Terror*, London, Weidenfeld and Nicolson.

Levy, R. (2002), 'Corruption in Popular Culture', P. Link, R.P. Madsen and P.G. Pickowicz (eds), *Popular China: Unofficial Culture in a Globalizing Society*, Oxford, Rowman and Littlefield, pp. 39–56.

Leys, C. (1996), 'The Labour Party's Transition from Socialism to Capitalism', *Socialist Register*, London, Merlin Press.

Lim, L. (2004a), 'China Boom Leaves Many Behind', *BBC News Online*, 19 July.

—— (2004b), 'Chinese Muslims Forge Isolated Path', *BBC News Online*, 15 September.

Lindblom, C. (1977), *Politics and Markets*, New York, Basic Books.

Lingle, C. (1997), *The Rise and Decline of the Asian Century*, Hong Kong, Asia 2000 Limited.

Link, P., Madsen, R.P. and Pickowicz, P.G. (eds) (2002), *Popular China: Unofficial Culture in a Globalizing Society*, Oxford, Rowman and Littlefield.

Lindsay, J.M. (2000), 'The New Apathy', *Foreign Affairs*, September–October.

Lipset, S.M. (1963), *Political Man*, New York, Doubleday.

Lister, R. (1998), 'Fighting Social Exclusion ... With One Hand Tied Behind Our Back', *New Economy*, 5, 1.

Luard, T. (2004a), 'Paying the Price for China's Growth', *BBC News Online*, 14 October.

—— (2004b), 'Looking for China's Culture', *BBC News Online*, 19 October.

Lynch, P. (1993), 'Europe's Post-Maastricht Muddle', *Politics Review*, 3, 2, pp. 2–5.

Maalouf, A. (2000), *On Identity*, London, Harvill.

Magnette, P. (2003), 'European Governance and Civic Participation: Beyond Elitist Citizenship?', *Political Studies*, 51, 1, pp. 144–60.

Makiya, K. (2001), 'Fighting Islam's Ku Klux Klan', *Observer*, 7 October.

Malcolm, N. (1998), *Kosovo: A Short History*, London, Papermac.

Mann, M. (1997), 'Has Globalization Ended the Rise and Rise of the Nation-State?', *Review of International Political Economy*, 4.

Matthews, K. (1993), *The Gulf Conflict and International Relations*, London, Routledge.

McDowall, D. (1995), *The Palestinians: The Road to Nationhood*, London, Minority Rights.

McGrew, A. (1996), 'A Global Society?', S. Hall, D. Held, D. Hubert and K. Thompson (eds), *Modernity: An Introduction to Modern Societies*, Oxford, MA., Blackwell, pp. 466–503.

McLuhan, M. (1964), *Understanding Media*, London, Routledge.

McNeill, W.H. (1986), *Polyethnicity and National Unity in World History*, Toronto, University of Toronto Press.

McRae, H. (2004), 'The Biggest Boom in History Could See China Overtake the UK by Next Year', *Independent*, 8 April, p. 40.

Meiksins Wood, E. (1998), 'Labour, Class, and State in Global Capitalism', E. Meiksins Wood, Peter Meiksins and Michael Yates (eds), *Rising from the Ashes? Labor in the Age of "Global" Capitalism*, New York, Monthly Review Press, pp. 3–16.

Mekata, M. (2000), 'Building Partnerships Toward a Common Goal: Experiences of the International Campaign to Ban Landmines', A.M. Florini (ed.), *The Third Force: The Rise of Transnational Civil Society*, Washington DC, Carnegie Endowment for International Peace.

Melucci, A. (1989), *Nomads of the Present: Social Movements and Individual Needs in Contemporary Society*, London, Hutchinson Radius.

Merkel, W. (2001), 'The Third Ways of Social Democracy', A. Giddens (ed.), *The Global Third Way Debate*, Cambridge, Polity, pp. 50–73.

Merkl, P.H. and Weinberg, L. (eds) (1997), *The Revival of Right-Wing Extremism in the Nineties*, London, Frank Cass.

Meyer, A.E. (1995), *Islam and Human Rights: Tradition and Politics*, Boulder, Westview Press.

Meyer, B. and Geschiere, P. (eds) (1999), *Globalization and Identity*, Oxford, Blackwell.

Michael Reisman, W. (1999), 'The United States and International Institutions', *Survival*, 41–4, pp. 62–80.

Michel, F. and Bouvet, L. (1998), 'Paris, Bonn, Rome: A Continental Way?', I. Hargreaves and I. Christie (eds), *Tomorrow's Politics*, London, Demos, pp. 140–8.

Milward, A., Sorensen, V. and Ranieri, R. (1993), *The Frontier of National Sovereignty*, London, Routledge.

Minkenberg, M. (1997), 'The New Right in France and Germany: *Nouvelle Droite, Neue Rechte*, and the New Right Radical Parties', P.H. Merkl and L. Weinberg (eds), *The Revival of Right-Wing Extremism in the Nineties*, London, Frank Cass, pp. 65–90.

Mohammad, M. (2001), *Islam and the Muslim Ummah*, Prime Minister's Office, Putrajaya, Malaysia.

Moore, T.G. (2002), *China in the World Market*, Cambridge, Cambridge University Press.

Navias, M.S. (2002), 'Finance Warfare as a Response to International Terrorism', L. Freedman (ed.), *Superterrorism: Policy Responses*, Oxford, Blackwell, pp. 57–79.

Nederveen Pieterse, J. (2004), *Globalization or Empire?*, London, Routledge.

Neocleous, M. and Startin, N. (2003), '"Protest" and Fail to Survive: Le Pen and the Great Moving Right Show', *Politics*, 23, 3, pp. 145–55.

Newhouse, J. (1998), 'Europe's Rising Regionalism', N. Malcolm, T. Garton Ash and J. Heilbrunn, *A New Europe?*, A Foreign Affairs Reader, Council on Foreign Relations, New York, pp. 19–36.

Nolan, P. (2004), *China at the Crossroads*, Cambridge, Polity.

Norton-Taylor, R. (2001), 'Bleak New World, as Seen by the MoD', *Guardian*, 8 February.

Nussbaum, M.C. (1996), 'Patriotism and Cosmopolitanism', M.C. Nussbaum, *For Love of Country*, Boston, Beacon, pp. 2–17.

Nye, J.S. Jr. (2002), *The Paradox of American Power*, Oxford, Oxford University Press.

Nye, J.S. Jr. and Ovens, W.A. (1996), 'America's Information Edge', *Foreign Affairs*, March–April.

O'Brien, R., Scholte, J.A., Williams, M. and Goetz, A.M. (2000), *Contesting Global Governance*, Cambridge, Cambridge University Press.

Oakes, T. (2000), 'China's Provincial Identities: Reviving Regionalism and Reinventing "Chineseness"', *Journal of Asian Studies*, 59, 3, pp. 667–92.

Offe, C. (1996), *Varieties of Transition: The East European and East German Experience*, Cambridge, Polity.

Ohmae, K. (1990), *The Borderless World*, London, Collins.

—— (1995), *The End of the Nation State*, New York, The Free Press.

—— (2000), 'The Rise of the Region State', P. O'Meara, H.D. Mehlinger and M. Krain (eds), *Globalization and the Challenge of the New Century*, Bloomington, Indiana University Press, pp. 93–100.

Oliveti, V. (2002), *Terror's Source: The Ideology of Wahhabi-Salafism and its Consequences*, Birmingham, Amadeus.

Oppenheim, C. (2001), 'Enabling Participation? New Labour's Welfare-to-Work Policies', S. White (ed.), *New Labour: The Progressive Future?*, Basingstoke, Palgrave, pp. 77–92.

Ougaard, M. and Higgott, R. (eds) (2002), *Towards a Global Polity*, London, Routledge.

Özkirimli, U. (2000), *Theories of Nationalism: A Critical Introduction*, Basingstoke, Macmillan.

Panitchpakdi, S. and Clifford, M.L. (2002), *China and the WTO*, Singapore, John Wiley.

Paton Walsh, N. (2003), 'US Looks Away as New Ally Tortures Islamists: Uzbekistan's President Steps up Repression of Opponents', *Guardian*, 26 May, p. 13.

Pei, M. (2002), 'China's Governance Crisis', *The Rise of China*, New York, Foreign Affairs, pp. 121–34.

Perkins, D. (1957), 'What is Distinctly American About the Foreign Policy of the United States?', G. Van Dusen and R. Wade (eds), *Foreign Policy and the American Spirit*, Ithaca NY, Cornell University Press, pp. 3–15.

Perraton, J. (2000), 'Hirst and Thompson's "Global Myths and National Policies": A Reply', B. Holden (ed.), *Global Democracy: Key Debates*, London, Routledge, pp. 60–72.

Persson, G. (2001), *2001 Congress Opening Speech*, Stockholm, SAP.

Petras, J. and Veltmeyer, H. (2001), *Globalization Unmasked: Imperialism in the 21st Century*, London, Zed.

Pieterse, J.N. (2004), *Globalization and Culture*, Oxford, Rowman and Littlefield.

Plant, R. (2001), 'Blair and Ideology', A. Seldon (ed.), *The Blair Effect*, London, Little, Brown and Co.

Pratt, A. (2001), 'Towards a "New" Social Democracy', M. Lavalette and A. Pratt (eds), *Social Policy: A Conceptual and Theoretical Introduction*, London, Sage, pp. 11–31.

Preston, P. (2003), 'Hope in the Carnage of Casablanca', *Guardian*, 19 May, p. 17.

Preuss, U.K. (1993), *Constitutional Aspects of the Making Democracy in the Post-Communist Societies of Eastern Europe*, Bremen, Centre for European Law and Policy.

Price, S. (2001), 'Pakistan Tackles Sectarian Violence', *BBC News Online*, 15 March.

Pye, L.W. (2000), '"Asian Values": From Dynamos to Dominoes?', L.E. Harrison and S.P. Huntington (eds), *Culture Matters*, New York, Basic Books, pp. 244–55.

Rashid, A. (2003), *Jihad: The Rise of Militant Islam in Central Asia*, New Haven, Yale University Press.

Rawski, T. (2002), 'Where's the Growth?', *Asian Wall Street Journal*, 19 April.

Reich, R. (1999), 'We Are All Third Wayers Now', *American Prospect*, 43, pp. 46–51.

Reilly, J.E. (ed.) (1999), *American Public Opinion and U.S. Foreign Policy*, Chicago, Chicago Council on Foreign Relations.

Reus-Smit, C. (2004), *American Power and World Order*, Cambridge, Polity.

Rhodes, M., Heywood, P. and Wright, V. (eds) (1997), *Developments in West European Politics*, Basingstoke, Macmillan.

Richmond, A. (1984), 'Ethnic Nationalism and Postindustrialism', *Ethnic and Racial Studies*, 7,1, pp. 5–16.

Rieger, E. and Leibfried, S. (2003), *Limits to Globalization*, Cambridge, Polity.

Ritzer, G. (1998), *The McDonaldization Thesis*, London, Sage.

Robbins, K. (2000), 'Encountering Globalization', D. Held and A. McGrew (eds), *The Global Transformations Reader*, Cambridge, Polity, pp. 195–201.

Robertson, R. (1992), *Globalization*, London, Sage.

Rogers, P. (2002), *Losing Control*, London, Pluto Press.

Rosenau, J. (1997), *Along the Domestic–Foreign Frontier*, Cambridge, Cambridge University Press.

—— (2002), 'Governance in a New Global Order', D. Held and A. McGrew (eds), *Governing Globalization*, Cambridge, Polity, pp. 70–86.

Rosenau, J. and Czempiel, E.O. (1992), *Governance without Government*, Cambridge, Cambridge University Press.

Rosendorf, N.M. (2000), 'Social and Cultural Globalization: Concepts, History, and America's Role', J.S. Nye and J.D. Donahue (eds), *Governance in a Globalizing World*, Washington DC, Brookings Institution Press, pp. 109–34.

Ross, G. (1998), 'European Integration and Globalization', R. Axtmann (ed.), *Globalization and Europe*, London, Pinter, pp. 164–83.

Rothkopf, D. (1997), 'In Praise of Cultural Imperialism? Effects of Globalization on Culture', *Foreign Policy*, 107, pp. 38–53.

Roudometof, V. (1999), 'Nationalism, Globalization, Eastern Orthodoxy: "Unthinking" the "Clash of Civilizations" in Southern Europe', *European Journal of Social Theory*, 2, 2, pp. 233–47.

Rouse, R. (2002), 'Mexican Migration and the Social Space of Postmodernism', J. Xavier Inda and R. Rosaldo (eds), *The Anthropology of Globalization: A Reader*, Oxford, Blackwell, pp. 157–71.

Roy, O. (1999), *The Failure of Political Islam*, London, I.B. Tauris.

—— (2002), *Globalized Islam: The Search for a New Ummah*, London, Hurst.

Rubinstein, D. (2000), 'A New Look at New Labour', *Politics*, 20, pp. 161–7.

Ruggie, J.G. (1996), *Winning the Peace: America and World Order in the New Era*, New York, Columbia University Press.

—— (2003), 'Taking Embedded Liberalism Global: the Corporate Connection', D. Held and M. Koenig-Archibugi (eds), *Taming Globalization: Frontiers of Governance*, Cambridge, Polity, pp. 93–129.

Ruthven, M. (1995), 'The West's Secret Weapon Against Islam', *Sunday Times*, 1 January, p. 6.

—— (2002), *A Fury for God: The Islamist Attack on America*, London, Granta.

Ryosei, K. (2004), 'Globalizing China: The Challenges and the Opportunities', K. Ryosei and W. Jisi (eds), *The Rise of China and a Changing East Asian Order*, Tokyo, JCIE, pp. 23–35.

Sadkovich, J.J. (1996), 'The Response of the American Media to Balkan Neo-Nationalism', S.G. Mestrovic (ed.), *Genocide After Emotion: The Postemotional Balkan War*, London, Routledge, pp. 113–57.

Saich, T. (2000), 'Globalization, Governance and the Authoritarian State: China', J.S. Nye and J.D. Donahue (eds), *Governance in a Globalizing World*, Washington DC, Brookings Institution Press, pp. 208–28.

Said, E. (2001), 'Islam and the West are Inadequate Banners', *Observer*, 16 September.

Saikal, A. (2003), *Islam and the West: Conflict or Cooperation?*, Basingstoke, Palgrave.

Saleh, H. (2004), 'A Victory for the Status Quo', *BBC News Online*, 9 April.

Sardar, Z. (2001), 'Islam has Become its Own Enemy', *Observer*, 21 October.

Sardar, Z. and Wyn Davies, M. (2002), *Why Do People Hate America?*, Cambridge, Icon Books.

Sassoon, D. (1998), 'Fin-de-Siècle Socialism: The United, Modest Left', *New Left Review*, 227, pp. 88–96.

—— (1999a), 'European Social Democracy and New Labour: Unity in Diversity?', A. Gamble and T. Wright (eds), *The New Social Democracy*, Oxford, Blackwell, pp. 19–36.

—— (1999b), 'Introduction: Convergence, Continuity and Change on the European Left', G. Kelly (ed.), *The New European Left*, London, Fabian Society.

Scheffler, S. (1999), 'Conceptions of Cosmopolitanism', *Utilitas*, 11, 3, pp. 255–76.

Scheve, K. and Slaughter, M. (2001), *Globalization and the Perceptions of American Workers*, Washington, DC, Institute for International Economics.

Schirm, S.A. (2002), *Globalization and the New Regionalism*, Cambridge, Polity.

Schlesinger, A. (1998), *The Disuniting of America: Reflections on a Multicultural Society*, rev. ed., New York, W.W. Norton.

Schlesinger, P. (1991), *Media, State and Nation: Political Violence and Collective Identities*, London, Sage.

—— (1994), 'Europeanness: A New Cultural Battlefield?', J. Hutchinson and A.D. Smith (eds), *Nationalism*, Oxford, Oxford University Press, pp. 316–25.

Scholte, J.A. (2002), 'Civil Society and Governance in the Global Polity', M. Ougaard and R. Higgott (eds), *Towards a Global Polity*, London, Routledge, pp. 145–65.

Schöpflin, G. (1996), 'Nationalism and Ethnic Minorities in Post-Communist Europe', R. Caplan and J. Feffer (eds), *Europe's New Nationalism: States and Minorities in Conflict*, Oxford, Oxford University Press, pp. 151–68.

Schwartz, T.P. (2002), 'Terror and Terrorism in the Koran', H.W.Kushner (ed.), *Essential Readings on Political Terrorism*, Lincoln, Gordian Knot, pp. 22–34.

Schweitzer, Y. and Shay, S. (2003), *The Globalization of Terror*, London, Transaction Publishers.

Seager, A. (2004), 'Fear Infects Flexible Workplaces', *Guardian*, 2 September, p. 22.

Segal, G. (1999), 'Does China Matter?', *Foreign Affairs*, 78, 5.

—— (2000), 'East Asia and the "Constrainment" of China', M.E. Brown, O.R. Coté, S.M. Lynn-Jones and S.E. Miller (eds), *The Rise of China*, Cambridge MA, MIT Press, pp. 237–65.

Senghaas, D. (2002), *The Clash within Civilizations*, London, Routledge.

Shambaugh, D. (2000), 'Containment or Engagement of China? Calculating Beijing's Responses', M.E. Brown, O.R. Coté, S.M. Lynn-Jones and S.E. Miller (eds), *The Rise of China*, Cambridge MA, MIT Press, pp. 207–36.

Shaw, E. (1996), *The Labour Party since 1945*, Oxford, Blackwell.

Shen, S. (2004), 'Nationalism or Nationalist Foreign Policy? Contemporary Chinese Nationalism and its Role in Shaping Chinese Foreign Policy in Response to the Belgrade Embassy Bombing', *Politics*, 24, 2, pp. 122–30.

Shih, C. (2002), *Negotiating Ethnicity in China*, London, Routledge.

Shikaki, K. (2002), 'This is a War on Islam', *Guardian*, 11 September.

Shore, C. (2000), *Building Europe*, London, Routledge.

Sklair, L. (1991), *Sociology of the Global System*, London, Harvester.

—— (1998), *Transnational Practices and the Analysis of the Global System*, ESRC Transnational Communities Programme Seminar Series, 22.

—— (2002), *Globalization: Capitalism and its Alternatives*, 3rd edition, Oxford, Oxford University Press.

Slater, D. and Taylor, P.J. (eds) (1999), *The American Century: Consensus and Coercion in the Projection of American Power*, Oxford, Blackwell.

Smith, A.D. (1995), *Nations and Nationalism in a Global Era*, Cambridge, Polity.

Smith, J. and Edmonston, B. (eds) (1997), *The New Americans: Economic, Demographic, and Fiscal Effects of Immigration*, Washington DC, National Academy Press.

Smith, M.J. (1994), 'Understanding the "Politics of Catch-up": The Modernization of the Labour Party', *Political Studies*, 43, 4.

—— (2004a), 'Conclusion: The Complexity of New Labour', S. Ludlam and M.J. Smith (eds), *New Labour in Government*, Basingstoke, Macmillan.

—— (2004b), 'Conclusion: Defining New Labour', M.J. Smith and S. Ludlam (eds), *Governing as New Labour*, Basingstoke, Palgrave, pp. 211–25.

Smith, S. (2002), 'Unanswered Questions', K. Booth and T. Dunne (eds), *Worlds in Collision*, Basingstoke, Palgrave, pp. 48–59.

Smythe, E. (1999), 'State Authority and Investment Security: Non-State Actors and the Negotiation of the Multilateral Agreement on Investment at the OECD', R. Higgott, G. Underhill and A. Bieler (eds), *Non-State Actors and Authority in the Global System*, London, Routledge.

Song, Q., Zhang, C. and Qiao, B. (1996), *Zhongguo Keyi Shuobu (China Can Say No)*, Hong Kong, Mingpao Publishing.

Soysal, Y.N. (1994), *Limits of Citizenship: Migrants and Postnational Membership in Europe*, Chicago, University of Chicago Press.

Starr, A. (2000), *Naming the Enemy: Anti-Corporate Social Movements Confront Globalization*, London Zed.

Stiglitz, J.E. (2003), 'Globalization and Development', D. Held and M. Koenig-Archibugi (eds), *Taming Globalization*, Cambridge, Polity, pp. 47–67.

Stone, D. (2002), 'Knowledge Networks and Policy Expertise in the Global Polity', M. Ougaard and R. Higgott (eds), *Towards a Global Polity*, London, Routledge, pp. 125–44.

Strange, S. (1995), 'The Limits of Politics', *Government and Opposition*, 30, 3, pp. 291–311.

Szayna, T.S. (1997), 'The Extreme-Right Political Movements in Post-Communist Central Europe', P.H. Merkl and L. Weinberg (eds), *The Revival of Right-Wing Extremism in the Nineties*, London, Frank Cass, pp. 111–48.

Talbott, S. and Chanda, N. (eds) (2001), *The Age of Terror: America and the World after September 11*, Oxford, Perseus Press.

Taylor, P.J. (1999), 'Locating the American Century: A World-systems Analysis', D. Slater and P.J. Taylor (eds), *The American Century: Consensus and Coercion in the Protection of American Power*, Oxford, Blackwell, pp. 3–16.

—— (2001), 'Izations of the World: Americanization, Modernization and Globalization', C. Hay and D. Marsh (eds), *Demystifying Globalization*, Basingstoke, Palgrave, pp. 49–70.

Thakur, R. and Malley, W. (1999), 'The Ottowa Convention on Landmines: A Landmark Humanitarian Treaty in Arms Control?', *Global Governance*, 5, July/September.

The Economist (1998), 'Culture Wars', Editorial, 12 September, pp. 97–99.

Thomas, C. (2000), *Global Governance, Development and Human Security*, London, Pluto Press.

—— (2002), 'Global Governance and Human Security', R. Wilkinson and S. Hughes (eds), *Global Governance: Critical Perspectives*, London, Routledge, pp. 113–31.

Thompson, G. (2000), 'Economic Globalization?', D. Held (ed.), *A Globalizing World? Culture, Economics, Politics*, London, Routledge, pp. 85–126.

Thompson, M.J. (ed.) (2003), *Islam and the West: Critical Perspectives on Modernity*, Oxford, Rowman and Littlefield.

Tibi, B. (2002), *The Challenge of Fundamentalism: Political Islam and the New World Disorder*, Berkeley, University of California Press.

Tickell, A. (1999), 'European Financial Integration and Uneven Development', R. Hudson and A.M. Williams (eds), *Divided Europe*, London, Sage, pp. 63–78.

Tolz, V. (1997), 'The Radical Right in Post-Communist Russian Politics', P.H. Merkl and L. Weinberg (eds), *The Revival of Right-Wing Extremism in the Nineties*, London, Frank Cass, pp. 177–202.

Tomaney, J. (1994), 'A New Paradigm of Work Organization and Technology?', A. Amin (ed.), *Post-Fordism: A Reader*, Oxford, Blackwell, pp. 157–94.

Tomlinson, J. (1991), *Cultural Imperialism*, London, Pinter.

—— (1997), 'Internationalism, Globalization and Cultural Imperialism', K. Thompson (ed.), *Media and Cultural Regulation*, London, Sage/Open University, pp. 117–62.

—— (1999), *Globalization and Culture*, Cambridge, Polity.

Touraine, A. (1997), *What is Democracy?*, Boulder, Westview Press.

Travis, A. (2004), 'Desire to Integrate on the Wane as Muslims Resent the "War on Islam"', *Guardian*, 16 March, p. 6.

Traynor, I. (2003), 'How American Power Girds the Globe with a Ring of Steel', *Guardian*, 21 April, p. 5.

Turner, B.S. (ed.) (1990), *Theories of Modernity and Postmodernity*, London, Sage.

UN Association of the USA (2000), *A Global Agenda: Issues before the 55th General Assembly of the UN*, Oxford, Rowman and Littlefield.

Urry, J. (2000), *Sociology Beyond Societies*, London, Routledge.

—— (2002), *Global Complexity*, Cambridge, Polity.

US Census Bureau (2000), 'The Foreign Born Population in The United States', *Current Population Reports*, 1, March.

—— (2001), 'Diversity of the Country's Hispanics Highlighted', <http://www.census.gov>.

Van Hemel, A. H. Mommaas and C. Smithuijsen (eds) (1996), *Trading Culture: GATT, European Cultural Policies and the Transatlantic Market*, Amsterdam, Boekman Foundation.

Vandenbroucke, F. (1998), *Globalization, Inequality and Social Democracy*, London, IPPR.

—— (2001), 'European Social Democracy and the Third Way: Convergence, Divisions, and Shared Questions', S. White (ed.), *New Labour: The Progressive Future?*, Basingstoke, Palgrave, pp. 161–74.

Vartiainen, J. (1998), 'Understanding Swedish Social Democracy: Victims of Success?, *Oxford Review of Economic Policy*, 14, 1.

Venables, T. (2001), 'The EU Charter: A Missed Opportunity to Respond to Citizens' Concerns', K. Feus (ed.), *The EU Charter of Fundamental Rights: Text and Commentaries*, London, Kogan and Federal Trust.

Vidal, J. (2004), 'Fair Trade Sales Hit £100m a Year', *Guardian*, 28 February, p. 13.

Vujacic, V. and Zaslavsky, V. (1991), 'The Causes of Disintegration in the USSR and Yugoslavia', *Telos*, 88, pp. 120–40.

Wallerstein, I. (2003), *The Decline of American Power*, New York, The New Press.

Walter, A. (2001), 'NGOs, Business, and International Investment: The Multilateral Agreement on Investment, Seattle and Beyond', *Global Governance*, 7, January/March.

Waltz, K. (1999), 'Globalization and Governance', *Political Science and Politics*, December.

Watson, M. (2004), 'Endogenous Growth Theory: Explanation or *Post Hoc* Rationalization', *British Journal of Politics and International Relations*, 6, 4, pp. 543–51.

Watts, J. (2004a), 'China Orders TV Stars to Stop "Queer" Western Behaviour', *Guardian*, 5 May, p. 18.

—— (2004b), 'China Admits First Rise in Poverty since 1978', *Guardian*, 20 July, p. 11.

—— (2004c), 'China's Farmers Cannot Feed Hungry Cities', *Guardian*, 21 August, p. 19.

Weber, H. (2002), 'Global Governance and Poverty Reduction: The case of microcredit', R. Wilkinson and S. Hughes (eds), *Global Governance: Critical Perspectives*, London, Routledge, pp. 132–51.

Wechsler, W.F. (2001), 'Strangling the Hydra: Targeting Al Qaeda's Finances', J.F. Hoge and G. Rose (eds), *How Did This Happen? Terrorism and the New War*, Oxford, Public Affairs, pp. 129–43.

Werbner, P. and Modood, T. (eds) (1997), *Debating Cultural Hybridity: Multi-Cultural Identities and the Politics of Anti-Racism*, London, Zed.

White, S. (1998), 'Interpreting the Third Way: Not One Road, but Many', *Renewal*, 6, 2, pp. 17–30.

—— (ed.) (2001), *New Labour: The Progressive Future?*, Basingstoke, Palgrave.

Wickham-Jones, M. (1995), 'Recasting Social Democracy: A Comment on Hay and Smith', *Political Studies*, 43, pp. 698–702.

—— (1997), 'Social Democracy and Structural Dependence: The British Case – A Note on Hay', *Politics and Society*, 25, pp. 257–65.

Wieviorka, M. (1994), 'Racism in Europe: Unity and Diversity', A. Rattansi and S. Westwood (eds), *Racism, Modernity and Identity on the Western Front*, Cambridge, Polity, pp. 173–88.

Williamson, C. Jr. (1996), *The Immigration Mystique: America's False Conscience*, New York, Basic Books.

Wolf, M. (2004), *Why Globalization Works*, New Haven, Yale University Press.

Wolfe, A. (ed.) (1991), *America at Century's End*, Berkeley, University of California Press.

—— (1998), *One Nation After All*, London, Viking.

Woods, N. (2002), 'Global Governance and the Role of Institutions', D. Held and A. McGrew (eds), *Governing Globalization*, Cambridge, Polity, pp. 25–45.

Woollacott, M. (2003), 'Al-Qaida is Spending its Men and Blowing its Networks', *Guardian*, 23 May, p. 28.

Wriston, W. (1992), *The Twilight of Sovereignty*, New York, Charles Scribner.

Xavier Inda, J. and Rosaldo, R. (eds) (2002), *The Anthropology of Globalization: A Reader*, Oxford, Blackwell.

Yan, Y. (2002), 'State Power and Cultural Transition in China', P.L. Berger and S.P. Huntington (eds), *Many Globalizations*, Oxford, Oxford University Press, pp. 19–47.

Yang, M.M. (2002), 'Mass Media and Transnational Subjectivity in Shanghai: Notes on (Re) Cosmopolitanism in a Chinese Metropolis', J. Xavier Inda and R. Rosaldo (eds), *The Anthropology of Globalization: A Reader*, Oxford, Blackwell, pp. 325–49.

Younge, G. (2003), 'Hispanics Set to Transform US Politics', *Guardian*, 15 October, p. 18.

—— (2004), 'Black Americans Move Back to Southern States', *Guardian*, 25 May, p. 13.

Zheng, Y. (1999), *Discovering Nationalism in China: Modernisation, Identity, and International Relations*, Cambridge, Cambridge University Press.

—— (2004), *Globalization and State Transformation in China*, Cambridge, Cambridge University Press.

Index

Information in notes is indexed in the form 153n.8: i.e. note 8 on page 153. Where there is more than one note with the same number on a page, it is indexed as 154n.4(ii): i.e. the second note 4 on page 154